CW00369975

JAZZ ON
CD

Jazz on CD
A Mitchell Beazley Pocket Book

First published in Great Britain in 1995
by Mitchell Beazley
an imprint of Reed Consumer Books Limited
Michelin House
81 Fulham Road
London SW3 6RB
and Auckland, Melbourne, Singapore and Toronto

Editor:	Mike Evans
Assistant Editor:	Michelle Pickering
Art Director:	Jacqui Small
Art Editor:	Sue Michniewicz
Production:	Michelle Thomas

CONTRIBUTORS
Roy Carr *(Consultant Editor)*; Linton Chiswick; Fred Dellar;
John Fenton; Mark Gilbert; Tony Hall; Barry McRae; John Martin;
Chris Sheridan.

A CIP catalogue record for this book is available from the British Library
ISBN 1 857 32499 4

Set in Caslon 540 and Gill Sans
Produced by Mandarin Offset
Printed in Malaysia

JAZZ ON
CD

Compiled by
Roy Carr

MITCHELL BEAZLEY

How To Use This Book

CD REFERENCE NUMBERS

Once upon a time a record would be given a catalogue number and that would be the end of it. Nowadays, records are deleted only to re-appear a couple of years later boasting a new bar code number or, in some instances, a whole selection of numbers to choose from. Furthermore, due to the free movement of goods throughout the Common Market and the availability (via specialist distributors) of US and Japanese imports, it's possible that the same album could appear in the racks sporting individual catalogue numbers that stem from numerous countries of origin.

However, we are optimistic that if ordering a record you use the catalogue numbers provided in this guide, you will receive the album of your choice. However, we can take no responsibility of cataloguing changes that individual labels may choose to introduce at any given time.

Throughout *Jazz On CD* you will observe that many CDs on labels such as Contemporary, Fantasy, Good Time Jazz, New Jazz, Pablo, Prestige, Riverside etc, carry an 'OJC' CD catalogue number as well as the catalogue number that record was given in its original vinyl form. OJC is an abbreviation of *Original Jazz Classics* the overall re-issue programme instigated by Fantasy who have purchased these and other legendary companies and their catalogues.

Note: *[L]* after a catalogue number denotes a live recording.

ABOUT THE RECOMMENDATIONS

Whereas, other guides to music on CD are often concerned with state-of-the-art digital stereo recordings to the exclusion of almost everything else (sometimes even the actual merits of the performance) and therefore have no interest in monaural performances, *Jazz On CD* places the performance at the very top of its agenda.

Remember, when seeking specific titles, the likelihood of the sales assistant informing you that the record is no longer available is always a reality. However, that doesn't mean that you still can't obtain a copy. The experienced collector is fully aware that a trawl around specialist shops, mail order catalogues and record fairs will often unearth even the most hard-to-find CD.

Finally, we have informed your bank manager that you are about to indulge in some reckless spending.

Roy Carr

KEY TO ABBREVIATIONS

h

as	alto saxophone	p	piano
b	bass (acoustic)	perc	percussion
bjo	banjo	ss	soprano saxophone
bs	baritone saxophone	tba	tuba
clt	clarinet	tpt	trumpet
cnt	cornet	tmb	trombone
d	drums	ts	tenor saxophone
e-b	electric bass	v	vocal
f	flute	vln	violin
gtr	guitar	v-tmb	valve trombone
org	organ	xy	xylophone

Foreword

I think it was in 1945 that I first heard Charlie Parker. I was eighteen years old and it was in the basement flat of Carlo Krahmer who was later to found the Esquire record label. The record was a ten-inch acetate, illegally smuggled from America and the reproduction was primitive and the music was glorious. Fifty years later and the spectrum of jazz music is available on superbly produced compact discs with near perfect sound quality.

Miles Davis (who once said to me 'get out of the way'), maintained that the history of jazz could be summed up in four words – 'Louis Armstrong' and 'Charlie Parker', but I'm sure he would have agreed that a great deal has happened between and since, and here's an extremely comprehensive and compact reference book that both informs and guides. The information consists of records listed alphabetically under the artist's name and – a most welcome rarity – comments on the music and musicians that are erudite, revealing and witty. Whilst I can't agree with all the opinions expressed – jazz is, after all, one of the most subjective art forms – at the same time the mini resumes and critiques contain some excellent and insightful writing on jazz music.

The range of inclusions is, to say the least, eclectic. From the Original Dixieland Jazz Band through Louis Armstrong, the Mills Blue Rhythm Band, Bob Crosby, Ellington, Basie, Charlie Parker, Coltrane, Miles Davis to avant-gardists like Cecil Taylor, Albert Ayler and Ornette Coleman. And a fair selection of singers – the immortal Billie Holiday, Ella, Mark Murphy, Billy Eckstine.

There's also considerable coverage of musicians who are less than household names – Jon Faddis, Lars Gullin, J.R. Monterose, Marilyn Crispell. Marilyn Crispell ??

The bottom line is that this pocket diary sized book is a superior addition to the jazz library – of interest not only to the tyro who wants information and guidance but to any seasoned jazz musician or collector looking for a tiny but perfectly formed reference book.

Ronnie Scott

MUHAL RICHARD ABRAMS

BLU BLU BLU
(Black Saint 120 117-2)

FAMILYTALK
(Black Saint 120132-2)

Founder of the influential Association for the Advancement of
Creative Musicians (see Anthony Braxton, Roscoe Mitchell &
Henry Threadgill), Muhal Richard Abrams is probably the most
important post-Ornette Coleman jazz figure apart from Albert
Ayler. His career began as a member of the Chicago bop band,
MJT+3, but Abrams felt restricted by bebop routines. Working
from the most minimalist basis – solo piano – he went on to
develop a thoroughly orchestral voice which can express the most
radical developments in jazz in readily accessible terms. Using
groups ranging from sextet to ten-piece or larger, he continually
marks major new steps along the music's frontiers while referring
to traditional elements as disparate as Jelly Roll Morton, Duke
Ellington, Count Basie, Dizzy Gillespie, Charles Mingus and the
seminal influence in post-war Chicago blues Muddy Waters, all fil-
tered into an entirely personal shape. Its basis in Chicago is important. People and places figure largely in his music, however abstract
its appearance, as does humour, because what began as a clearly
introspective means of expression has become outgoing and risk-
taking, notably in its dependency on soloists' spontaneity to carry
the development of Abrams' compositions. CS

LEVELS & DEGREES OF LIGHT
(Delmark DD 413)

1-OQA+19
(Black Saint 120017 2)

GEORGE ADAMS

BREAKTHROUGH
(Blue Note BT 85122)

SONG EVERLASTING
(Blue Note BLJ 46907)

George Adams, ultimately – like so many of his profession over the
years – a victim of hard living, was a most audacious tenor sax stylist
who, be it with Charles Mingus, Gil Evans, McCoy Tyner or, more
famously, the quartet he co-lead with pianist Don Pullen (for close
to a decade) never attempted to disguise his deep-rooted Rhythm
and Blues sensibilities and wicked sense of humour. For most of
the time, the pair were relentless driven by Cameron Brown (b)
and Dannie Richmond (d). Few partnerships, in recent times, have
produced such a highly charged signature or such flambouyant
musical punctuation. Adams' loud whirlwind rushes welded
together elements of Ayler and Rollins, leaving the more puckish
Pullen to break ranks and freely pound from one end of the keyboard to the other whenever the mood took him. Though a pair of
Live At The Village Vanguard albums recorded for Soul Note are
worth close inspection, the two Blue Note albums marginally have
the edge. RC

LIVE AT THE VILLAGE VANGUARD
(Soul Note SN1094/1095) [L]

JULIAN 'CANNONBALL' ADDERLEY

SOMETHIN' ELSE
(Blue Note CDP 7 46338 2)

AT THE LIGHTHOUSE
(Landmark CD 1305) [L]

He may have originally been hailed as the new Bird, but in the final reckoning, Cannonball was more blues than bop, more sanctified than speed crazy, more commercial than contrite. From the same 'church' as Eddie 'Cleanhead' Vinson, Louis Jordan, Hank Crawford etc, Cannonball proved himself to one in an impressive line of alto blowin' popularizers that run from Earl Bostic and Tab Smith through Lou Donaldson up to David Sanborn and Everett Harp. Except for a time when he was bookended by Coltrane and Miles in the latter's sextet (1957-59), Cannonball (in cahoots with cornet playing brother Nat) lead his own wildly popular quintet/sextet until his death in 1975, at the age of 46. Much of his success was due to the skillful deployment of power-driven rhythm sections lead by a succession of pianist/composers: Bobby Timmons (*In San Francisco*), Victor Feldman (*At The Lighthouse*), Joe Zawinul (*In Europe*) and, later, George Duke. By any standards, an impressive career, that not only produced a string of bona fide jazz hits such as 'This Here', 'Sack O'Woe', 'Dat Dere', 'Work Song', 'Jive Samba', 'Mercy, Mercy, Mercy', 'Country Preacher' but saw Cannonball cameo'd in Clint Eastwood" *Play Misty For Me*. Elsewhere he was usually found in the company of Davis band pianists Bill Evans (*Know What I Mean*) or Wynton Kelly (*Things Are Getting Better*). Taped just prior to Cannonball signing with Riverside, a one-off Blue Note date *Somethin' Else*, has Miles as his frontline foil and Jones' Hank (p) and Sam (b) plus Art Blakey behind drums. With *At The Lighthouse* (featuring a blistering 'Sack O'Woe') running a close second, it's by far his most satisfying account of his craft and, in every way, superior to his work within Davis' own band. Meanwhile, *In San Francisco* (inc 'This Here'), *Them Dirty Blues* (inc 'Dat Dere', 'Work Song', 'Jeanine') and *Cannonball In Europe* (recorded during a continuous rain storm), are gilt-edged examples of Cannonball's joyous noise.   RC

IN SAN FRANCISCO
(Riverside 1157/OJC CD 035) [L]

THEM DIRTY BLUES
(Landmark CD 1301)

CANNONBALL IN EUROPE!
(Landmark CD 1307) [L]

TOSHIKO AKIYOSHI

COLLECTION (RCA/NOVUS ND 83106)
(Columbia 472925 2)

Toshiko Akiyoshi is an unusually international phenomenon: a Manchurian-born Japanese woman, writing in an American art form, for an American orchestra based in New York, successfully mixing oriental and western traditions and selling best in Europe and Japan. She is also one of the handful of major arranger/composers to have emerged in jazz. Her music is less predictable than many jazz band composers: it often changes meter several times, her accents are often unusually placed and her voicings are quite personal. She often writes extended pieces, complex in detail, which require considerable doubling in the saxophone section. Some are conceptualised in their entirety, others develop organically. They may be inspired by experiences, like 'Studio J' (the Berklee classroom where Toshiko learned improvisation), events, like 'After Mr Teng' (celebrating the USA's recognition of Red China), or people, like 'Kogun' ("one who fights alone": dedicated to the Japanese soldier found in a Philippine jungle over thirty years after World War Two), which blends western instrumentalism, Japanese music and Noh theatre. If the Thad Jones-Mel Lewis big band was the great modern jazz orchestra of the late 1960s and 1970s, then it was Toshiko Akiyoshi who took up the baton thereafter. CS

SUMI-E
(Insights 32CJ-1)

WISHING PEACE
(Ken 660.56.001)

MONTY ALEXANDER

THREESOME
(Soul Note SN 1152 CD)

JAMBOREE
(Concord Picante CCD 4359)

Threesome, from 1985, is a flawless example of the hard-swinging, virtuoso piano style that made this Jamaican-born pianist's name when he moved to American at the beginning of the '60s. The star bass and drums team of Niels-Henning Ørsted-Pederson and Grady Tate help make this special amongst Alexander's many fine trio recordings. *Jamboree* is one of a number of albums reflecting Alexander's own cultural background. The band, known as Monty Alexander's Ivory & Steel, augments the piano trio format with extra percussion and two steel drums. Othello Molineaux and Len 'Boogsie' Sharpe give the steel drums a contemporary phrasing that works well in the context, and help add life to a number of Alexander's fine original compositions, a jaunty version of Joni Mitchell's 'Big Yellow Taxi' and two Jamaican folk songs. And it's his dynamic and versatile in-person performances that has made Monty Alexander such a popular attraction on the international club and festival circuit. LC

GERI ALLEN

LIVE AT THE VILLAGE VANGUARD
(DIW 847) [L]

MAROONS
(Blue Note CDP 7 99493 2)

The current practice of surrounding young hopefuls with seasoned professionals has led to some 'new stars' sounding out of their depth. No such problem has occured with Geri Allen because her status as a reliable team player was established in the workplace. Her piano credentials were nailed down with Oliver Lake, Ralph Peterson and Dewey Redman but, more significantly, by her association with New York's M-Base movement and the likes of Steve Coleman and Gary Thomas. *The Village Vanguard* examines her under fire in a trio with Charlie Haden (b) and Paul Motian(d) and she performs admirably. The subtleties of her style are not in doubt but she flaunts her rhythmic unpredictability on 'Fiasco', her natural control of rubato on 'Mumbo Jumbo' and her acquaintance with the medium 12 bar on 'Vanguard Blues'. As a fine alternative, *Maroons* features her with various sized groups. It offers a mixture of youth and experience with thirteen original compositions to show how she supports her own sidemen. Allen is on the brink of becoming a seasoned professional in her own right. BMcR

HENRY 'RED' ALLEN

WORLD ON A STRING
(Bluebird ND 82497)

Red had power. Not many trumpeters of his day (except for Louis) could compete on that level. Hailed as the last great trumpet star to make it out of New Orleans, he swung his way through the late '20s and '30s, working with Luis Russell and others bands, occasionally fashioning solo classics such as the Ellington-like 'Feeling Drowsy' *Great Trumpets* (Bluebird ND 86753). A swing-era mainstay on New York's 52nd Street, he lined up alongside anybody as an equal or superior, albeit a bop or mainstream gig and, in common with Roy Eldridge, can be considered as a link between Armstrong and Gillespie. This 1957 session, which has Allen trading licks with Coleman Hawkins (ts), Buster Bailey (clt) and J.C.Higginbotham (tmb) is a casual joy, sparked by a memorable version of 'I Cover The Waterfront', that contains one of the great all-time trumpet solos, full of quirky runs, muffled growls and a final reach for the stars. Powerful. And then some. FD

HENRY 'RED' ALLEN AND HIS ORCHESTRA 1929-1933
(Classics 540CD)

MOSE ALLISON

BACK COUNTRY SUITE
(Prestige 7091/OJC CD 075)

GREATEST HITS
(Fantasy/OJC CD 6004)

ALLISON WONDERLAND
(Rhino/Atlantic 71689)

Currently, there's more activity surrounding Mose Allison's back-catalogue than at almost any period in a career spanning four decades. While his Prestige material has been sensibly restored, highlights of his lengthy association with Atlantic (1962-1976) boxed, (likewise a trio of mid-'60s album on Columbia) and those early '80s Elektra-Musician albums transferred to CD, there are also newly recorded albums (*The Earth Wants You*) for Blue Note to be heard. If Hoagy Carmichael's deadpan crackerbarrel vocals directly influenced Allison then, in turn, this Mississippi-born musical maverick's nasal whine served Ben Sidren but more so Georgie Fame to perfection, as well as leaving its mark on two generations of Brit Rock frontrunners; John Mayall ('Parchman Farm'), The Who ('Young Man Blues') The Yardbirds ('I'm Not Talking'), The Clash ('Look Here'), Elvis Costello ('Everybody Is Cryin' Mercy') and Van Morrison with whom he's toured. *Back Country Suite* (1957) was a bold album debut, relying upon a single concept and evocatively illustrated by Allison via a string of instrumental minatures performed at the piano. Both a perceptively, quick-witted lyricist and a barrelhouse-to-bop pianist, the full extent of Allison's Prestige-era minimalistic virtues are best encapsulated on *Greatest Hits* while a much wider career retrospective is the come-on from *Allison Wonderland*. RC

LOCAL COLOR
(Prestige 7121/OJC CD 457)

GENE AMMONS

YOUNG JUG
(Chess GRP 18012)

BOSS TENOR ✰
(Prestige 7180/OJC CD 297-2)

The wayward tenor playing son of boogie pianist Albert Ammons, 'Jug' (as he became nicknamed), combined the essential elements of swing and bop with R&B directness to create a free booting style that found a mass jukebox audience. It was later to prove a building block for future Chicago tenors Johnny Griffin, Clifford Jordan, Eddie Harris. All these elements are vividly assembled on the Chess set. Covering the years 1948 to 1952, only half-a-dozen of the 20 tracks exceed three minutes, yet sufficient enough for Jug to state his case. Though he later recorded extensively for Prestige, a chronic lifelong drug dependency which, kept him in jail from 1964 until 1969, meant that he seldom stretched his abilities. Prestige's *The Gene Ammons Story* trilogy goes part way to fixing his place in the scheme of things with *The 78 Era* (Prestige PRCD 24058), *The Organ Combos* (Prestige PRCD 24071) and *Gentle Jug* (Prestige PRCD 24079), but 1960's *Boss Tenor* (with Tommy Flanagan at the piano) is probably the most satisfying available showcase. mixing standards ('Close Your Eyes' and 'Canadian Sunset') with groove juicers ('Hittin' The Jug' and 'Blue Ammons'). Recorded the following year *Boss Tenors* (Verve 837440) successfully reunited Jug with Sonny Stitt (with whom he co-lead a combo a decade earlier) and proves to be friendly fixture as opposed to a grudge match. Also worth investigating is a one-off with Richard 'Groove' Holmes for Pacific Jazz (*Groovin' With Jug*). Ultimately, Ammons can be seen as knocking out as many albums as any label could handle in order to bankroll his debilitating habit which finally felled him in 1974 at the modest age of 49. RC

RAY ANDERSON

RIGHT DOWN YOUR ALLEY
(Soul Note 121087)

Trombone virtuoso or clown prince, Ray Anderson is good at all he does. As comfortable with 'free' as with 'changes', his style is located in a self made zone between the precision of Britt Woodman and the rustic bombast of Roswell Rudd. Chicago born, he emerged into New York's loft scene in the seventies and remains a first call player in that City. Leading his own combo on *Right Down Your Alley*, he shows his composing talents with a satirical funeral march on 'Portrait Of Mark Dresser' and a non stomping 'Stomping On Enigmas' that shows his awareness of the European school. His funk, dance band Slickaphonics was formed in 1984. He and his sidemen sang and jived like sidewalk buskers and it was a group that accommodated the light hearted side of his personality. Not that his music was ever predictable. His regular unit on *Wishbone* (Gramavision GV 79454 2) shows his adaptability, with Anderson's solo on 'Gathooze' full of gut bucket swing, 'Sound Of Love' treated with Lawrence Brown-like candour and the title track showing his frenetic side. It is the work of an impressive jazzman, one with more than a little ragtime in his soul. BMcR

LOUIS ARMSTRONG

HOT FIVES & SEVENS VOL.1
(JSP CD 312)

HOT FIVES & SEVENS VOL. 2
(JSP CD 313)

HOT FIVES & SEVENS VOL. 3
(JSP CD 314)

RHYTHM SAVED THE WORLD
(MCA/GRP 16022)

SATCH PLAYS FATS
(CBS 450980 2)

LOUIS ARMSTRONG/DUKE ELLINGTON:
THE COMPLETE SESSIONS
(EMI/Roulette CDP 7 93844 2)

Genius is an overworked word, yet, for all his popular personae, Daniel Louis Armstrong was the first of a few true geniuses who shaped the course of jazz. It was undoubtedly unplanned. But, such was the young trumpeter's force of musical personality that a breakout from the customary ensemble-based jazz to provide a platform for virtuosic solos was inevitable. It can be detected in embryo in several areas of his recorded work prior to the truly revolutionary Hot Five and Hot Seven performances. In King Oliver's Creole Jazzband, he breaks through ensembles in unprecedented manner; in accompaniment to blues singers like Bessie Smith the idea of instrumental solo is seized without artifice.

Yet Armstrong's first impact was on the ensemble practices of embryo big band jazz. Packed off to New York by his ambitious wife in 1924, Louis found himself a country boy among the city slickers of the Fletcher Henderson Orchestra. But it was they who were old fashioned and, to their staid dance-band structures, Armstrong brought harmonic, melodic and, above all, rhythmic revolution. From the moment he stood to take his first break, arrangers Henderson and Don Redman – to their eternal credit – recognised a new musical language which they hastened to incorporate into their scores. These arrangements, especially for trumpets, gradually took on Armstrong mannerisms that were retained right through to the Swing Era and the advent of South Western Swing in the form of Count Basie. Armstrong's lessons were also heeded by Coleman Hawkins, enabling him to find a developed jazz voice for the tenor saxophone.

The apotheosis of Armstrong's revolution was to be found after he left Henderson – fronting a studio recording group named by OKeh A&R man Richard M Jones as the Hot Five (and later Hot Seven). It is said that listening to their 'West End Blues' for less than three minutes tells one more about Louis' genius than reading every word ever written about him. The harmonic revolution is continued from Henderson through outrageous reworkings of pop songs, and solos freed from ties to chord sequences, allowing him to extend the trumpet style to levels of *bravura* that no contemporary could match. The rhythmic revolution applied parallel freedoms to existing practices which, based on ragtime, stressed alternate beats. Armstrong's phrasing cut across this to imply more supple rhythms, bringing further freedom to his melodic developments. The Hot Five and Hot Seven recordings are a treasure trove, from the early virtuosic style of 'Cornet Chop Suey', through 'Potato Head Blues', 'Twelfth Street Rag' (an exercise in the impossible), 'SOL Blues' and 'Hotter Than That', to the crowning 'West End Blues', 'Weatherbird Rag', 'Tight Like This' and 'Skip The Gutter'.

At the end of the 1920s, with the Wall Street Crash still ringing in the nation's ears, Armstrong moved on to front a big band, ultimately ensuring his popularity and fame as the 'Mr. Entertainer' of jazz. Yet even the most dated of the arrangements used – often flimsy platforms for spectacular trumpet displays – threw Armstrong's overall contribution to jazz into even sharper focus. Above all, they also underlined his fatherhood of the jazz vocal, drawn from his trumpet style and bequeathed most notably to Billie Holiday.

By the end of the 1930s, newer forces were at play and the knell of the big band was being rung. Armstrong soon reverted to his small group 'All Stars' format and would never again scale the dizzy heights of the mid 1920s, when he was challenged by musicians similarly at the cutting edge, notably Earl Hines (p), Johnny Dodds (clt) and Kid Ory (tmb). Comfortable as an old slipper they might have been, but they frequently provided the platform for intensely inventive Armstrong trumpet. This in turn only enhances the fact that snatches of Armstrong can be heard in every trumpeter who has played a note of jazz. Even Dizzy Gillespie's manner of articulation and staccato forays into the upper register are distant relations of Armstrong's innovations, for he was the first to break loose from the structures of mere thematic variation. He was not simply *avant garde* for his day, he was *avant garde* period.

N.B. Though Armstrong's Hot Five and Hot Seven recordings are available on a number of labels, the JSP releases are recommended above all others for their superior sound quality. CS

LOUIS WITH FLETCHER HENDERSON
(Forte F-38001/2/3)

HOT FIVE & SEVENS VOL. 4
(JSP CD 315)

BIG BANDS VOL. 1 & 2
(JSP CD 305 & 306)

HEART FULL OF RHYTHM
(MCA/GRP GRD-620)

POPS, THE 1940S SMALL BAND SIDES
(RCA/Bluebird ND 86378)

TOWN HALL CONCERT PLUS
(RCA 13036-2) [L]

CALIFORNIA CONCERTS
(MCA GRP4-6132) [L]

COMPLETE ALL-STARS ON DECCA
(Mosaic MD6-146) 6-CD Box

LOUIS ARMSTRONG PLAYS W.C. HANDY
(CBS 450981 2)

THE ART ENSEMBLE OF CHICAGO

THE ART ENSEMBLE 1976/8
(Nessa NCD 2500 A/B/C/D/E)

URBAN BUSHMEN
(ECM 1211/12) [L]

DREAMING OF THE MASTERS SUITE
(DIW 854)

To appreciate the full scope, creative challenge and sheer icona-clastic determination of the group, it is essential to fully digest *The Art Ensemble* 1967/8, five CD set made, not entirely for publication, before the 'Of Chicago' was added in Paris. Saxophonist Roscoe Mitchell emerges as the motivator but this remarkable document presents music in the making. Some of the material has appeared on LP but here we have the embryonic progression, via orthodox horns, 'little instruments' and brave silences to the fully mature Art Ensemble of Chicago style. Old is funky in a way that Miles would have hated, the Tatas-Matoes rehearsal reminds us that Phillip Wilson was house drummer for Stax, Mitchell taunts 'Oh Susannah' for thirty one minutes, a 'Warm Up' deserves posterity and gets it and there are delicious solo moments from Mitchell on 'Solo' and 'Tkhke', bassist Malachi Favors on 'Tutankhamen' and trumpeter Lester Bowie on 'Jazz Death' but the whole package is irresistible!

Paris did produce some remarkable work but too little is on com-pact disc, while the seventies found the Ensemble rather less than frequently recorded. Fortunately, they often toured and their shows were masterpieces of theatre as well as full of uncompromis-ingly free jazz. *Urban Bushmen* came from two concerts in 1980 and they capture the mood of the live performances splendidly. In some ways, they are like a musical ghost train journey. a snippet of melody brushes by, a haunting theme rises suddenly from nowhere, an historical figure is briefly recognised and there are changes of direction so sudden as to suggest a melodic derailment. The whole trip is from the orthodox jazz tradition to the brink of free anarchy. Quality recordings continued to appear in the eight-ies, on one occasion with African guests and with the group making a courtesy change to their name on *Art Ensemble Of Soweto* (DIW 897). A more challenging item was *Dreaming Of The Masters Suite*, an excellent tribute to John Coltrane. Only three 'Trane originals are used but the drastic mood changes throughout its ten titles provide a rich diet for listeners who enjoy strong flavours. Undoubtedly the Art Ensemble of Chicago are an acquired taste, but certainly one worth cultivating. BMcR

ROY AYERS

A SHINING SYMBOL
(Polydor 519 378)

GET ON UP GET ON DOWN
(Polydor 519 918)

Lionel Hampton was the man who originally turned Roy Ayers onto the vibraphone sometime around 1960, but his influence over Ayers's music was soon far less obvious than over his choice of instruments. Ayers became a prime mover in the burgeoning jazz/funk scene – developing, after a series of collaborations with Chico Hamilton, Hampton Hawes and Herbie Mann, into a top-selling crossover artist, with a series of popular albums on the Polydor label. Because Ayers's music is so far removed from the jazz mainstream, with its soulful vocals and disco beats, it is common for his not inconsiderable achievements to be overlooked by jazz 'purists'. But his vibraphone was fluent, imaginative and exciting; and some of his compositions and arrangements in a jazz/funk style, like 'Everybody Loves The Sunshine' and 'We Live In Brooklyn Baby', have a sharp, powerful edge that elevate them above the competition. These two Polydor collaborations contain all Ayers's '70s hits, and much of the best material from the period. There are contributions by vocalist Dee Dee Bridgewater, saxophonist Sonny Fortune, bassist Ron Carter, trumpeter Jimmy Owens and drummer Billy Cobham. With the advent, in Britain and Europe, of the Acid Jazz movement, Ayers has experienced yet another turn in fortune, being elevated to 'Godfather' status, signed to Ronnie Scott's Jazz House label (*The Essential Groove-Live* (Jazz House CD 035)), teaming up with Donald Byrd to tour with rapper Guru (*Jazzamatazz*) and enjoying the time of his life. LC

ALBERT AYLER

SPIRITUAL UNITY
(ESP 1002)

IN GREENWICH VILLAGE
(Impulse 254635) [L]

In terms of influence and stylistic identification, Albert Ayler must rate with Hawkins, Young, Rollins and Coltrane as one of jazz's five most important tenor saxophonists. His earliest CD from 1962 displayed a bumbling incompetence. It implied that he had a style in his head but could not get it through the bell of his horn. Two years later *Spiritual Unity* (which premiered 'Ghosts') proclaimed his true arrival. His style was in place, his music delivered with astonishing power. With Gary Peacock (b) and Sunny Murray (d) tuned into the same wavelength, it screamed that 'black was beautiful' and, in concentrating on his own method of motivic development and employing a wide vibrato, it challenged many previously incontrovertible tenets. Disappointingly, few LPs followed but *In Greenwich Village* was his finest outside the studio. As with earlier works, its themes were a mixture of naivety and magniloquence, 'For John Coltrane' wisely featured his alto, while 'Change Has Come' and 'Truth Is Marching In' present his line pared to the bone and delivered with a vocalised dialect going back to Congo Square. Flirtations with R&B elements on the 1968 *New Grass* and elsewhere added nothing to his reputation but *Fondation Maeght Nights Vols. 1 & 2* (Jazz View COD 004/5) showed that even till the last he was capable of superb jazz performances. Pulled from New York's East River, in November 1970, at the age of thirty four, Ayler had already made a massive contribution to jazz progress. BMcR

DEREK BAILEY

SOLO GUITAR VOL. 2
(Incus CD 09)

A man that surrenders a comfortable career in popular music to take on the vagaries of free music must be either totally sincere or mad. Guitarist, Derek Bailey, a-down-to-earth Yorkshireman, is certainly not the latter and his sincerity and commitment has never been in doubt. At the age of thirty one he sat down and re-examined the musical rules that he had previously accepted without question and he evolved a style of free form guitar that became a model of its kind. A stalwart of the Spontaneous Music Ensemble, Music Improvisation Company and Iskra 1903, he was there at the start of the British free movement. His superbly abstract style, perfectly presented on *Solo Guitar Vol. 2* is not for the feint hearted. There is no traditional jazz 'story telling'. Bailey is concerned with the beauty of sound and the space around it. His music has a splintered glass angularity about it but, within his own rules, he plays with scrupulous accuracy. His group recordings offer a surfeit of riches and to hear him pitting his musical wits against Hugh Davis (electronics) and soprano saxist Evan Parker with the Music Improvisation Company is to hear musical interaction in its finest form. BMcR

MUSIC IMPROVISATION COMPANY 1968-1971
(Incus CD 12)

CHET BAKER

LET'S GET LOST/THE BEST OF CHET BAKER SINGS
(Pacific Jazz CDP 7 929932 2)

THE BEST OF CHET BAKER PLAYS
(Pacific Jazz CDP 7 97161 2)

LIVE AT NICK'S
(Criss Cross Jazz Criss 1027) [L]

LIVE AT FAT TUESDAY'S
(Fresh Sound FSR CD 131) [L]

BLUES FOR A REASON WITH WARNE MARSH
(Criss Cross Jazz Criss 1010)

CHET'S CHOICE
(Criss Cross Jazz Criss 1016)

Even by pop's instant-fame standards, Chet Baker's success was of the overnight variety. Within 12 months (1952-53) Chet found himself catapulted from obscurity to partnering Bird for a West Coast tour prior to becoming Gerry Mulligan's front-line accomplice in the baritone saxman's innovative piano-less quartet; an association that dissolved within a year. If that wasn't sufficent, young Chet (23) leapfroged Dizzy and Miles to scoop the most prestigious popularity jazz polls as top trumpet. Simultaneously smothered and damned with praise (and secretly plagued with self-doubt), Chet commenced his career at the very top and, to his credit, earned his merit badge under the glare of the most fierce spotlight. Despite constant digs from those who resented such 'undeserved' success, the boxed 4-CD overview of his five year association with the label *The Pacific Jazz Records Years* (CDP 7-89292) puts paid to the myth that Baker had a 'glass' lip. Quite the contrary, Baker's post-Mulligan work with pianist Russ Freeman repeatedly affirmed his abilities. An inspired collaboration every bit as productive as that with Mulligan, the pair interacted with immense skill and attention to detail ('Bea's Flat', 'Maid In Mexico'etc). One of the great unsung partnerships, it is documented in full on two 3-CD boxes from US mail order specialist, Mosaic: *The Complete Pacific Jazz Live Recordings Of The Chet Baker Quartet with Russ Freeman* (MD3 113), which includes much hitherto unreleased material plus *The*

Complete Pacific Jazz Studio Recordings Of The Chet Baker Quartet with Russ Freeman (MD3 122).
Furthermore, Chet's finest vocal recordings were cut for Pacific. Plaintive, introspective – an extension of his familiar trumpet style ('But Not For Me', 'My Funny Valentine'). Seldom has anyone ever had as much going for them as Chet did in the mid-'50s: a distinctive trumpet signature, a little-boy-lost voice and doomed-youth looks that positioned him as James Dean, Sinatra and Bix all rolled into one. Sadly, they would soon be accompanied by a monkey on his back the size of King Kong.

If Baker's good looks prematurely deserted him, his music continued to haunt. By the end of the '70s, Baker began to ressurect his faultering career on various European labels but such was the proliferation of 'live' sessions, that it seemed that part of his overall appearance fee was a rider allowing the promoter to tape Mr. Chet's performance. As a journeyman soloist he would often find himself fronting players whose skills didn't come close to matching their enthusiasm. However, there were always exceptions. As the lines on his face deepened so to did the intensity of his playing and when sympathetically produced by Criss Cross *Blues For A Reason* (an inspired pairing with tenorman Warne Marsh) or broadcasting from *Fat Tuesday's* (alto sax ace Bud Shank renewing an old friendship), Baker explored emotional depths beyond the grasp of most players. As in life, Baker's death, in 1988, age 58, was melodramatic. Whether he was pushed or accidentally fell out of an Amsterdam hotel window has never been clarified. RC

AND CREW
(Pacific Jazz CDP 7 81205 2)

WITH STAN GETZ/TOGETHER FOR THE FIRST TIME
(Fresh Sound FSCD 1022)

CHET BAKER IN PARIS VOL. 1
(EmArCy 837474)[L]

KENNY BALL

STRICTLY JAZZ
(Kaz CD 19)

NOW 2
(SRT 1993)

Ball is a good British trumpet player who, stylistically, might well have fitted in on any Eddie Condon session and walked away with the honors. But he led a band in the era when Trad was the fad and thereafter got stuck with a novelty tag, his links with Pye Records (owned at that point by ATV) ensuring a spot on scores of TV shows, usually of the family kind. His 'Midnight In Moscow', a well-shaped worldwide hit that sticks in the memory, is probably the most prominent recorded achievement on his personal CV though his cover of 'March Of The Siamese Children' reiterates his love of the Yank Lawson sound, the Rodgers-Hammerstein favourite having been earlier recorded in dixieland style by the Lawson-Haggart Jazzband. A household name he may well be, but Ball never deserted his jazz roots. Therefore it's not surprising that from a man who cites both Satchmo and Brownie as lasting influences, the territory covered by his Jazzmen encompasses Armstrong's 'Wild Man Blues', Duke's 'Black & Tan Fantasy', Berigan's 'I Can't Get Started' and Gerry Mulligan's ultra cool 'Walkin' Shoes'. FD

CHRIS BARBER

40 YEARS JUBILEE VOLS. 1 & 2
(Timeless CDTTD 586) [L]

30 YEARS CHRIS BARBER
(Timeless CDTTD 517/8)

Chris Barber's another who helped break the mould. He was there amid the original British trad boom of the '50s but while the critics and those raised on genuine New Orleans sounds copped an approving ear to what he and his band did, unlike the Balls and the Bilks, Chris flunked out popwise, only a version of 'Petite Fleur' (a feature for Monty Sunshine's clarinet) really making any chart impact. Meanwhile, a spin-off skiffle group headed by Lonnie Donegan, notched a hit of its own with a version of Leadbelly's 'Rock Island Line' (cut as part of a Barber album) and Donegan quit to become a near-superstar by combining blues and vaudeville and shaping the result for mass consumption.

Barber, a trombonist of great merit, whose marriage to the blues-bawling Otillie Patterson meant that the band never suffered from shortcomings in the vocal department, didn't hang around to see the scene fold on him. His music began incorporating elements of swing, jump, bebop even, his sidemen encompassing the likes of altoist Joe Harriott, probably the nearest thing to a Charlie Parker that Britain ever possessed. Whereas previously, Barber had introduced blues legends Muddy Waters and Otis Spann to an uncaring British audience, at one point during the '70s Barber toured with an Ellington-styled outfit and there were links with such as Dr John and Louis Jordan both of whom recorded with the British band.

From a collection of private recordings made during concert tours of Holland and Germany, *40 Years* stems from 1954-1956 and on 'Magnolia's Wedding Day', 'Bogalusa Strut' and 'Panama' delineates exactly why Barber's band received those early nods of approval from the pundits, while *30 Years* attempts to present a wider spectrum by linking cuts from 1956 with others recorded in 1984. Neither therefore, is the sampler that the titles would appear to indicate. Even so, as examples of Barber's work they're worth a place on any shelve, though, regrettably, the wonderfully eclectic 'Battersea Rain Dance', which decorated the late' 60s, has not yet re-appeared in CD form.. Shame, that. FD

ALAN BARNES

BRUCE ADAMS & ALAN BARNES: SIDE-STEPPIN'
(Big Bear CD 38)

ALAN BARNES & DAVID NEWTON: LIKE MINDS
(Fret FJCS 105)

The difference between American and British musicians isn't necessarily ability, rather attitude. Stateside, the misplaced careerist ethos currently emasculates more young artists than it promotes. In many instances the image projected being identical to that employed to promote male cosmetics and designer underwear; ignoring that hipness is acquired naturally, not an off-the-peg commodity. If most artists subjected to big-spend marketing campaigns possessed half the ability of multi-saxist Alan Barnes, then the ratio of style over content would produce records that warranted more than a cursory audition. Perhaps, it's not so much a question of British reserve as a vocational approach. The music still matters: a charts over cheque book situation. Stateside, points of reference have become so narrow you couldn't even slip a Rizla paper inbetween them. In contrast, Alan Barnes, moves effortlessly from genre to genre like the proverbial fish-through-water. Be it a jaunty post-hard bop quintet co-headed with trumpeter Bruce Adams, a reflective duo situation with pianist David Newton, or, his past association in the company of the Jazz Renegades and the Humphrey Lyttleton Band, this self-effacing pollwinner is a world-class player. As *Like Minds* demonstrates, be it alto or tenor sax or various clarinets, Barnes possesses the strength of character to investigate material associated with someone of Stan Getz's magnitude ('The Peacocks' and 'Nobody Else But Me') yet not have the listener grab for the originals. As an altoist who can be as fragile as Desmond or as gritty as Bostic, his knowing tip of the beret to a fellow altoist 'Waltz For Sonny Criss', again affirms that Barnes truly is a man for all seasons. RC

CHARLIE BARNET

DROP ME OFF IN HARLEM
(MCA GRP 16122)

With a whole slew of wives to his credit, it's little wonder that Barnet had the strength to blow thrusting sax. But he did, heading a band that owed something to Ellington musically and a lot more financially to Barnet's father, who happened to be a millionaire. A life of two halves, one spent on Bluebird for whom Barnet provided over a score of hits including the booting 'Cherokee' and the more relaxed 'Pompton Turnpike', the band arguably peaked during its era with US-Decca (now MCA) when it boasted such trumpet aces as Roy Eldridge and Al Killian along with brilliant bop pianist Dodo Marmarosa, whose 'The Moose' feature (named after Dodo's profile) penned by Ralph Burns, is considered to be a watershed in big-band arrangments. Later, Barnet was to move to Capitol and become almost a secondary Kenton (featuring high note trumpet ace Maynard Ferguson) but here's where to dig first. FD

CHEROKEE
(Bluebird ND 90632)

GARY BARTZ

THERE GOES THE NEIGHBOURHOOD
(Candid CCD 79506)

Whereas many former Miles sidesmen turned their association into full blown solo careers, Gary Bartz – having scooped all the major polls as ace altoman – promptly lost direction in '70s jazz disco goo. Perhaps, from Bartz's viewpoint it seemed the right option, though it ultimately led up a blind alley. But then, to all but a charmed few,'70s jazz life wasn't nearly as lucrative as one would have wished. With the prospects of non-musical day jobs looming, a number of name players became University educators or sought more secure means of musical employment anywhere from Dixeland to Disneyland. While the insatiable jazz-dance fraternity are presently excavating his funk tracks, Bartz has chosen to return to the more Bird-based roots still favoured, by (sacred) flamekeepers Phil Woods, Frank Morgan, Bobby Watson, Donald Harrison, Charles McPherson and Jackie McLean. This quartet date shared with Kenny Barron shows his ability to push his way to the front of the pack – though never quite past McLean. RC

COUNT BASIE

THE COMPLETE DECCA RECORDINGS
(MCA/GRP GRD 3 611)

THE GOLDEN YEARS VOL. 1
(Jazz Archives VILCD 073)

THE GOLDEN YEARS VOL. 2
(Jazz Archives VILCD 074)

BASIE IN LONDON
(Verve 833 805 2) [L]

THE COMPLETE ATOMIC MR BASIE
(EMI/Roulette CDP 8 28635 2)

KANSAS CITY EIGHT – GET TOGETHER
(Pablo PACD 2310 924 2)

More influential than Ellington, more genial than Armstrong, almost as *avant-garde* as Parker, whom he twice declined to employ, Count Basie was the music's true King Of Swing, leading two of the best big bands in jazz and paving the way for modern jazz, both hot and cool. At the same time, Basie himself was also one of its most important pianists. Ironically, he didn't set out to be a piano player; his original ambition was to be a drummer. But virtuosic near-neighbour, Sonny Greer, put him off percussion, leaving Basie the pianist with a perfectly-informed sense of rhythm. Influenced by Fats Waller, touring took him to Kansas City, where he worked with Walter Page's Blue Devils, then the area's big name, Bennie Moten. Here in a city where corruption kept the depression at bay, Basie finally organised his own orchestra, the 'Old Testament' band which played its first big time dates in Chicago, then New York at the end of 1936. Within two years, Basie had established his initially raggedy outfit as one of the three best bands of the day (alongside Ellington and Lunceford), turning out some of the most brilliant big band jazz recordings, not least the *sine qua non* of Basiana, 'One O'Clock Jump', and other hits like 'Jumpin' At The Woodside' and 'Swingin' The Blues'. But a sharp deal by Decca denied Basie any royalties.

If Basie's ensembles lacked others'. polish, the band as a whole gained immense drive and momentum from its ability to build riffs, usually spontaneously, from ideas passed along the reeds from Jack Washington to Lester Young, or ignited among the trumpets by Buck Clayton. Basie was also redefining jazz piano in a way that, especially in accompaniment to soloists, would usher in the Bebop Era, while organising his orchestra's dynamics to maximise the impact of his soloists. And they were remarkable. Lester Young produced a body of work that remains almost without parallel. Jack Washington, much underrated, achieved a similar distinction for the baritone sax, influencing Serge Chaloff and Gerry Mulligan. Herschel Evans found an individual voice in the Coleman Hawkins legacy and, with Young, maintained Basie's love of tenor 'battles' in his music. Trumpeters Buck Clayton and Harry Edison produced highly individual and contrasting interpretations of Armstrong, and Dicky Wells made the trombone laugh and joke in a way that is still felt in contemporary playing. After the slump in big band fortunes of the late 1940s, he ran a combo for eighteen months before re-forming his New Testament band in late 1951. Though often dubbed an 'arrangers' band', and thus a departure from previous glories, it was in fact a *development* of the Old Testament orchestra. Its arrangements continued a process already started, becoming sharply-etched sculptures in dynamics, distilling ensemble practices of riff, call-and-response and linear melody, just as Basie had distilled his own piano style. It is a key fact that, whether from inside the band (Ernie Wilkins, Thad Jones, Frank Foster, Frank Wess) or from outside (Neal Hefti, Quincy Jones, Buster Harding, Jimmy Mundy), no arranger's work was immune to remoulding by Basie or his 'committee', bringing simplification and the unwritten rhythmic nuance that made a Basie ensemble instantly indentifiable (and inimitable).

Their finest recordings – the *Dance Sessions*, *Atomic Mr Basie*, *Basie Plays Hefti* and *One More Time* (among others) amply bear this out, being among the finest of *all* big band recordings of the 1950s. Nor was it devoid of eloquent soloists. The boss remained a seminal pianist and, in trumpeter Thad Jones and trombonist Al Grey, it had men the equal of many in the Old Testament line-up. Other soloists of character included trumpeter Joe Newman (who played in both Old & New), trombonist Quentin Jackson, and tenor saxists Eddie 'Lockjaw' Davis, Frank Foster and Frank Wess, who should be credited for giving the flute a mature role as a jazz voice.

In his last decade, Basie subtly reshaped the New Testament sound in the looser style of Kansas City days. The band played with renewed vigour, pushing its ever more functional arrangements to the limit. He increasingly took the spotlight, and it was the small groups built around his minimalist piano that caught the ear, while two trio sessions provided this shy man's first recorded solos since 1939! By his death in April, 1984, Basie had shown that, no less than Ellington, he was a musician who had two instruments, his piano and his band. The latter was simpler, more basic than Duke's, but remains pre-eminent in the history of jazz. CS

THE JUBILEE ALTERNATIVES
(HEP CD 38)

COUNT BASIE & HIS ORCHESTRA 1944
(Circle CCD 60)

COUNT BASIE & HIS ORCHESTRA 1944-1945
(Circle CCD130)

THE COMPLETE ROULETTE LIVE RECORDINGS
(Mosaic MD8-135) 8-CD Box

THE COMPLETE ROULETTE STUDIO RECORDINGS
(Mosaic MD10-149) 10-CD Box

COUNT ON THE COAST VOL. 1 & 2
(Phontastic CD 7555 & 7575)

THE BASIE BIG BAND
(Pablo PACD 2310 756 2)

KANSAS CITY 3 - FOR THE SECOND TIME
(Pablo 2310 878/OJC CD600)

DJANGO BATES

SUMMER FRUITS (AND UNREST)
(JMT 514 008 2)

A ubiquitous figure on the British jazz scene and one time member of Loose Tubes, Bates is very much his own man. A facile pianist and general keyboard man, he has continued to develop his technique on peck horn. Both are in evidence on *Summer Fruits*, an album that also affords the listener a chance to compare his Human Chain combo with his big band Delightful Precipice. Bates writes appropriate arrangements for both outfits and uses charts that make Precipice sound a lighter unit and Chain, in its non-augmented form, take on the illusion of being more full than a mere quartet. The broad scope of his instrumental horizons is also apparent when comparing the jaunty cut of his peck horn on 'Food For Plankton' with the sinuously, late night feeling of his piano on 'Little Petherick'. Django Bate's music already seems to be reaching out beyond jazz. It could be that he is now ready for more international exposure. BMcR

SIDNEY BECHET

THE BLUEBIRD SESSIONS
(RCA/Bluebird ND 90317)

JAZZ CLASSICS VOL. 1
(Blue Note CDP 7 89384 2)

SIDNEY BECHET & HIS AMERICAN FRIENDS VOL. 2
(Vogue 600173 2)

Like Louis Armstrong, Sidney Bechet was too big to be confined within the New Orleans regimen. He was one of the earliest jazz messengers, having been introduced into the famous Eagle Band of New Orleans by Bunk Johnson in 1912 before touring Texas and other southern states during World War I. He was among the first black musicians to migrate to Chicago and, in 1919, departed for Britain with Will Marion Cook's Southern Syncopated Orchestra. It was in London that he bought his first soprano saxophone, and it quickly became evident that, whereas he had always been able to use his clarinet to pierce an ensemble, his soprano completely dominated its surroundings, usurping the trumpet to upstage everyone in sight. Possibly this is because, while his style on both instruments was essentially the same, it was better suited to the saxophone. He was the first to produce mature and durable jazz on the saxophone, which he invested with an heraldic voice of romantic exuberance, pigmented by a broad and fierce vibrato. Every solo told a story, wherein were balanced swooping and sliding lines of great melodic and rhythmic intensity. But his impact on the general jazz scene was initially limited by long absences abroad, and he exerted little direct influence on the course of jazz, mainly because he was such a powerful and inimitable musical personality. His only major disciple was alto saxophonist Johnny Hodges, who rapidly imposed his own individuality on his instrument anyway. Bechet's own work in fact drew rigorous rhythmic and harmonic lines beyond which his music never developed. Thus, at any stage of his career, the music played is always loosely based upon New Orleans principles, though, unlike the revivalists, without conscious archaicism. Bechet returned to France after World War II, where his popularity was equal to that of any pop star, and remained there until his death in 1959. CS

THE KING JAZZ STORY VOL. 1-4
(Storyville STCD 8212 5)

SIDNEY BECHET & HIS AMERICAN FRIENDS VOL. 1
(Vogue 600122 2)

RECONTRES
(Vogue 600186 2)

BIX BEIDERBECKE

VOL. 1 SINGING THE BLUES
(CBS 466309)

The first white jazz legend (and still the most enigmatic), the ill-starred Bix virtually invented the original cool school. A cornet player from Iowa, he ditched the heated, epic approach of such as Armstrong and, instead, opted for a more crystalline tone and a lyrical approach , as much ice as fire, as much head as heart. Yet everything he created possessed a certain beauty which has remained unblemished by time. At one point a sideman with plodding big bands (Paul Whiteman and Jean Goldkette), Bix had the ability to instill even their elephantine arrangements with magic via solos often so brief that, in any other hands, they might have gone unnoticed. Hoagy Carmichael stated nothing but the truth when he claimed: "four notes of Bix could change your life". *Singing The Blues* possesses a title track that changed many lives. It's one of those melodies that has become a trumpeter's test piece, yet most of those who add it to their repertoire chose to simply repeat Bix's chorus on the basis that you can't change that which is perfect. Elsewhere on the album are some of Bix's finest tracks with the Frankie Trumbauer Orchestra and others, plus 'In A Mist', a remarkable piano solo that owes more to Debussy than to any jazz keyboardist. The search for Chet and Miles starts here. N.B. The prototype for a dynasty of live-fast-die-young icons, Beiderbecke (who died in 1931, age 28) was romaticised in Dorothy Baker's fictional novel *Young Man With A Horn* later to be turned into a movie starring Kirk Douglas. However, a little-seen documentary *Bix*, directed by Brigitte Berman is a more accurate accounting. FD

THE BIX BEIDERBECKE LEGEND
(RCA 74321-13037-2)

BIX LIVES
(Bluebird ND86845)

GEORGE BENSON

IT'S UPTOWN WITH THE GEORGE BENSON QUARTET
(Columbia 476902)

COMPACT JAZZ: GEORGE BENSON
(Verve 833292)

Bursting on to the scene in the early '60s as a sideman with organist Brother Jack McDuff, 19-year-old George Benson was very clearly a young guitarist of uncommon promise, playing a fluent, bluesy and melodic Wes Montgomery-inspired semi-acoustic guitar with show-stopping panache and imagination. But Benson's jazz instrumental career soon became held in check by the bigger commercial success he found when he introduced his super smooth soul-orientated singing. *It's Uptown* is a typical horn 'n' Hammond soul-jazz date from 1966, featuring organist Lonnie Smith and contains a long, imaginative version of 'Willow Weep For Me', a swinging 'Foggy Day' and some exemplary high-speed bop guitar on 'Myna Bird Blues'. The following year, Benson and Smith cropped up on Blue Note for Lou Donaldson's big selling *Alligator Bogaloo* and when, during the making of *Miles In The Sky*, the great trumpeter introduced a guitar into his line-up for the first time, he chose Benson. The Verve set is at its best on a handful of inspired small group performances with Herbie Hancock (p), Ron Carter (b) and

Billy Cobham (d), but there is some masterful playing in a big band setting, in a similar style to Wes Montgomery's own big band work with Verve. And, a surrogate Montgomery was how he was viewed when Benson moved over to CTI. By the mid-70s, George Benson was on Warner Brothers, an international superstar and responsible for the first jazz album to go platinum with *Breezin'* (Warner Brothers 2561992) which, for years to come, would become the soundtrack for hotel chain coffee shops the world over. Nowadays, not so much the pop chart crooner, Benson has become a fixture on the jazz festival circuit. LC

BUNNY BERIGAN

PORTRAIT OF BUNNY BERIGAN
(ASV CD AJA 5060)

If he had recorded nothing else, then Berigan's 1937 version of Gershwin's 'I Can't Get Started' would have assured him of a place in jazz history. A trumpet-player with a wonderfully warm and full tone, he somehow filled the niche between Bix and Louis Armstrong, as romatically lyrical as the former and nearly as heated as the latter in full flight. *Portrait* neatly encapsulates most of the Berigan career; the early gigs with bands headed by Paul Hamilton, Frank Trumbauer, Gene Gifford and Glenn Miller, the later high times with Benny Goodman, Tommy Dorsey and his own popular big band. Also present are those mid-'30s jaunts with his first and unsuccessful swing oufit plus other rewarding stopovers. Ever-exciting and able to deliver solos that seemed almost written to fix (it's hard to image Dorsey's 'Marie' kitted out with any trumpet solo other than Bunny's so-right, hotter-than-that few bars) Berigan is the legend that never quite made it and arguably the finest white trumpeter of them all. But regrettably, he followed the Bix path to failure, initially following Beiderbecke first into the Paul Whiteman band, then into an early grave, an abundance of bad booze putting an abrupt end to an equal abundance of classic choruses. FD

BUNNY BERIGAN 1935-1936
(Classics 734CD)

THE COMPLETE BUNNY BERIGAN VOL. III
(Bluebird NL 90439) 2-CD

LEON 'CHU' BERRY

A GIANT OF THE TENOR SAX
(Commodore CD8.24293)

Another of the many jazz musicians fated to die young, Leon 'Chu' Berry achieved perhaps the most opulent of all tenor sax tones, equally rich throughout the instrument's range. He came to prominence after travelling from his native Wheeling, West Virginia, to New York, where he rapidly built his reputation, first with Benny Carter's Chocolate Dandies, then with the bands of Teddy Hill, Fletcher Henderson and finally Cab Calloway. At a time when Coleman Hawkins was away in Europe, Chu became the leading tenor star of the day; Lester Young, who was with the fledgeling Count Basie Orchestra, was yet to be widely appreciated.

Chu's recordings reveal a *sans pareil* ability to build rhythmic excitement, avoiding any stickiness of phrasing his rich tone might have imposed. However, it did introduce an occasional sentimentality, and the superb 'Body & Soul' reveals both sides – the latter in the slow intro. Berry influenced a range of good Swing players and remained with Calloway until, late in 1941, he elected to travel ahead of the band bus on a trip from Ohio into Canada. His colleagues found his car crashed on the road 30 minutes out of town, but could not find a doctor in time to save him. CS

FLETCHER HENDERSON: A STUDY IN FRUSTRATION
(Columbia C3K 57596)

RED NORVO: KNOCK ON WOOD
(Affinity CD AFS 1017)

CAB CALLOWAY FEATURING CHU BERRY
(Columbia 471657 2)

CAB CALLOWAY: PENGUIN SWING
(Archives Of Jazz 380108 2)

ACKER BILK

THE TRADITIONAL JAZZ SCENE VOL. 1
(Teldec 43996)

THE VERY BEST OF ACKER BILK
(Pickwick PWKM 91)

He's billed as Mr Acker Bilk and once headed the Paramount Jazz Band, doyens of the 'late '50s and early '60s Brit Trad scene. Like Bob Wallis' Storyville Jazzmen and others of the ilk, Bilk's band wore the kind of vaudevillian bowlers and Edwardian silk waist-coats that ensured a place on prime-time TV shows. And often the show-biz thing and the comedic Wurzel-like approach disguised the fact that both Bilk and the various members of his band were musicians who knew their trade. A clarinet player of distinctive tone, with a perchant for middle-register work, Acker led his band to chart glory on such Top 20 sides as 'Summer Set', 'Buona Sera', 'That's My Home', 'Lonely' and 'A Taste Of Honey' but hit real paydirt by linking with the Leon Young String Chorale on 'Stranger On The Shore' and creating a quality easy-listening multi-million selling monster which he's been forced to constantly reprise ever since. A later (1976) hit in similar vein with 'Aria', just confirmed the view that Bilk's future was as an MOR icon and there has been little in the way of real jazz from him in recent years, although the Teldec collection reflects his leanings in an era (1959-63) when 'The Saints' still meant more than the cents, the Pickwick release mainly showcasing the later, ambient armchair attitude. FD

ED BLACKWELL

ED BLACKWELL PROJECT VOL. 1: "WHAT IT IS?"
(Enja ENJ 7089) [L]

ED BLACKWELL PROJECT VOL. 2: "WHAT IT BE LIKE?"
(Enja ENJ 8054) [L]

This New Orleans drummer was playing with Ornette Coleman as far back as 1951. However, by the time anyone (Contemporary's Lester Koenig) was interested in affording Coleman studio time (1958), Blackwell had returned to the Crescent City participating in countless R&B record dates. He rejoined Coleman in 1960 (*This Is Our Music*) and again for two further stints (1967-68 and 1970-73).

Inbetween, Blackwell toured with Coltrane, Dolphy, Cherry, Monk and Randy Weston. With Dewey Redman filling Ornette's vacant chair, Blackwell banded together with Don Cherry (tpt) and Charlie Haden (b) in 1976 as Coleman repertory players Old And New Dreams. To many, Blackwell (along with Tony Williams) is regarded as the most important of post-Hard Bop sticksmen. Drawing heavily on the directness of his R&B heritage, Blackwell often instilled his logical approach with almost vocal-like qualities. Taped live just two months prior to his death in October 1992, (and three days short of his 63rd birthday), the Project recordings further highlight his richness of style, affirming the belief that Ed Blackwell never made a bad record. RC

OLD & NEW DREAMS
(ECM 1154)

PLAYING
(ECM 1205)

ONE FOR BLACKWELL
(Black Saint 120113)

ART BLAKEY

A NIGHT AT BIRDLAND VOL. 1 & 2
(Blue Note CDP 7 46519/20 2) [L]

CAFE BOHEMIA VOL. 1 & 2
(Blue Note CDP 7 46521/22 2) [L]

WITH THELONIOUS MONK
(Atlantic 781332)

MOANIN'
(Blue Note CDP 7 46516 2)

A band on the threshold of greatest. The 1954 Birdland session had Clifford Brown (tpt) and Lou Donaldson (as) producing fiesty front line fireworks while pianist Horace Silver frantically drove the rhythm section equally as hard as Blakey. The Bohemia date (of a year later) now had Silver vigourously shaping the group from within (though not contributing any originals) as Kenny Dorham (tpt) and Hank Mobley (ts) fixed the Hard Bop house-style for the next three generations of conscripts that followed with 'Minor's Holiday' and 'Sportin' Crowd'. Soon, differences of opinion caused Silver to quit taking Dorham, Mobley, and bassist Doug Watkins with him, leaving Blakey alone with just the name and the task of restocking both personnel and repertoire. Saxmen Jackie McLean and Johnny Griffin passed rapidly through the ranks, but it wasn't until (1959) when Benny Golson (ts) was hired as MD along with Lee Morgan (tpt) and Bobby Timmons (p) that the Messengers regained a real sense of purpose. However, prior to that, there was one truly memorable event.
Of all drummers, nobody attended to Thelonious Monk's rhythmic needs more perceptively than Blakey. Nobody else came near. With Bill Hardman on trumpet and Johnny Griffin on tenor, their solitary meeting (convened in 1957) proved to be of master-class dimensions. Never again would Monk's 'Evidence', 'In Walked Bud', 'I Mean You' etc, be given such an invigorating rub-down. A spell in Paris, knocked the Morgan-Golson-Timmons line-up into shape with Golson scoring the soundtracks for movies *Des Femmes Disparaissent* (Fontana 834 752 2) and *Les Liaisons Dangereuses*

(Fontana 812 017 2), adding 'Blues March (for Europe)' and 'Whisper Not' to the book. By now, Blakey's Messengers were on permanent overdrive while his awesome press rolls had reached China syndrome proportions. Back on Blue Note, 1959's *Moanin'* charts the rebirth of the band just prior to Golson handing over to Wayne Shorter and with *Big Beat* (Blue Note CDP 7 46400 2) – to which Shorter contributed 'The Chess Players' and 'Lester Left Town' – established the Messengers as Hard Bop's undefeated heavyweights. *The Complete Blue Note Recordings of Art Blakey's 1960 Jazz Messengers* (Mosaic MD6 141) gives the full breath-taking picture by installing eight classic albums on six-CDs. (*The Big Beat, A Night In Tunisia, Like Someone In Love, Meet You At The Jazz Corner Of The World Vol. 1 & 2, Roots And Herbs, The Witch Doctor* and *The Freedom Rider*).

In 1961, a drastic overhaul which saw the departure of Morgan and Timmons and the introduction of Freddie Hubbard and Cedar Walton plus trombonist Curtis Fuller as extra man, again revitalized the band. For some, this even takes precedence over the Morgan/Shorter line-up. It was also the last great Messengers line-up until 1979, when Blakey discovered teen trumpeter Wynton Marsalis, the wheel turned full circle and for a new generation of musicians such as saxmen Bobby Watson, Branford Marsalis, Jean Toussaint, Donald Harrison, trumpeters Terence Blanchard, Wallace Roney and pianists Mulgrew Miller, Benny Green, the Messengers became the centre of the universe. For a band with such an illustrious recording career, the 2-CD *The Best Of Art Blakey & The Jazz Messengers* (Blue Note CDP 793205 2) is highly recommended in that it covers the group's entire career right up to Marsalis and Blanchard. RC

MOSAIC
(Blue Note CDP 7 46523 2)

BUHAINA'S DELIGHT
(Blue Note CDP 7 84104 2)

FREE FOR ALL
(Blue Note CCP 7 84170 2)

LIVE IN STOCKHOLM 1959
(Dragon DRCD 182) [L]

LIVE IN STOCKHOLM 1960
(Dragon DRCD 160) [L]

UGETSU
(Riverside 9464/OJC CD 145) [L]

TERENCE BLANCHARD

TERENCE BLANCHARD
(Columbia 468388)

SIMPLY STATED
(Columbia 471364)

A stipulation for any out-going Messenger graduate was that they had to nominate their own successor. Wynton Marsalis chose fellow New Orleanian, 20-year old Terence Blanchard to replace him as both trumpet player and musical director in the Jazz Messengers. It proved a wise choice; *Art Collection* (Concord CCD 4495). After four productive years (1982-1986) – during which he doubled the front line to four horns – Blanchard left to kicked off a solo career by first, co-leading a spirited quintet with fellow-Messenger, altoist Donald Harrison. Soon an association with moviemaker Spike Lee resulted in Blanchard soundtracking *Mo' Better Blues* and *Malcolm 'X'* (Columbia 473676) while elsewhere he is responsible for the incidental non-rock film score for the pre-Beatlemania *Backbeat*.

Having taken the pilgrim's trail that leads from Dizzy Gillespie – by way of Freddie Hubbard to Woody Shaw, *Simply Stated* proved Blanchard to be a much finer player than often given credit for, if slightly eclipsed (critically) by the more higher-profiled Wallace Roney and Roy Hargrove. RC

THE BILLIE HOLIDAY SONGBOOK
(Columbia 475926)

CARLA BLEY

ESCALATOR OVER THE HILL
(ECM 839 310 2)

DUETS
(Watt 20)

FLEUR CARNIVORE
(Watt 21)

A perennial pollwinner, no evaluation of Carla Bley's music would be complete without drawing attention to her incredible 'chrono-transduction' *Escalator Over the Hill*. It is an opera with a score full of atmospheric defiance and chuckle tune flippancy. The jazz solos tell their own story; Roswell Rudd (tmb) is outspoken, Gato Barbieri (ts) garrulous,. Don Cherry (tpt) humorous and John McLaughlin (gtr) full of Eastern promise. Probably the best chronotransduction you will hear. As a pianist, in her own right, she is something of an 'after hours' entertainer. She is rhythmically mobile but her solos and her counterpoint with Steve Swallow on *Duets* take her momentarily into musical cul-de-sacs. Her spatial awareness, cunning use of dissonance and her conscious rubato guarantee her a way out. Many of her smaller touring bands of the eighties had a circus tent quality, with trombonist Gary Valente sometimes exploiting his instrument's association with the sawdust ring. He avoids those extremes on the 1988 *Fleur Carnivore* and is one of several soloists who enhance a superb Bley exercise in fine composing and outstanding arranging. BMcR

PAUL BLEY

IN THE EVENINGS OUT THERE
(ECM 1488 517 469 2)

Paul Bley was that rare animal, an Ornette Coleman pianist. He also worked with Charles Mingus, married Carla and was a founder member of the Jazz Composer's Guild. In between times, he was also a highly original pianist in a style that fell between Mal Waldron and Muhal Richard Abrams but owed nothing in detail to either. When it was fashionable (early seventies), he plugged into the electric instrument but his strong linearity and refined rhythmic sense hurried him back to acoustic reality and so he has remained. Fortunately, it was an all purpose style and *The Paul Bley Quartet* (ECM 1365) and the atonal based *12 (+6) In A Row* (hat ART CD 6081) show how well he wrote for and supported horns. The 1991*In The Evenings* only makes it ahead of these because, as a representative issue, it offers Bley in various hats, from solo to quartet. His absence on three of the twelve titles might deter some listeners but this is a superbly atmospheric set. To paraphrase Lord Buckley (of 'The Naz'), 'Bley never did anything simple'. BMcR

ARTHUR BLYTHE ✗ Tone

THE GRIP
(India Navigation IN 1029 CD)

One senses that altoist Arthur Blythe gives little for what critics may opine. He arrived, Black Arthur a ready cut stone, in New York in 1974. Little was known about him but he was accepted by his peers because he was good! Furthermore, as he rapidly demonstrated in the groups of Chico Hamilton, Gil Evans and in the jam sessions of the loft movement, he was a highly original stylist. His wide vibrato and strongly rhythmic approach were from an earlier era. He shunned open ended or abstract playing but the manner in which he worked with 'themes' fully justified the claim that he was involved in freer attitudes.

His finest work, orginally on two LP's and recorded live in 1977 is merged on *The Grip*. It confirms him as one of the most rhythmically secure saxophonist since Sonny Rollins; his solos a mixture of richly decorated runs, pertinent, single notes, rumbustous riff figures and a little warm hearted r & b for good measure. Following his more commercial flotations in the eighties, he returned to more creative waters later in the decade and the 1991 *Hipmotism* (Enja 6088 - 2) presents these righteous values. Could be the thinking man's David Sanborn – just a touch older. BMcR

LESTER BOWIE

THE 5TH POWER ✗ Trumpet ?
(Black Saint 120020)

ALL THE MAGIC!/THE ONE AND ONLY
(ECM 1246/47 810 625)

I ONLY HAVE EYES FOR YOU
(ECM 1296 825 902)

Lester Bowie is one of a number of contemporary and free jazz musicians who have used elements of R&B and gospel music to re-inject jazz with the earthy individualism that had originally distinguished the music. A founding member of the Art Ensemble Of Chicago, Bowie is a trumpeter who specialises in an often demanding, post-Ayler free-jazz language, based around a funky thesaurus of growls, smears, roars and cracked notes. *The 5th Power* dates from 1978, and features brilliant bassist Malachi Favors, Arthur Blythe (as), pianist/vocalist Amina Myers and Philip Watson (d) playing some fragmented but exciting free improvisations with an unusual rapport. The ECM box set contains discs from 1983. *All The Magic!* features an uplifting slow blues dedicated to Louis Armstrong, with words by Fontella Bass, and a version of Ayler's famous 'Ghosts'; while *The One And Only* is a daring solo recording, pitting Bowie's expressive trumpet with various percussive and natural sounds. An enjoyable 1985 date by Bowie's celebrated 9-piece Brass Fantasy (trumpets, trombones, French horn, tuba and drums) produced *I Only Have Eyes For You* featuring subtle, bluesy arrangements, and some fine soloing by Bowie himself. LC

RUBY BRAFF

MEL POWELL TRIOS
(Vanguard CD 662223)

THE BEST I'VE HEARD
(Vogue CDVJD 519)

SAILBOAT IN THE MOONLIGHT
(Concord CCD 296)

Back in the less articulate days of jazz criticism appreciation of a musician was frequently summed up in the expression 'he really wails' Ruby Braff really wails. Those long, expressive squeezed out notes bent into long glissandos, falling away into flurries of fast runs (almost as though he was afraid of being caught out in an excess of feeling) are hallmarks of Braff's unmissable cornet playing.

If personal sound is any mark of a musician's standing then Braff's instantly recognisable style puts him up there with Louis, Miles and Dizzy. His path has been a hard one – working (or rather mainly not working) in Mainstream in the Bop Era. At heart the tough, little, no compromise cornettist is a Romantic cynic. He has survived illness, lack of work and neglect to champion his kind of jazz. Until the arrival of Scott Hamilton and the New England Gang twenty years later Braff was the only new boy in Mainstream City.

The superb double album *The Best I've Heard* with the George Barnes Quartet 1973-75 provides him with a Musical Twin. The telepathic interplay on 'Looking At You' is comparable with the best of any other jazz duo. Barnes was a fast player with a prodigious technique. His zippy runs where the notes seem to balance precariously, hovering at the end of each phrase, lend an unpredicable excitement to his playing and Braff responds with typical aggression. 'It Don't Mean A Thing' is taken at breakneck tempo but with no sense of tension and Braff is never happier than when challenged. He produces some outrageous inventions.

Date-stamped 1954, *Mel Powell Trios*, highlights the early Braff, with eight tracks from the *Thigamagig* album which established him as a player of astonishing maturity. His bright, yet mellow, tone with frequent plunges into the lower register stamp him as a great original. 'Your'e My Thrill' is worth the price of admission alone and the roller coaster version of 'Button Up Your Overcoat' is a joy. *Sailboat in the Moonlight* pairs him with fellow-traveller Scott Hamilton on tenor and some of the New England team of John Bunch (a first choice of such players) on piano Chris Flory (gtr) Phil Flanagan (b) and Chuck Riggs (d) in an invigorating set which drives both players into toe-to-toe duels the apogee of which is the electrifying 'Lover Come Back to Me'. Braff still remains, arguably, the most underated musician in jazz. JM

ANTHONY BRAXTON

THREE COMPOSITIONS OF NEW JAZZ
(Delmark DS 423)

PERFORMANCE (QUARTET) 1979
(hat ART CD 6044)

The 1968 *Three Compositions* was Anthony Braxton's first recording as a leader. It conferred the same value on both space and sound in the jazz making tapestry. It used the human voice, encouraged the vocalisation of instrumental tones and was distinguishable as a product of the sixties Chicago free school. Braxton followed the Art

Ensemble Of Chicago to Europe in 1969 and became enamoured of the experiments in free improvisation that were going on there. He formed Circle (ECM 843 163) with Chick Corea and pursued a policy divided between the free and the orthodox. *In The Tradition* (SteepleChase 1015) was Braxton's obligatory answer to the sceptics. Yes! He could play standards but it was the likes of *Performance* that best described what he did. Braxton called it 'continual evolution' rather than thematic development because there was no sequential progress. Braxton's most successful group of the eighties teamed him with Marilyn Crispell (p), Mark Dresser (b) and Gerry Hemingway (d). *Quartet (London)*, essential listening when reading Graham Lock's *Forces In Motion* book, presented continually changing moods in each of its twelve titles and, although all concerned played well, Braxton's stunning clarinet on 40F is the work of a major jazzman. Braxton did serve a probation in big band experiments and his unique combo style did translate, often via notation, quite successfully. *Composition No 96* (Leo LRCD 169), dedicated to Karlheinz Stockhausen, was a modest success and best described as an extension of his normal, improvisational process. *Eugene* is included because the failures of outstanding players are often more significant. He used the Northwest Creative Orchestra and they claimed to find the music 'difficult'. Only on one title do they achieve the momentum Braxton surely had in mind and a doomy atmsophere too often prevails. BMcR

QUARTET (LONDON) 1985
(Leo LRCD 200/1)

EUGENE (1989)
(Black Saint 126062)

MICHAEL BRECKER

NOW YOU SEE IT. . . (NOW YOU DON'T)
(GRP GR 922)

THE MICHAEL BRECKER BAND LIVE - 1989
(Jazz Door JD 1230) [L]

Michael Brecker may well be regarded as one of the most influential of post-Coltrane tenormen, but the paradox is that (too often) he gives the impression of preferring to work in the shadow of others as a highly sought-after sessioneer rather than holding centre stage. Perhaps, aware of his value, Brecker is more attracted to the kind of pay-cheque (and prestige) that recording and touring with artists of the calibre of Paul Simon brings. Similarly, he and trumpet playing brother Randy, probably made far more off their commercially successful/technically brilliant jazz-funk band, The Brecker Brothers (1975-81) than from sorties into straight-ahead jazz. But then, when did Michael Brecker ever sign a blood-pact stipulating that he would only perform in a single style. As things stand, since his promising eponymous debut on Impulse in 1987, Brecker hasn't pursued a solo recording career with the kind of vigour one would have hoped for. Perhaps, because in his role as session star, Brecker is (often) only required to fashion a short, focused solo, there's a reluctance to make the necessary commitment as a leader. For most of the *Now You See It* sessions there's too much borrowing from other (familiar) sources and, it's only on 'Meaning Of The Blues' and 'Minsk', that Brecker truly gives the impression that he's breaking sweat. In person, it's an entirely different matter. *Live* goes some way to blowing holes in such theories. Recorded at the 1989 Montreux Jazz Festival, Brecker is captured in the go-for-broke mood that was once exclusive to Sonny Rollins. ferociously slugging it out with guitarist Mike Stern (transformed from reviled smacked-our jazz metal grunger to muso role model), Joey Calderazzo on piano and synthesizers while Jeff Andrews (b) and Adam Nussbaum (d) rock the rhythms and the house. Subtle it isn't – Calderazzo's sonic synthe surfing on the closing 'Original Rays' – may well evoke the kitchen sink scenario, but in terms of energy expounded, overall Brecker's band is nothing short of impressive. RC

COLLECTION VOL. 1
(RCA Novus 90442)

THE COLLECTION VOL. 2
(RCA Novus 83076)

BOB BROOKMEYER

JIMMY GIUFFRE: HOLLYWOOD & NEWPORT 1957-58
(Fresh Sound FSR CD 1026) [L]

BOB BROOKMEYER & FRIENDS
(Columbia 468413)

THE QUINTETS
(Vogue 7432111503 2)

GERRY MULLIGAN: LIVE AT STORYVILLE
(Pacific Jazz CDP 7 94472 2) [L]

With *Traditionalism Revisited*, *The Street Swingers* and *Kansas City Revisited* still awaiting widespread CD reissue, Brookmeyer's best available work is in the company of others; most notably Gerry Mulligan, Stan Getz, Clark Terry, Zoot Sims and Jimmy Giuffre.
A product of Kansas City, Brookmeyer has more or less made (the seldom used) valve trombone his very own while his piano playing is best exemplified on the two-pianos-and-rhythm, *The Ivory Hunters* (Blue Note CDP 8 27324 2) where he duets with uncanny rapport with Bill Evans on a six-pack of standards from 'Honeysuckle Rose' to 'I Got Rhythm'. Having a perfected a rustic, dry-roasted tone, Brookmeyer seems to constantly look back (almost wistfully) to past times.
No more so than on the Newport section of the Fresh Sound release which features Giuffre's *Jazz On A Summer's Day* soundtrack and the memorable 'The Train And The River', which accompanied the opening credits. The line-up of just saxophone, valve trombone and Jim Hall's guitar would appear to be courting disaster, but in a succession of complex criss-cross manoeuvre's and split-second timing this all-swinging threesome avoid any head-on collisions. Recorded at a time when the Mulligan Quartet were the hit of the 1954 Paris Jazz Festival, *Quintets* finds Brookmeyer effectively utilising rhythm pals Red Mitchell (b) and Frank Isola (d) plus Henri Renaud (p) and Jimmy Gourley (gtr) for coherent readings of '9.20 Special' and 'Loverman' etc. Ten years later *Friends* proves a more satisfactory excursion in that Stan Getz (ts), Gary Burton (vib), Herbie Hancock (p), Ron Carter (b) and Elvin Jones (d) never attempt to wrestle the date away from Brookmeyer. Also worth checking are records by the Thad Jones-Mel Lewis Orchestra and Mulligan's Concert Big Band for which Brookmeyer wrote arrangements. RC

TINA BROOKS

TRUE BLUE
(Blue Note B2 28975)

FREDDIE HUBBARD/OPEN SESAME
(Blue Note CDP 7 84040 2)

When not kicking around New York with local Latin bands, Tina (Harold Floyd) Brooks probably spent as much time blowing tenor behind R&B hitmakers Sonny Thompson, Charles Brown, Joe Morris and Amos Milburn as he did scratching a living on the city's competative jazz scene. While making good account of himself on Blue Note dates fronted by Jimmy Smith *The Sermon*, Kenny Burrell *Live At The Five Spot*, Freddie Hubbard *Open Sesame*, Freddie Redd *Shades Of Redd*, Jackie McLean *Jackie's Bag* and understudying for the alto star in the New York stage production of the controversial drugs drama *The Connection* (and also cutting a stage score album with Howard McGhee), this was the only album to be issued under Brooks' own name during his all-too-short lifetime: drugs terminated his career in 1961 and his life in 1974 at the age of 42. It was following the emergence of two posthumous albums in Japan (later collated with further material on Mosaic's vinyl-only box *The Complete Blue Note Recordings Of Tina Brooks Quintets*) that Brooks' neglected skills could be placed into reasonable perspective.

Recorded in June 1960, *True Blue* featured Freddie Hubbard on whose *Open Sesame*, Brooks had appeared a week earlier; even composing the title track. Both albums are exceptional, awash with fine playing from both hornmen while Brooks' dead-centre originals including 'Miss Hazel' 'Good Old Soul' (released as a single) and 'True Blue' itself should have had him off and running.

As with Hank Mobley, with whom he shares understated stylistic traits, Brooks' approach was somewhat at odds with the en vogue hard tenor approach of Rollins and Coltrane and didn't capture the immagination of the public in the same way as those who hired his services. RC

CLIFFORD BROWN

PARIS COLLECTION VOL. 1-3
(Vogue 74321154612/54622/54632)

IN CONCERT
(Vogue 655602) [L]

BROWNIE
(EmArCy 838306-16) 10-CD box

AT BASIN STREET
(EmArCy 814648) [L]

When, in 1950, Fats Navarro's personal excesses felled him at 26, it was left to Clifford Brown (20) to further articulate the new gospel according to Diz. As fate decreed, Brownie's lifespan may have amounted to one year less than Navarro's but still time enough to prove himself one of the undisputed greats before perishing in a fatal autosmash in June 1956.

Viewed in total, the three volume *Paris Collection* (covert recordings made in 1953 by almost all of Lionel Hampton's band against his expressed wishes) amount to a remarkable tribute to the art of moonlighting. Here, Brownie fronts a quartet then, with altoist Gigi

Gryce supplying the charts a sextet and finally a swaggering Big Band with a sense of purpose that belies his age and experience.

The first part of '54, found Brownie on Blue Note alongside Lou Donaldson (as) and Horace Silver (p) in Art Blakey's pre-Messengers quintet (*A Night At Birdland Vol. 1 & 2*) but by mid-year he switched coasts to co-lead a quintet in Los Angeles with bop's other master drummer, Max Roach. It was here that his (still) unmatched brilliance blossomed to where a Hard Bop trumpet dynasty that began with Donald Byrd and Lee Morgan by way of Freddie Hubbard, Blue Mitchell, Booker Little, Bill Hardman, Woody Shaw through to Wynton Marsalis, Terence Blanchard, Tom Harrell, Roy Hargrove and Wallace Roney continues to owe more to Brownie than probably anyone else.

Brownie's range was expansive and as such, was never in danger of being compromised into sacrificing tonal quality in pursuit of speed: an eloquent player, his fluency of thought, puckish humour, the on-the-hoof dexterity with which he constantly formulated his ideas, the melodic invention of his compositions ('Joy Spring', 'Daahoud', 'Sandu'), but above all the sheer beauty of his exhuberant full-bodied brassy tone elevated the star-crossed trumpeter to fully paid-up God-like status. Equal to any other similar unit of the time, Max Roach-Clifford Brown Incorporated was fortunate to have such frontline partners as tenormen Teddy Edwards, Harold Land (*In Concert*) and, finally, the great Sonny Rollins. Indeed, Land's role has become overshadowed due to him abdicating his position to Rollins who took over for what were to be the last six remaining months of Brownie's short life to create such master-pieces as 'Love Is A Many Splendoured Thing'. As the 10-CD *Brownie* box set substantiates, this is state-of-the-art hard bop which has become an even more enticing experience than when it was first recorded. RC

JAZZ IMMORTAL
(*Pacific Jazz CDP 7 46850 2*)

COMPACT JAZZ
(*EmArCy 842933*)

MARION BROWN

SONGS OF LOVE AND REGRET
(*Freelance FRL CD 006*)

Like many of the second generation of free form players, Marion Brown's career has been a retreat from revolution. The sixties albums for ESP and Impulse had demonstrated him capable of bringing adventurous, free elements to his own very deliberate compositions but they have not yet made it to the CD racks. Having said this, the ZYX company's reissue programme may yet see the release of *Marion Brown Quartet* (ESP 1022). A pre-view of Butch Morris' 'conduction' principles coloured some of his seventies work but his solo playing became more conservative. *Reeds 'N' Vibes* (IAI 123 855 2) with Gunter Hampel endorsed this trait, pointing him into a chromatically realised hinterland in which melody lines are 'gently' fractured. The process continued in the eighties with *Songs Of Love*, where his wispy persuasiveness on the solo Hurry Sundown and on duets like Blue Monk and Golden Lady, with Mal Waldron, took him back to near orthodox improvisational methods. There would seem to be some merit in viewing his career in reverse. BMcR

DAVE BRUBECK

JAZZ AT OBERLIN
(Fantasy 3-245/OJC CD 046) [L]

JAZZ AT COLLEGE OF THE PACIFIC
(Fantasy 3-223/OJC CD 047) [L]

STARDUST
(Fantasy FCD 24728)

TIME OUT
(Columbia 62068)

TIME SIGNATURES: A CAREER RETROSPECTIVE
(Columbia 472776) 4-CD Box

Jazz fans can sometimes prove to be amongst the most intolerant of people. Forget Modern vs Trad, as fame beckoned, hatred of McCarthyite intensity was aimed at Brubeck. His crime? There were those blow-hards who had convinced themselves that the pianist's classically-inclined stance, his penchant for two-fisted bombast when matched to the ethereal sound of his alto blowing cohort, Paul Desmond, was openly subverting the true essence of jazz. This (not rock 'n' roll) was the Devil's music! Quite the contrary, Brubeck was a time traveller and musical adventurer. And, one of the most successful of all jazz popularizers. Some have preference for the Quartet's earlier and less self-conscious days on Fantasy and a musical cache mainly comprised of standards 'The Way You Look Tonight', 'All The Things You Are', 'These Foolish Things' 'Perdido' (*Jazz at Oberlin*), 'For All We Know', 'I'll Never Smile Again', 'Trolly Song', (*College Of The Pacific*), that made this particular Fab Four the undisputed darlings of the Oxford loafers generation. It was this loyal Campus following that Brubeck took with him when moving to Columbia Records.

As events demonstrated, an even wider audience would soon favour Brubeck's more adventurous excursions. Sensing now was the moment to progress away from such standard fare and 'old school' time signatures, Brubeck and Desmond (now, with drummer Joe Morello) didn't anticipate what a quantum leap his 1959 album *Time Out* would prove. The quartet already enjoyed pop-like acceptance, but it was to be both this album plus international jukebox smashes 'Take Five' (composed by Desmond) with its then-innovative 5/4 rhythm, 'It's A Raggy Waltz' and 'Blue Rondo A La Turk' followed by a succession of concept albums *Dave Digs Disney* (Columbia 471250), *Gone With The Wind* (Columbia 450984) and much-covered compostions ('In Your Own Sweet Way' and 'The Duke') that made them life-long media superstars. As the success enjoyed by Gerry Mulligan, Chico Hamilton, Chet Baker, George Shearing, Shorty Rogers, Red Norvo, Oscar Peterson, Cal Tjader, Jay & Kai, Jimmy Smith, Thelonious Monk, Miles Davis, Jimmy Giuffre plus The Jazz Messengers and the Modern Jazz Quartet clearly demonstrated, the Dave Brubeck Quartet emerged during a period when it was essential that the overall sound of a combo and not just its featured soloists had to be uniquely distinctive. As the title implies, the 4-CD box *Time Signatures: A Career Retrospective* offers such detailed coverage with tracks cherry-picked from 1946 through to 1991 (encounters as diverse as those with Leonard Bernstein, Charles Mingus, Gerry Mulligan, Jimmy Rushing, Louis Armstrong etc,) that it should seriously be considered as a first purchase. RC

THE DAVE BRUBECK OCTET
(Fantasy 3-239/OJC CD 101)

THE DAVE BRUBECK QUARTET
FEATURING PAUL DESMOND IN CONCERT
(Fantasy 60-013) [L]

THE GREAT CONCERTS
(Columbia 462403) [L]

RAY BRYANT

MONTREUX 77
(Pablo Live 2308 201/OJCCD 371) [L]

60TH BIRTHDAY SPECIAL VOL. 2
(EmArCy 512 933-2)

To some extent, Ray Bryant's recording career is divided in two. The important point is that both sections offer superb piano playing by a man habitually taken for granted. House pianist at Philadelphia's Blue Note in the fifties, he worked with the greats. His backings for singers like Carmen McRae and Ella Fitzgerald were examplary and there is something about his relaxed, rolling sense of delivery and his unique manipulation of bebop that defies catagory. His excellent output for Pablo and his legendary *Alone With The Blues* set await ratification on CD but the fine *Montreux 77* live performance is available to display his talents to the full.

Following this productive period, he dropped out of the recording limelight. He claimed to be less than satisfied with himself and vowed that he would wait until the moment was right before returning. That moment was certainly right when he recorded his 1992 *60th Birthday Special Vol. 2* (*Vol. 1* is EmArCy 512 764-2). The recommendation of volume two is based purely on its programme and the way that material as different as Oleo, Lil' Darlin', Whisper Not and Round Midnight can be splendidly Bryantized. Both albums are rather special. BMcR

KENNY BURRELL

ON VIEW AT THE FIVE SPOT CAFE VOL. 1
(Blue Note 46538 2) [L]

GUITAR FORMS
(Verve 825576 2)

As a guitarist, Kenny Burrell is equipped with the most mellow of tones, a genuine feeling for the blues and a grasp of bop principles that make him the consummate performer. He is also the musical version of the character actor who ruthlessly steals scenes from the star. With him as leader, *The Five Spot*, from 1959, reverses that role. It finds him playing superbly and himself having to accommodate the forceful drumming of Art Blakey and the insinuating talent of tenor saxophonist Tina Brooks.

Burrell's sheer professionalism has meant that he has been sideman on more than 200 record dates, supporting legendary artists such as Billie Holiday, Stan Getz, John Coltrane, Sonny Rollins and Jimmy Smith. Topping these, if possible, is his own date in collaboration with master arranger, Gil Evans. *Guitar Forms* has him solo, or with a rhythm team, on four titles but it is the remainder that counts. It presents a superb wedding of Kenny Burrell's caressing guitar lines, and a musical backdrop to enhance their graceful flight. At the same time it perhaps passes the character actor's cap back to Gil Evans. BMcR

GARY BURTON

THE NEW QUARTET
(ECM 1030)

TIMES SQUARE
(ECM 1111)

Beginning in the early sixties, Burton by-passed the horn-derived style of Lionel Hampton, Red Norvo and Milt Jackson, developing instead a pianistic, four-mallet approach influenced technically and aesthetically by pianist Bill Evans. The result could be cloyingly insubstantial, but *The New Quartet*, with Burton's favourite guitarist Mick Goodrick (a model for later Burton guitarists John Scofield and Pat Metheny), produced a rich yet uncluttered texture in which Abraham Laboriel's bass and Goodrick's chunky guitar acted as welcome ballast for Burton's featherweight vibes. Ever unsure of his writing ability, Burton came by some excellent tunes here too, with Keith Jarrett's beautiful 'Coral' and Carla Bley's 'Olhos De Gato' outstanding numbers in a distinguished pad. Despite his rejection of bebop convention, Burton showed on the 1978 *Times Square* that he could swing as fiercely as the rest. His sound vaporises as readily as ever, but the hard bopping team of Steve Swallow (b) and Roy Haynes (d), plus Tiger Okoshi's joyful trumpet work, provide the perfect foil. Swallow wrote half of the numbers here, and another fine reading of 'Coral' does not come amiss. MG

HOTEL HELLO
(ECM 1055)

REUNION
(GRP 9598 2)

DONALD BYRD

AT THE HALF NOTE CAFE VOL. 1 & 2
(Blue Note CDP 7 46539 2/46540 2) [L]

BLACK BYRD
(Blue Note CDP 7 84466 2)

The fact that at one time trumpeter Byrd had the distinction of being one the most recorded jazzmen ever, doesn't necessarily equate such Herculean prowess with artistic achievments. In many instances, it was the kind of jobbing sessions common to Blue Note, Prestige, Savoy and other East-Coast labels using Rudy Van Gelder's studio in the mid-to-late fifties. Brief stints with The Jazz Messengers and Horace Silver's Quintet empowered Byrd with disciplinary skills which he brought to the successful hard bop quintet he organised with baritone saxist Pepper Adams of which the 1960 'live' Half Note Cafe date has the slight edge with 'My Girl Shirl' being the highlight of Vol. 1 while Duke Pearson's sprightly 'Jeannine', which opens Vol. 2 has become a much-used jazz-dance floor-filler. A Doctor of Ethnomusicology, the early '70s saw Byrd undergoing a drastic personality change translating his awareness of Black America's social dilemmas and the importance of both James Brown and Motown, into a passionate pursuit of fusioneering. This resulted in Blue Note's first million-selling LP, *Black Byrd* and the trumpeter abandoning jazz for a band of young funketeers of the same name. A recent return to playing has seen Byrd dividing his activities between sessions for Landmark and collaborations with rapper Guru and the Jazzamatazz project. RC

CAB CALLOWAY

THE KING OF HI-DE-HO 1934-1947
(Giants Of Jazz CD 53096)

Though the Calloway big band featured its fair share of great musicians, everthing eventually came down to the showmanship and charisma of its larger-than-life leader. The arrangments might be fine but his suits were more impressive. Drape-shaped and boasting sufficient excess cloth to supply enough tux's for your average sextet, they occupied general game-time till the first three or four tunes had rattled round the Cotton Club or whichever upmarket venue the band was playing. Cab's vocals too were startling. Full of dipstick nonsense, demanding crowd response – with Cab yelling 'Hi-de-hi-de-ho' and the believers echoing 'Ho-de-ho-de-ho'. Additionally there was a smattering of scat and tunes meant to trouble. And when jumpin' jive led to rock 'n' roll Cab just tuned in, no problem at all. Everything's here – the crowd-pleasing 'Minnie The Moocher', a 1942 reprise of Cab's 1932 No.1, through to 'The Calloway Boogie', a 1947 roots of rock heat-raiser on which the hip one reveals 'We play waltzes, bebop and jive, but here's the kind of music that keeps you alive.' Names that include ill-fated tenorman Chu Berry (magnificent on 'Ghost Of A Chance') Dizzy Gillespie, Jonah Jones (tpt), Tyree Glenn (tmb) and drummer Cozy Cole indicate why the pay-roll was higher than most. Cab was still making movies (*The Blues Brothers*) and drawing capacity crowds up until his death in 1994, at the age of 87. FD

BEST OF THE BIG BANDS
(CBS 466618 2)

BENNY CARTER

THE CHRONOLOGICAL BENNY CARTER 1936
(Classics 541CD)

THE CHRONOLOGICAL BENNY CARTER 1940-41
(Classics 631CD)

JAZZ GIANT
(Contemporary 7555/OJC CD 167)

3, 4, 5 THE VERVE SMALL GROUP SESSIONS
(Verve 849 395 2)

COSMOPOLITE – THE OSCAR PETERSON SESSIONS
(Verve 521 673 2)

Pick a record. Any record. And as long as it's by Benny Carter, you've an ace in your hand. Benny's done everything that's worth doing in jazz and, amazingly for someone born in a tough New York neighbourhood in 1907, is still doing it. Though mainly considered as an altoist who, stylistically, has much in common with the swing era approach of Willie Smith and Johnny Hodges, he's played trumpet, clarinet, tenor, trombone and piano, while he's also an oustanding writer and arranger, who's shaped everything from charts for the BBC Dance Orchestra through to scores for such films as *Stormy Weather*, *A Man Called Adam* and *Buck And The Preacher*. Not surprisingly, his records are diverse, spanning many eras and many fashions. The 1936 set is basically the old *Swingin' At Maida Vale* session, made with the cream of Brit-jazz during Benny's days at the Beeb while the 1940-41 dates represent some of the finest of Carter's pre-Pearl Harbour playing. *Jazz Giant* has the then mere 50 year-old chummying-up with tenorist Ben Webster against a late '50s West Coast setting, kinda Benny Goes Lighthouse with a ye-olde songbook, the band (Frank Rosolino (tmb), Barney Kessel (gtr), Andre Previn (p), Leroy Vinnegar (b) , Shelly Manne (d)) swinging on such rusty gates as 'Blue Lou', 'I'm Coming Virginia' and 'Blues My Naughty Sweetie Gives To Me'. And nothing sounds in the least incongruous. *3, 4, 5: The Verve Small Group Sessions* and *Cosmopolite*, stem from earlier in the '50s but might just as well have been recorded yesterday, such is the vitality displayed in the exchanges between Carter, Oscar Peterson (p) and other visiting JATP well-wishers. The material is immaculate, spanning such as Alfred Newman's 'Street Scene' Hollywood hurrah through to pages ripped from the Ellington, Burke and Van Heusen, Gershwin, Kern and Porter songbooks. And thoughout, Carter is searing, sophisticated and scintillating, creating the perfect mood for the subject in hand. Then, the same could be said for just about everything he's ever tackled and it would be difficult to select a lack-lustre Carter compilation on even the cheapest of budget albums (test drive *These Foolish Things* on Tring GR087). Which says much about the measure of the man. FD

ALL OF ME
(Bluebird ND 83000)

THE KING
(Pablo PACD 2310 768)

LIVE AND WELL IN JAPAN
(Pablo 2308 216/OJC CD 736) [L]

HARLEM RENAISSANCE
(Limelight 844 299)

BETTY CARTER

DROPPIN' THINGS
(Verve 843 991 2) [L]

FEED THE FIRE
(Verve 523 600 2) [L]

No other jazz vocalist has dared to treat the music's mainstream repertoire with such harmonic and melodic sophistication as Betty Carter. Once nicknamed 'Betty Bebop' for her adaption of complicated instrumental modern jazz techniques into her vocals, she has developed an expressive, intensely musical and sometimes challenging approach to phrasing and improvisation. *Droppin' Things*, recorded live in New York in 1990, captures her at her brilliant best, accompanied by Marc Cary (p), Tarus Mateen (b) and Gregory Hutchinson (d), and with guest contributions by pianist Geri Allen, trumpeter Freddie Hubbard and saxophonist Craig Handy. The session comes alive with a loose, creative feel. *Feed The Fire* is the result of a live, all-star concert at London's Royal Festival Hall in 1993. The combined genius of pianist Geri Allen, bassist Dave Holland and drummer Jack DeJohnette inspires one of Carter's classic performances. Highlights include Allen's dynamic 'Feed The Fire', in which Carter matches any contemporary jazz instrumentalist for imagination and virtuosity, and a compelling duet with Holland on 'All Or Nothing At All'. LC

THE AUDIENCE WITH BETTY CARTER
(Verve 835684 2) [L]

SERGE CHALOFF

BLUE SERGE
(Capitol TOCJ 5431)

Even at vastly inflated import prices this Japanese reissue is one of those rare albums genuinely worth going without food to acquire. What's more, this session taped in L.A. a year prior to his undignified death, in 1957, age 33, now comes with one extra track, 'How About You'. It was as baritone saxman in Woody Herman's celebrated 'Four Brothers' sax team (1947-49) that this Bostonian carved out his reputation as the instruments first bona fide bopper. In doing, Chaloff grabbed the pole position previously exclusive to Harry Carney. More than any other player, Chaloff mastered what in most other hands was a cumbersome instrument. However, his virtuosity wasn't obsessed with speed but in exploring the textural light and shade the instrument had to offer. 'A Handful Of Stars', as much as any track, reveals him to be a most expressive soloist capable of great lyricism; compare it to the Stan Getz version on Verve. There's no contest! In terms of technical dexterity. He could be as agile as Konitz while his considered use of dynamics and breathless tone placed Serge Chaloff on a par with his one-time Herdsman 'Brother', Stan Getz. Hopefully, as you read this, *Blue Serge* will have effected a domestic (and much less expensive) CD release. RC

THE FABLE OF MABEL
(Black Lion BLCD 760923)

MEMORIAL/WE THE PEOPLE BOP
(Cool N' Blue CD 102)

DON CHERRY

THE COMPLETE BLUE NOTE RECORDINGS
OF DON CHERRY
(Mosaic MD 2-145)

MU (THE COMPLETE SESSION)
(Affinity AFF 774)

Don Cherry is an outstanding trumpeter with the capacity to play with mind blowing brilliance or what, at least, sounds like joyless languor. His recorded work with Ornette Coleman from 1958 to 1961 was superb. The tight, tonal quality of his pocket instrument had just the expressiveness that Coleman required. Furthermore, he grasped the implications of the music and was able to complement the leader's improvisational style. He played his part in Sonny Rollins' *On the Outside* (RCA Bluebird ND 82496), an affaire de coeur not entirely escorted to artistic consummation. Far more important were the three sessions from 1965/61 superbly presented by Mosaic on two CDs re-issuing albums originally titled *Complete Communion, Symphony For Improvisers* and *Where Is Brooklyn*. Cherry plays with complete authority and no little excitement, while in Gato Barbieri and Pharoah Saunders he has two saxophonists at slightly different stages of development but both coming to terms with the music effectively. The compositions are challenging and the Henry Grimes, Ed Blackwell rhythm section on two of the three sessions is magnificent.

While in Paris in 1969, Cherry and Blackwell recorded as a duet. *Mu*, the outcome, must rate as one of jazz's finest duo performances. Cherry's trumpet uttered a stream of meaningful ideas, tenuously related thematically and self suffiencient in their own right, while Blackwell, one of the most musical of all drummers, breezed through his kit in complete support. Cherry also introduced his flute and piano to demonstrate his growing versatility.

In 1976 that duo got together with tenor saxophonist Dewey Redman and bassist Charlie Haden to form Old & New Dreams. An album with that name (ECM 1154) documents their personal look at the music of the Ornette Coleman Quartet and Cherry shows on the old Coleman tune Lonely Woman that he still has things to say. Unfortunately, Cherry's activities away from the group where less effective and his move toward World Music not always flattering. The best moments on the 1988/90 *Multi Kulti* are when he uses trumpet and not flute, voice or novelty instruments. He is better when able to concentrate on his first choice horn and on *Dona Nostra* it is steadfast trumpet readings on Fort Cherry, What Reasons Could I Give and Prayer that best serve his fine reputation. BMcR

MULTI KULTI
(A & M 395323)

DONA NOSTRA
(ECM 1448 521727-2)

CHARLIE CHRISTIAN

GENIUS OF THE ELECTRIC GUITAR
(CBS 460612)

SWING TO BOP
(Natasha NL 4020) [L]

Charlie Christian was the first 'father' of modern jazz. Texas born and Oklahoma raised, he emerged from the south west with a blues-steeped guitar style of complete originality, inspired by the legato phrasing of Lester Young. Although Eddie Durham had first developed means to amplify the guitar, it was Christian's virtuosity that made it such an important voice. His playing was movingly expressive, deceptively easy, using single-note lines in the manner of a saxophone. Although his long, probing, harmonically progressive phrasing, with its fascinating rhythmic variations, paralleled earlier guitarists' work, the blues gave it an inner intensity missing from the playing of Django Reinhardt or Eddie Lang. Benny Goodman's Sextet provided an unbeatable public platform for these innovations; as a result, Christian made his instrument a complete frontline instrument, laying the ground rules for a generation of guitarists. Much of this work being preserved intact on the weekly broadcasts made by Goodman.

Eventually, however, the high-living Christian felt limited by the Goodman format and, in the last months of his short life, frequented a drab little room in Harlem called Minton's Playhouse. Christian's version of 'Topsy' recorded at Minton's *Swing To Bop* is one of the greatest of all guitar solos; here, alongside such as Dizzy Gillespie, Thelonious Monk and Kenny Clarke, bop was turned from theory into fact. A few weeks later, aged only 25, he was claimed by TB and high times. CS

SOLO FLIGHT
(Vintage Jazz Classics VJC 1021)

BENNY GOODMAN SEXTET
(Columbia CK 45144-2)

JUNE CHRISTY

SOMETHING COOL
(Capitol CDP 7 96329 2)

THE MISTY MISS CHRISTY
(Capitol CDP 7 98452 2)

The queen of cool, Christy was the Kenton band's ice-lady. No matter how the trumpets flared and the rest of the brass team stoked the fire, June's vocals always provided the adequate cubes in the Southern Comfort. *Something Cool*, boosted to a 24 track affair by the inclusion of a generous helping of bonus tracks, contains a selection of mainly Pete Rugolo cuts that range from the gentle jive of 'Whee Baby' and 'Kicks' through to the sublime intimacy of the title song. *The Misty Miss Christy* a similar cable-car to icy climes, pans out as more cohesive proposition because only two additional songs to send the original concept awry. In a way it's daring stuff because June often hangs and extends lines over the merest of backdrops. And it works because when it comes to control, Christy once had it all.   FD

THE BEST OF JUNE CHRISTY
(Capitol CDP 7 92588 2)

EARLY JUNE
(Fresh Sound FSR CD 1011)

SONNY CLARK

COOL STRUTTIN'
(Blue Note CDP 7 46513 2)

LEAPIN' AND LOPIN'
(Blue Note CDP 7 84091 2)

Sonny Clark often gets mistakenly lumped in with beautiful-losers Herbie Nichols, Carl Perkins, Elmo Hope and Richard Twardzik. Granted, Clark may not have been recognised outside of a small coterie of musicians but, unlike the others, he was never short of work and recorded extensively. When, after years on the road with clarinettist Buddy DeFranco, Clark decided to settle in New York in 1957, he practically became Blue Note's house pianist. *Cool Struttin'* as with *Leapin' And Lopin'* (recorded three years later in 1961) have come to represent the more enduring elements of New York Hard Bop. Throughout, grooves are hit with sure-footed confidence by Paul Chambers (b) and Philly Joe Jones (d), while the evenly matched front line of Jackie McLean (as) and Art Farmer (tpt) cut and thrust with speed and accuracy. In contrast, the two horn players enlisted for *Leapin' And Lopin'*, Tommy Turrentine (tpt) and Charlie Rouse (ts) flex a different kind of muscle. Speed not always being of the essence, Clark rises to the occasion by making you forget that anyone else ever attempted 'Deep In A Dream' with one of his incredible long-lined solos. Years later, 'Voodoo' re-emerged as the centrepiece for jazz magpie, altoist John Zorn's Sonny Clark Memorial Quintet recorded tribute. In August 1962, Clark accompanied Dexter Gordon on a Blue Note session that produced both *Go!* and *A Swingin' Affair*, but by January the usual jazz-related causes forever silenced Clark at 32. TH

SERGE CHALOFF – BLUE SERGE
(Capitol TOCJ 5431)

BUCK CLAYTON

COMPLETE JAM SESSIONS
(Mosaic MD6-144) 6-CD Box

A SWINGIN' DREAM
(Stash STCD 281) [L]

'The prettiest cat I ever saw' was Billie Holiday's verdict – and trumpeter Wilbur 'Buck' Clayton also proved to be one of the music's prettiest players, and most consistently expressive.

Though drawing on identical resources, his style contrasted sharply with that of Hot Lips Page, whom he replaced in Count Basie's 1936 band. Armstrong's achievements were tempered, distilled, creating a style of great melodic clarity and coherence that is a major milestone in the development of a 'cool' approach. From the start, Clayton's playing was subtle and understated in a way that set its face directly against fashionably *bravura* trends. He preferred the middle register, fashioning singing solos that were remarkably free of cliche; indeed, Clayton was rare in developing no litany of personal mannerisms, which may explain why he founded no school of trumpet playing (though men like Ruby Braff and Warren Vache owe a clear debt). Open or muted, his sound was instantly identifiable, the former relying far more on the development of deceptively simple melodic fragments than on vocal effects, the latter often creating an eery distance, with the cup used to bend notes in a way that continues the melodic development of his solo. Such gifts played a major part in making masterpieces of many recordings by Count Basie, Billie Holiday and Lester Young.

In the post-war period, they underpinned the organisational band leading abilities that established 'mainstream' jazz through his now-classic *Jam Sessions*; one track-per-side albums ('All The Cats Join In' etc) originally recorded for CBS in the mid-fifties and boasting collective personnels that included Billy Butterfield, Ruby Braff (tpt), Tyree Glenn, J. C. Higginbotham (tmb), Coleman Hawkins, Buddy Tate (ts) and Basie-branded rhythm sections that were second to none.

The last 20 years of his life were marred by an inability to play for health reasons, which he overcame by re-establishing himself as a significant swing arranger with a completely individual touch, the live Stash recordings revealing an important lost piece in the post-Swing jigsaw. CS

THE CLASSIC SWING OF BUCK CLAYTON
(Riverside 142/OJC CD1709)

BUCK 'N' THE BLUES
(Vanguard 662225)

COPENHAGEN CONCERT
(SteepleChase SCCD 36006/7)

OLYMPIA CONCERT
(Vogue 600160)

BUCK & BUDDY
(Swingville 2017/OJC CD 757)

BILLIE HOLIDAY: QUINTESSENTIAL VOL. 5 1937-1938
(CBS 465190 2)

LESTER YOUNG & FRIENDS
(Commodore CCD 7002)

AL COHN

BODY AND SOUL
(Muse MCD 5356)

STANDARDS OF EXCELLENCE
(Concord CCD 4241)

Al Cohn spread his career equally between playing and arranging. As a player, he nodded toward Lester Young, mixed in his own, warmed-up edition of the cool school and delivered his solos with a distinctive 'dark brown' tone. He worked effectively as an arranger for groups of all sizes and also contributed charts for several musicals. Even his smallest combos worked with good arrangments, with soloists always creatively accommodated.

Cohn was, for a short time, one of Woody Herman's 'Four Brothers' but his most successful, musical association was a co-leader of a quintet with Zoot Sims. The 1973 *Body And Soul* is a perfect example, with both men at their cooperative best. Sims was the lighter toned and certainly the more swinging of the two but it was a partnership that succeeded because it fostered genuine, creative interaction. Later in his career (Sims died in 1985), Cohn made impressive recordings with other and very different soloists. His aptly titled *Standards Of Excellence* with guitarist Herb Ellis was particularly succcessful and perhaps suggests that Cohn had been slightly inhibited by his friend Sims. BMcR

NAT COLE

THE BEST OF THE NAT 'KING' COLE TRIO
(Capitol CDP 7 98288 2)

THE COMPLETE AFTER MIDNIGHT SESSIONS
(Capitol CDP 7 48328 2)

Through the corn eventually grew high in terms of the Cole songbook, nobody ever questioned Nat's piano-playing ability. Originally, a pianist who, now and again, sang for his supper-clubs, rather than a pop vocalist who also played keyboards, Nat was basically an R&B smoothie whose vocal style influenced post-war West Coast-based 'club blues' performers Charles Brown, Ray Charles and a zillion lesser talents. Instrumentally, he owed much to Earl Hines, but rejigged Fatha's 'trumpet' style into something more fluid, more of a reedman's approach. His trio (with guitar and bass) was tight, tasty and riff-ready, Cole's 'I Like To Riff' (*Trio Days*) nailing his whole early '40s formula and acting as a catalyst for the Oscar Peterson Trio a decade later. A few pretty ballads were often inserted as a change of pace and these led to a more commerical career, though even 1959, Nat was still demonstrating how he won numerous Down Beat, Esquire and Metronome awards for his piano playing by linking with such style-wise musicians as Harry 'Sweets' Edison (tpt), Willie Smith (as), Juan Tizol (tmb) and violinist Stuff Smith to create the *After Midnight* sessions and provide what many feel was his definitive jazz album. Those who yearn for trio overkill are directed towards Mosaic's *The Complete Capitol Recordings Of The Nat King Cole Trio* (Mosaic MD 18 138). This all-embracing 18-CD box set, comprises 349 songs (over 100 previously unissued) covering every recording from Cole's first seven years at Capitol (1943-49) including radio transcriptions, plus everything released afterwards (up to 1956) that can reasonably be considered jazz based. Less expensive are the excellent series of radio takes on the budget label (Laserlight 15746/47/48/49/50). FD

TRIO DAYS
(Charly QBCD 4)

HIT THAT JIVE JACK: THE EARLIEST RECORDINGS
(MCA MCAD 42350)

BIG BAND COLE
(Capitol CDP 7 96259 2)

BILL COLEMAN

BILL COLEMAN IN PARIS 1936/1938
(DRG/Swing CDSW 8402)

Paris had a double influence on William Johnson Coleman's fortunes. Born in Paris, Kentucky, he would spend the best part of his life based in Paris, France, tiring of the racism in American music as early as 1935 to settle in the French capital after touring there with Lucky Millinder. He also broke early from the all-pervading Armstrong trumpet style, developing an audibly 'cool' approach – pure of tone and avoiding excessive vibrato and precipitous dynamic contrasts. Often his melody lines float over the beat with a rhythmic freedom and melodic invention that combine irresistably in his *tours de force*, 'I'm In The Mood For Love' and 'After You've Gone'. Rarely does he lean on the beat in the manner of a 'hot' player, even when his inventions take on a more Romantic shape. Undoubtedly he would have had a more prominent career had he not remained in Europe, but Coleman's conversational style told a new story from early on. CS

REALLY I DO
(Black & Blue 59.162 2)

GEORGE COLEMAN

BIG GEORGE
(Charly 83)

CONVERGENCE
(Richie Beirach/Coleman – Triloka 185-2)

There is something distinctly muscular about George Coleman's approach. He is a forthright soloist and is cognisant of all that has gone on in the sixties, seventies and eighties. His impressive CV includes work with B.B. King, Max Roach, Slide Hampton and Miles Davis and he has an impressive record in his own right. He encountered the octet while with Hampton and has frequently formed his own during the eighties. *Big George* is a fine example and, if unable to match his stunning, live performances, still affords the opportunity to value Coleman's arranging skills. It has a Body And Soul that owes nothing to other versions and a title track on which Coleman shows his driving attack in a solo that has an architect's logicality and a painter's passion. Similar creative talents are shown in a quartet line-up on *Amsterdam After Dark* (Timeless SJP 129) and *Play Changes* (Jazz House JHCD 002) but the duo circumstances of the 1990 *Convergence* make it a special release. The mood is one of reasoned musing. The two men stimulate and provoke, producing a transcendental plain that massages their creative processes. It may be a far cry from the headlong Coleman in other circumstances but the full, emotional depth of this man has, perhaps, still to be heard. BMcR

ORNETTE COLEMAN

TOMORROW IS THE QUESTION
(Contemporary 7569/OJC CD 342)

BEAUTY IS A RARE THING –
THE COMPLETE ATLANTIC RECORDINGS
(Rhino/Atlantic R2 71410)

AT THE GOLDEN CIRCLE
(Blue Note BCT 84224) [L]

Ornette Coleman stands, alongside Louis Armstrong and Charlie
Parker, as one of the most influential musicians in jazz history. He
was certainly not the first to introduce free form jazz but he was the
central figure and inspiration of a movement that provided it with a
valid, musical syntax and a real sense of direction. The 1959
Tomorrow Is The Question was one of Coleman's two first, commercial recordings and like *Something Else* (Contemporary 7551/OJCCD
163) offered many fine compositions dating back some seven or
eight years. They also presented the world with its look at the
Coleman style. It was a style that revered melody. Excellent
themes were provided and these were then used as launching pads
for totally free blowing. The harmonies of the theme did not direct
the solos and only oblique reference to them was maintained. In
some ways, these albums were flawed proclamations. Coleman had
moved to New York in 1959 and it was his recordings there that
became the jazz encyclical to influence the course of jazz for the
next twenty years.

The magnificent *Beauty* package contains every Atlantic track
recorded between 1959-61 including six items never issued before.
It is lavish and not a little expensive, some of the material is available on single Atlantic CD's but this is a magnificent package, a
'mortgage-the-house' set that should be in every collection. It contains the truly magical Peace, the haunting Lonely Woman, the
absolutely rollicking Blues Connotation and Ramblin' as well as
the deliciously irreverent Embraceable You. It has the two third
stream pieces from Gunther Schuller's Jazz Abstrations, all of
Coleman's tenor pieces and the seminal Free Jazz. It features
Coleman in sublime form, Cherry firing on all free with a touch of
bebop, cylinders and Charlie Haden, Jimmy Garrison and Scott
LaFaro making jazz bass history while supported by drum masters
Billy Higgins and Ed Blackwell. Coleman took a sabbatical from
1963 to 1965 during which time he self taught himself trumpet and
violin. These took him further into the abstract but are well featured on *Golden Circle*, recorded live in Stockholm. His also
remained unchanged and his ability to conjure up good compositions was unimpaired. The use of twelve year old son Denardo on
drums for the *New York Is Now* session in 1966 was consistent with
Coleman's ideal of playing without memory. He further extended
the testing process by recording with Coltrane alumnus Elvin Jones
in a session, presenting Coleman with less obvious climax points
and a swing cloaked in a shroud of subtle, rhythmic complexity.

The early seventies were a barren time for Coleman but he did
some important woodshedding. Later in the decade, he formed a
new group called Prime Time, began to describe his music as 'harmolodic' and with the 1976 *Dancing In Your Head* (unavailable on
CD) provided a blue print for the style. Prime Time's heavy rock
rhythms took much of the subtlety out of Coleman's music and,
perhaps predictably, the group's output has been slow to surface on
CD. There were important moments in the eighties, most in live
concerts and under Metheny's leadership on *Song X*. Coleman

wrote four tunes for the date and predictably stole all the solo honours. It is not nostalgia that suggests that currently he is heard to best advantage when he goes to work with an acoustic unit. Coleman's deft skills should be put on a better canvas than one painted by a funk band. BMcR

NEW YORK IS NOW
(Blue Note CDP 84287)

WITH PAT METHENY – SONG X
(Geffin 924096)

STEVE COLEMAN

DROP KICK
(Novus 01241 63144)

THE TAO OF MAD PHAT [FRINGE ZONES]
(Novus 01241 63160) [L]

One of contemporary jazz's true originals, alto saxophonist Steve Coleman has built a complex, demanding and often compelling music (known as M-Base) from a vast array of black music building blocks, including soul, jazz, funk, hip-hop and blues. The result is a rhythmically intricate, often harmonically enigmatic fusion that sits in its own strange groove and provides a showcase for Coleman's inspired, angular solos. *Drop Kick*, from 1992, features a leaner, more subtle sound than on previous outings, and benefits from a host of guests. 'The Journeyman' is a mesmerising duet with vocalist Cassandra Wilson, accompanied by percussion and bass; 'Bates Motel' is slow and sinister and the title track has a unique, funky momentum. *The Tao Of Mad Phat* (1993) has a slightly looser feel and more slack but, perhaps due to the presence of a 'live studio audience', contains some edgier, more exciting solo work, particularly by the leader. Those interested in Coleman's solo style should seek out his work under the leadership of bassist Dave Holland, who featured Coleman on essential albums on the ECM label. LC

STRATA INSTITUTE: CIPHER SYNTAX
(JMT 834 425)

JOHN COLTRANE

BLUE TRAIN
(Blue Note CDP 746095 2)

GIANT STEPS
(Atlantic 781337)

COLTRANE PLAYS THE BLUES
(Atlantic 1382)

FAVOURITE THINGS
(Atlantic 782346)

LIVE AT THE VILLAGE VANGUARD
(MCA MCAD 39136) [L]

A LOVE SUPREME
(MCA DMCL 1648)

THE MAJOR WORKS OF JOHN COLTRANE
(Impulse GRD 21132)

One does not so much select CD's to document the career of saxophonist John Coltrane as much as scrutinize the list to see just what items are indispensible. He joined Miles Davis in 1955 to a barrage of critical rejection and, on the surface, did seem to be an unlikely choice. The reality was something different and albums such as *Relaxin'* and *Workin'* are monuments to their unlikely compatability. Coltrane also fronted record dates of his own and the excellent *Blue Train*, with Lee Morgan (t) and Kenny Drew (p), certainly made its mark. It depicted a Coltrane already demanding his head, moving away from structures and declaiming every idea with a weather beaten hardness of tone and an already ineluctable power. *Giant Steps* was the real landmark. It turned hard fought acceptance into total maturity and completed a picture of remorseless leader, gifted composer and monster instrumentalist. On *Coltrane Plays The Blues* his classic quartet was McCoy Tyner (p), Steve Davis (b) and Elvin Jones (d); it worked superbly with all four able to sustain the most incredible energy levels. *Favourite Things* captured the public imagination but it was just one of several superb albums to chronicle the work of this magnificent unit. If anything, *Plays The Blues* gets top billing but then a concentration of Coltrane's blues playing does make it an unfair contest. Studio or live sessions, there was no let up and, with Reggie Workman for Davis and Eric Dolphy doubling the size of the reed section, the *Vanguard* performance was one of the great 'on location' records of all time. The sheer power of Chasin' The Trane was of almost apopletic proportions and from then on, understatement was an unlikely visitor.

It was a short step to *A Love Supreme* but a series of five recordings document the period from the 1961 *Vanguard* to this 1964 classic. There was the excellent *Ballads* and the strangely mixed collaboration with Johnny Hartman. There were countless concert recordings and the deeply moving *Crescent*. *A Love Supreme* said it all. It was Coltrane's transcendental affirmation, his spirituality there for eternity. Much of it was notated but the whole exercise celebrated his salvation. Drug addiction was behind him and he was at one with his god. In the following year, he completely broke the mould with *Ascension*. The Impulse *Major Works* compilation solves the two *Ascension* riddles and other discographical inconsistences. The real point is that *Ascension*, for all its alleged freedom, worked to a pre-designed arrangement. The licence was left to the individual soloists and to their 'instrument over ensemble' interludes. Whatever the practicalities of its performance, the outcome was a stunningly exciting work, its raw abandon a myth but its fierce jazz potency unquestionable. *Ascension* was Pharoah Sanders' first recording with Coltrane and from then to the time of Coltrane's death he was associated with the great man. Asking his disciple and 'rival' to join him repeated the King Oliver and Louis Armstrong legend of early history. *Live In Seattle* (Impulse WMC 5116) proved that throwing down the gauntlet worked. Two years later Coltrane was dead but, more than a quarter of a century later, he remains the roll model for a legion of aspiring saxophonists. BMcR

RELAXIN'
(Prestige 7129/OJC CD 190)

WORKIN'
(Prestige 7166/OJC CD 296)

BALLADS
(MCA MCAD 5885)

CRESCENT
(MCA MCAD 5889)

KEN COLYER

THE DECCA YEARS 1955-59: SENSATION!
(Lake LACD 1)

SERENADING AUNTIE
(Upbeat URCD 111)

Ken Colyer just wouldn't compromise. Known as 'The Guv'nor', he was raised on the sounds of Bunk Johnson and the ways of New Orleans (Ken was once jailed for overstaying his welcome in that city) he attempted to bring authenticity to the British jazz movement. The result was often primitive but such was the obsessive force of what he played that his following was among the most vociferous on the revival scene of the '50s. Religions have been founded on much less! A forceful trumpeter who led ensembles with tremendous flair even if his improvisation skills were limited, his glory years are best represented by *Sensation!* on which the band wheels through such great expecteds like 'Dippermouth Blues' and 'Maryland, My Maryland' plus some agreeable slices of ragtime. Had it not been for some enterprising company engineer preserving these BBC Jazz Club and TV broadcasts on acetate discs, they would have been forever lost to the company's policy of wiping tapes clean soon after transmission. Covering much the same period as the Decca material, 'Chrysanthemum Rag' and 'Goin' Home' alone are worth the price of admission. FD

EDDIE CONDON

DIXIELAND JAM
(Columbia 465680)

THE COMPLETE CBS JAM SESSIONS
(Mosaic MD5 152)

Even Damon Runyon would have been hard-pressed to create a wise-crackin' three-dimensional, street smart character as vivid as Eddie Condon. Synonymous with prohibition-era Chicago Jazz and the embodiment of the fast lane jazz life, Condon's true talent was not as a (rhythm) guitarist but as an inspired organiser, raconteur, author, coach, *bon vivant* and whisky drinker. Though fellow musicians spoke highly of his musical qualities, nobody can quite remember any of his solos (but then he seldom took any) but many will regale the listener with a selection of Condon's immortal one liners: "We don't flatten our fifths, we drink 'em" (being a barb aimed at beboppers). For more, read his autobiography We Call It Music (1948). From the McKenzie-Condon Chicagoans back in 1929, through to the pre-World War II Summa Cum Laude Orchestra and a personnel that included Pee Wee Russell (clt), Bud Freeman (ts), Gene Krupa (d) and Max Kaminsky (tpt) the style for all future Condon outfits was set in stone as these and a succession of high-profile individualists such as Wild Bill Davison (cnt), Billy Butterfield, Bobby Hackett, Jimmy McPartland (tpt) Cutty Cutshall, Lou McGarity (tmb), Ed Hall, Peanuts Hucko, Bob Wilber (clt), pianists Gene Schroeder and Joe Bushkin, and drummers George Wettling and Cliff Leeman took part in what, more often than not, appeared to be one long party.

A catalyst with few equals, by the mid-1940s, he was operating his own celebrity-packed club in Manhattan, hosting a regular series of all-star Town Hall Concerts (preserved on numerous Jazzlogy releases) while, in 1948, *The Eddie Condon Floor Show* made him a familiar TV personality, an outspoken columnist in the *New York*

Journal-American and, by virtue of a series of ads for Kellogg's All-Bran, a crusader against constipation! All this in turn lead to a fruitful association with CBS Records in the mid-'50s and, for the first time, listeners were able to evesdrop on the informal *bon homme* that existed everytime Condon and friends hosted a raucous studio party where inspiration flowed as freely as the liquor. Covering the period November 1953, through to September 1962 (taking in the 1956 Newport Jazz Festival in the process) all these CBS albums, *Jam Session: Coast To Coast, Jammin' At Condon's, Bixieland* plus much more have been painstakingly collated on Mosaic's five-CD package. It's a monument to 'Classic' jazz and, as with *Dixieland Jam* gleefully plunders a repertoire drawn from a portfolio that includes the likes of 'Wolverine Blues', 'When A Woman Loves A Man', 'Davenport Blues', 'That's A Plenty', 'Dippermouth Blues', 'Struttin' With Some Barbecue', 'Big Butter And Egg Man' etc. Setting aside styles, eras or tiresome trad vs modern prejudices, this amounts to some of the most exuberant music ever recorded. RC

CHICK COREA

NOW HE SINGS, NOW HE SOBS
(Blue Note CDP 7 90055 2)

COMPACT JAZZ: THE SEVENTIES
(Verve 517952 2)

THREE QUARTETS
(Stretch GRS 00032)

Before he got the message from L.Ron Hubbard to go forth and communicate, Corea led a blamelessly jazzy life, with the 1968 *Now He Sings, Now He Sobs* an example of his virtuosic Tyner-Evans pianism at its peak. 'Steps-What Was' is a comprehensive index of his interests, ranging from a freeish intro through a whirlwind blues to the Hispanism which was to inform much of his later work. In 1970, tiring of the circumscribed funk of Miles Davis's band, Corea and bassist Dave Holland fled to the improvising quartet Circle. However, Corea's discovery of Scientology coincided with a crisis of faith in free music and led to the formation of Return To Forever, best known for its polished version of Mahavishnu-style fusion. *Compact Jazz* summarises the style as well as demonstrating Corea's acoustic work with Stan Getz, Herbie Hancock and others. Much of Corea's eighties work amounted to occasionally glossy updates of RTF and *Sings/Sobs*, but the 1981 *Three Quartets*, a straightahead date with Michael Brecker (ts), Eddie Gomez (b) and Steve Gadd (d), restores faith in Corea's jazz credentials. 'Quartet No. 2' has Corea and Brecker in especially exhilarating form, and Gomez is singingly expressive throughout. The Stretch/GRP adds four previously unreleased numbers to the original album. MG

THE SONG OF SINGING
(Blue Note CDP 7 46401 2)

CIRCLE: PARIS CONCERT
(ECM 1018/19) [L]

TRIO MUSIC
(ECM 1232/33)

THE ELEKTRIC BAND
(GRP D 9535)

MARILYN CRISPELL

GAIA
(Leo Records CD LR 152)

A stunningly gifted avant-garde piano virtuoso, Crispell shares with free-piano pioneer Cecil Taylor an interest in the physicality of the instrument, its responses to energy, and a fearsome technique. Her position as one of the piano's most original voices has developed through periods of work with Andrew Cyrille (d), Leo Smith (tpt), Anthony Davis (p), Tim Berne and Oliver Lake (as), right through to her much-lauded duo with multi-instrumentalist Anthony Braxton. *Gaia*, one of a number of very fine Crispell releases on the Leo label, features here trio with bassist Reggie Workman and drummer Doug James, and runs the gamut of expression, from the introspective and pastoral to the violent and torrential. LC

LIVE IN SAN FRANCISCO
(Music & Arts 633 CD) [L]

SONNY CRISS

CALIFORNIA BOPPIN'
(Fresh Sound FSR 156)

A regular cast-member of California-based 'Just Jazz' shows (d.j. Gene Norman's mid-'40s localised JATP equivilant) where he frequently partnered Al Killian, Howard McGhee (tpt) Wardell Gray, Teddy Edwards and Dexter Gordon (ts), this energetic Memphis-born alto player sufficiently impressed overlord Norman Granz to become a regular Jazz At The Philharmonic firebrand (1948-49). Stints with The Lighthouse All-Stars, Billy Eckstine, Stan Kenton and Buddy Rich followed. Due to the period in which Criss surfaced, he possessed a tart, hyper-active brittle-sounding 'Bird'-cry laced with more than a passing reference to Willie Smith. *The Inglewood Jam* (Fresh Sound FSR CD 17) – a June 1952 date where he shares the frontline with Charlie Parker and Chet Baker – depicts a slightly manic Criss trying not to be overawed by the presence of his mentor. By the mid-'50s, Criss had formularized his style on three albums he recorded for Imperial *Jazz-USA, Go Man! It's Sonny Criss And Modern Jazz* and *Plays Cole Porter* but which, at the time of writing, are only available as Japanese imports.
As with so many of his generation, he drifted in and out of music for the remainder of his life, settled for sometime in Europe before staging a comeback in the mid-'60s under the auspices of Prestige. While *Portrait* is a straight ahead session focusing on his interpretative bop skills, *Sonny's Dream* (aka *Birth Of The New Cool*) is the revelation for here, Criss works with a medium-size ensemble on a number of arranger/composer Horace Tapscott's challenging charts. A further six year lay-off gave way to *Crisscraft* (Muse MCD 6015) and *Out Of Nowhere* (Muse MCD 5089) which both stem from the same 1975 and illustrate that he still had something interesting to say. It was but a short respite, for Sonny Criss fatally shot himself in 1977 aged 50. RC

PORTRAIT OF SONNY CRISS
(Prestige 7526/OJC CD 655)

SONNY'S DREAM
(Prestige 7576/OJC CD 707)

BOB CROSBY

STOMP OFF, LET'S GO!
(ASV CD AJA 5097)

Brother of supercrooner Bing, Bob Crosby was an unremarkable, pleasant voiced singer who discovered his true forte was heading a remarkable band. What made it so distinctive was that it was basically a dixieland outfit disguised as a regular big band of the late '30s and '40s. At every opportunity, the front-liners took off as drummer Ray Bauduc headed into two-beat, and whenever things got a little boring – the odd commercial ballad had to be thrust in to please sponsors and suchlike – The Bobcats, a small group, would break from the main band and play as if New Orleans was just two miles down the highway. The main contenders stuck pretty much together, with dynamic lead trumpet man Yank Lawson swapping choruses with reedmen Eddie Miller, Irving Fazola and Matty Matlock, trombonist Ward Silloway, pianists Bob Zurke or Jess Stacy and others who thought of the band as home. And the inherent happiness was reflected in such monster hits as 'South Rampart Street Parade', a jazz march for the masses, and 'Big Noise From Winnetka', a dotty duet between whistling bassist Bob Haggart and the irrepressable Baudauc who had a penchant for drumming on Haggart's bass string. Only World War II and the draft put an end to it all. Then war really never was much fun. FD

THE MARCH OF THE BOBCATS
(Jazz Hour JHR 73534)

THE (JAZZ) CRUSADERS

THE GOLDEN YEARS
(GRP 50072)

HOLLYWOOD
(MoJazz 530 306)

Whereas many players graduate from R&B to straight ahead jazz, the (Jazz) Crusaders enjoyed their biggest commercial success when taking the return trip. In a recording career that stretches way back to 1961 with *Freedom Sound* (Pacific Jazz CDP 7 96864 2) and takes in various labels including Motown, Chisa, Blue Thumb, MCA, it wasn't until the introduction of guitarist Larry Carlton and bassman Pops Popwell into their line-up (and the word 'Jazz' was dropped from their billing) that this cult attraction effected the longed-for cross-over success that had eluded them for almost a decade. Sure, they already had a loyal fan base, but up to this point, their wider reputation had been earned by virtue of association as L.A's most reliable and in-demand sessioneers. Legend has it, when their own career went into overdrive, in an effort to wind-down studio work, they decided to outprice themselves by doubling their individual session rate from one to two thousand dollars. It actually had the reverse effect; enquiries quadrupled. Consummate stylists as opposed to innovators, the Crusaders' importance is that without compromising their basic stance, the four founder-members Wilton Fielder (ts), Joe Sample (p), Wayne Henderson (tmb) and Stix Hooper (d) utilised the funk-pop sensibility that had always been an integral part of their vision and made jazz easy to access for the masses. In the process not only did many of their albums sell in six figures but they went Top 100 with such singles as 'Put It Where You Want It' (1972), 'Don't Let It Get You Down' (1973), 'Scratch' (1974) and 'Street Life' (1979) RC

PAQUITO D'RIVERA

WHO'S SMOKING?
(Candid CCD 79523)

40 YEARS OF CUBAN JAM SESSION
(Messidor 15826)

The political situation that exists between Cuba and the USA means that the only way that Cuban musicians can ever get to play in the States is by defecting. When, in 1980, Cuba's world famous jazz combo Irekere made a concert stopover in Spain, altoist Paquito D'Rivera immediately contacted the US Embassy to request political asylum. The following year, D'Rivera's fellow band member, trumpet player, Arturo Sandoval chose the same escape route. While the technical excellence and fiery disposition of both these flamboyant players is beyond question, finding the appropriate setting for their personalized approach still poses problems. Dizzy Gillespie's United Nations Orchestra may have proved a brief sanctuary, but for all his obvious virtues, previous albums have indicated that there is an inherent danger of D'Rivera becoming a over-seasoned hard bop caricature of himself as he hovers between styles. The 1993 Messidor recording with its flexible line-up of 20 assorted musicians (including movie actor Andy Garcia on conga) establishes that D'Rivera is most definitely at his best on both alto and clarinet ('Una Tarde') when pursuing his latin heritage as opposed to utilising it as mere decoration. Whether the public wants such a subtle blending of these ingredients or, as the super-charged *Who's Smoking?* suggests, more pyrotechnics than a Fourth Of July celebration is still open to debate and taste.   TH

TICO! TICO!
(Chesky CD 034)

TADD DAMERON

FATS NAVARRO
FEATURED WITH THE TADD DAMERON BAND
(Milestone M 47041)

FONTAINEBLEAU
(Prestige 7037/OJC CD 055)

Tadd Dameron was hardly a prodigious composer but his themes had the happy knack of appealing to major players and earning immortality due to their efforts. More significantly, bebop was emerging and Dameron had a feel of it. Initially an arranger for several territory bands, he read the new music well and was amongst the very first in providing it with a workable group vocabulary. As a pianist himself, he was a modest journeyman; he accepted an ensemble role but, as his work on the *Fats Navarro Featured* shows, he could often produce solos of shape and imagination. True, they were planted in a bop setting but viewed in isolation belonged to no specific era.

He took meticulous care over his arranging and *Fontainebleau*, an extended work, was fully written out. In a way, it is not unlike Duke Ellington's extended pieces; Henry Coker and Sahib Shihab present their own ideas but the essential, musical framework continually works for them. His only known solo album was made in 1961 but it has yet to reach CD and, despite three dates for Riverside in 1962, his health was failing. Still under 50, he died in 1965, a victim of circumstance as much as of drug addiction. BMcR

JOHN DANKWORTH

THE VINTAGE YEARS
(Sepia RSCD 2)

THE ROULETTE YEARS
(Roulette CDP 7 96566 2)

Shamefully ignored by those who shape jazz CD reissues, John Dankworth was one of the musicians who, after a stint playing clarinet with Freddie Mirfield's Garbage Men, helped shape the course of British jazz in the post-war years. It took just two quick moves. First, alto-bopping his way out of the Club Eleven (Britain's answer to Birdland) to form his groundbreaking Dankworth Seven (with wife-to-be Cleo Laine and Frank Holder handling vocals), then creating a big band of some difference by merely providing a brass wrapping (sometimes five trumpets and four trombones) around the basic structure of the Seven. Maybe too polite, too neat for some, this band (featured in its late '50s structure on the Sepia release and in lightly revised form on the early '60s Roulette outing) like most Dankworth outfits, thrived, not unlike that of Count Basie's, on the ability to mix light and shade, while the list of musicians involved on the later recording – Peter King (as), Kenny Wheeler (tpt), Ronnie Ross (bs) etc. reads more like a roll of honour than just a mere line-up. The repertoire is healthy too, an 'African Waltz'-styled 'Cannonball' rubbing shoulders with Dave Lindup's Hefti-ish 'New Forest', 'The Avengers Theme' (penned by Dankworth, remember ?) and pianist Dave Lee's wonderfully reflective 'Blue Furs'. And though Dankworth (who nowadays vies musically not only with his wife but also his siblings (*The Alec & John Dankworth Generations Big Band: Nebuchadnezzer* Ronnie Scott's Jazz House JHCD 029) has often moved on to become involved with other things, both records provide ample evidence of why the band was once invited to flag-wave at the Newport Jazz Festival at a time when the opposition was hot. FD

LIVE AT RONNIE SCOTT'S
(RSCD 2015) [L]

EDDIE 'LOCKJAW' DAVIS

VERY SAXY
(Prestige 7167/OJC CD 458)

THE COOKBOOK VOL. 1
(Prestige 7141/OJC CD 652)

SAVE YOUR LOVE FOR ME
(Bluebird ND 86463)

JAWS AND STITT – WITH SONNY STITT
(Roulette CDROU 1039)

Jaws was one of those tenormen who could be anything they choose to be. Placed in an R&B environment he could outblow just about any contender tossed in the ring with him. Equally, he could caress a ballad in masculine manner and turn it into something so romantic that, even today, the resulting off-record sound will virtually reach out of the speakers and pull the girl for you. The three volume *Cookbook* series stems from a period when the former 'Atomic'-period Basie-ite and Shirley Scott were doing their tenor-organ, Prestige-prompted, combo thing, bluesy and trend-setting, virtually establishing the way of things to come for Blue Note believers. *Very Saxy*, is from the same period but features Davis in the agreeably pushy company of fellow-tenorists Arnett Cobb, Coleman Hawkins and Buddy Tate, each urging the other on to more spectacular licks and party tricks. *Jaws And Stitt* being yet another '50s-set organ-assisted tenor joust that reiterates the pattern set by such as Dexter Gordon and Wardell Gray on 'The Chase'. However, it was a take-no-prisoners partnership with Johnny Griffin that kicked up the most dust, prompting all but the brave at heart or those with a self-destructive streak to take on these toughest of tenors (*Looking At Monk*). The 60s Bluebird set is more sedate, made just after Davis had enjoyed a two-year sojourn as a booking agent. Yet in its approachable, amiable way it's of equal value as Davis blows in almost Webster-like manner on such superior pops as 'Save Your Love For Me' and 'The Good Life', sometimes parading his breathy Ben approach with the aid of a rhythm section, at others moving outfront of a stellar big band, populated by such as Ernie Royal, Joe Newman (tpt), J.J.Johnson (tmb), Frank Wess, Frank Foster (ts) and other names that virtually glow when you type them. But the rule of thumb remains. If a record sleeve reveals the presence of Eddie 'Lockjaw' Davis, then it is to be acquired. Simple as that. FD

COOKBOOK VOL. 2
(Prestige 7161/OJC CD 653)

COOKBOOK VOL. 3
(Prestige 7219/OJC CD 756)

EDDIE 'LOCKJAW' DAVIS WITH MICHEL ATTENOUX
(Storyville STCD 5009)

MILES DAVIS

BIRTH OF THE COOL
(Capitol CDP 7 92862 2)

RELAXIN'
(Prestige 7129/OJC CD 190-2)

MILESTONES
(CBS 460827 2)

PORGY AND BESS
(CBS 450985 2)

KIND OF BLUE
(CBS 460603 2)

E.S.P.
(Columbia 467899 2)

IN A SILENT WAY
(CBS 450982 2)

WE WANT MILES
(CBS 466440 2)

If Miles Davis' s initial encounters with bebop were uncomfortable, it wasn't long before he reworked the style in his own image. His 1949-50 nonet enabled him to enjoy the essence of bebop without being a virtuoso, to turn his technical limitations to positive advantage, and to establish himself at the forefront of jazz innovation, a position he would maintain virtually for the rest of his career.

Indeed, in its use of rich chromatic harmony, nonstandard material and unu-sual instrumentation, the urbane, orchestrated bebop which came to be known as *Birth of the Cool* still sounds more modern (particularly in John Carisi's 'Israel')than Miles's work a few years later using a conventional quintet. The cascade of small group recordings which followed Miles's disentanglement from heroin in 1954 might seem to signal a new attempt at bebop, but they departed from bop convention in focusing on pop tunes rather than bop themes and in consolidating Miles's introspective 'walking on eggshells' aesthetic. The 1956 quintet with Coltrane produced four highly regarded albums for Prestige of which *Relaxin'* is perhaps the most confident, varied and atmospheric. As befits an album that marks the end of an era, the 1958 *Milestones* was at once retrospective and prophetic. The flaring, unreconstructed bop exchanges of 'Dr. Jekyll' actually say more about smashing eggs than walking on their shells, but the taut, three-chord title track outlined the harmonically sparse style Miles would unveil in *Kind of Blue* the following spring. Not before time, Miles was ready in 1957 for another taste of the orchestral style of *Birth of the Cool*. His first large-scale collaboration with Gil Evans, *Miles Ahead*, was a rather ordinary affair, not helped by a preponderance of bland material. *Porgy and Bess*, from the following year, thrives on a darker tonality and the unifying hand of Gershwin's fine writing. The effectively modal passages of 'The Buzzard Song' and 'Ain't Necessarily So' and the blues segment of 'Gone' draw some superb iazz from Miles. Inaccuracies in the orchestral playing have often been noted, but it was certainly near enough for iazz and for a soloist who was not noted for his technical infallibility.

The lyrical, minimalist approach Miles had been developing through the fifties was first officially expressed in the classic 1959 album *Kind of Blue*. The obvious examples of the style are the brooding two-chord vamp 'So What', and the impressionist ballads 'Blue in Green' and 'Flamenco Sketches', but even the two blues, 'All Blues' and 'Freddie Freeloader', are gospel-inflected versions of that venerable form, in which all harmonic superfluity has been pared away. Despite the slight musical substance on paper of *Kind of Blue*, it exercised an incalculable effect on music in the following decades. It's an indication of its wide and enduring appeal that George Russell later scored Miles's beautifully weighted 'So What' solo for big band, and shortly before Miles's death, the British guitarist Ronny Jordan, born some years after 'So What' was recorded, gave the tune the George Benson treatment and made the British top 40. Between *Kind of Blue* and the great sixties quintet, Miles's small group work consisted mainly of ever faster readings of his fifties triumphs. The excellent 1963 *Miles In Antibes*, with George Coleman, mapped out some of the territory the emerging quintet would cover, but it wasn't until the arrival of Wayne Shorter that all the elements were in place. An album of entirely new material, the 1965 *E.S.P.* stepped ahead of the quintet's live dates and presented a catalogue of the new band's methods – Tony Williams's exhilarating manipulation of time, dynamics and texture; Shorter's startlingly fresh writing; Herbie Hancock's oblique, lyrical pianism; and a breadth of expression that encompassed the crepuscular abstraction of 'Mood' and the incipient rock of 'Eighty-One'.

1969 was another pivotal year for Miles, his music changing but as ever remaining continuous with the past. The modal character of *In A Silent Way* and the lush impressionism of Zawinul's title track recall *Kind of Blue*, but there is not a moment of four-to-the-bar swing here. The transition to the rock pulse implied on *E.S.P.* was complete. However, where the form of Miles's seventies jazz-rock excursions was often vague (*Jack Johnson* was one clear exception),

In A Silent Way is a perfectly programmed sequence with clearly delineated dynamic variations – most effectively realised on the dramatic 'It's About That Time'.

Miles's 1980 comeback album, *The Man With The Horn*, showed him still hungover from the musical and personal dissipations of the seventies, but by the following year, as the electrifying *We Want Miles* showed, his playing and his band of versatile young sidemen were gathering a fearsome momentum. Too many assessors of this music, unable to grasp that a rock sound does not necessarily mean a rock vocabulary, have faltered at the opening bars of Mike Stern's guitar solo on 'Jean-Pierre', unable to proceed to the loose, spontaneous development, the subtle ensemble interplay, the acute dynamic awareness and crackling solo work which makes this one of Miles's most playable late records. Still, it wasn't the first time Miles had fallen foul of critical myopia. MG

MILES DAVIS 1945-1954
(Giants of Jazz CD 0221)

THE REAL BIRTH OF THE COOL
(Recording Arts JZCD 313)

WALKIN'
(Prestige 7076/OJC CD-213-2)

WORKIN'
(Prestige 7166/OJC CD-296-2)

STEAMIN'
(Prestige 7200/OJC CD-3912)

COOKIN'
(Prestige 7094/OJC CD-128-2)

IN ANTIBES
(CBS 462960 2) [L]

DAVISIANA
(Moon MCD 033-2)

NEFERTITI
(Columbia 467089 2)

BITCHES BREW
(CBS 460602 2)

A TRIBUTE TO JACK JOHNSON
(Columbia 471003 2)

DECOY
(Columbia 468702 2)

TUTU
(WEA 925 490 2)

BUDDY DeFRANCO

THE COMPLETE VERVE RECORDINGS OF THE BUDDY DEFRANCO QUARTET/QUINTET WITH SONNY CLARKE
(Mosaic MD4 117)

Frequently damned with feint praise, De Franco was the finest clarinettist of the bebop era. An undisputed virtuoso, he is the master of the shapely, personal oration, told over any chord sequence left at his mercy.During his career, he has jousted with Art Tatum,

Dizzy Gillespie and other masters and has always effortlessly held his own. *The Complete* represents him at his finest, confidently relaxed and very much at ease with Sonny Clark and Tal Farlow. If there is a problem it is that, even at his best, there is no sense of passion. His well-sculptured improvisations confirm his total involvement, yet they do not always communiate his emotional commitment and the superficial listener mistakes 'cool' for 'glib'. De Franco is not well represented on CD but *Five Notes Of Blues* (Musidisc 500302) is a typical, recent (1991) issue. There is not an ugly note on the entire album but, finally, there is a feeling of a gentle, musical coach ride from the comfort of the inside lane. Beware; this man can overtake when the traffic demands. BMcR

JACK DeJOHNETTE

NEW DIRECTIONS IN EUROPE
(ECM 11S7)

AUDIO-VISUALSCAPES
(Impulse 2558S1 2/MCAD 8029)

The 1979 *New Directions In Europe* confirmed drummer (and some-times pianist) DeJohnette as a master of percussive multi-skilling, equal conversant with jazz, rock and free improvisation and often integrating these and other techniques within a single piece. Perhaps the most complete performance here is 'Bayou Fever', where DeJohnette's reflective piano introduction prefaces sus-penseful pedal point, limber swing, fierce free playing and hints of R&B. However, the sinewy 'Salsa For Eddie G.', set alight by an exuberant trumpet-guitar dialogue between Lester Bowie and John Abercrombie, is the most satisfying piece. Apart from his role as sideman, DeJohnette's recent output as a leader has been domi-nated by curiously pedestrian rock and world music, but his late-80s band achieved an awesome intensity, thanks in large part to the presence of M-Base saxophonists Greg Osby and Gary Thomas, who darken an already grim harmonic style with sax-triggered synth dissonances. *Audio-Visualscapes* documents this formidable band, with Osby's 'Master Mind' and Thomas's tenor blizzard on Ornette Coleman's 'Sphinx' generating a diabolical head of steam, guitarist Mick Goodrick adding spice to the evil stew. MG

PAUL DESMOND

DAVE BRUBECK QUARTET:THE GREAT CONCERTS
(Columbia 462403 2) [L]

PAUL DESMOND: EASY LIVING
(BMG ND 82306)

If the word 'wit' had to be applied to any jazz person, it would have to be identified with Paul Desmond. His elegant urbane, high pitched, alto sound and sophisticated, graceful delivery, spiked with humorous asides and half quotes, offered another alternative to the Boppers. His greatest performances were probably with his friend and mentor Dave Brubeck, a serious absorbed musician whose percussive, often hectic, piano attracted a great deal of unfair criticism which often ended by suggesting that Desmond would be an even better player if he left the Brubeck Quartet. Perversely, it was the very contrast of the two musicians which accentuated Desmond's inventive flair. Although comfortable with fast tempos his temperament was especially suited to ballads which he graced with femininely delicate lyricism. *The Great Concerts* has a confident Desmond leading the way on three disparate appearances in Amsterdam, Copenhagen, and New York assisted by bassist Gene Wright and the effervescent Joe Morello on drums. The Quartet preferred to record before a live audience and from his exhilarating entrance on 'Pennies From Heaven', Desmond is in his finest form. The purity of his solo in 'For All We Know', at Carnegie Hall, suggest a private reverie so unusual at a Public Concert that listening is almost an intrusion. Also included is Desmond's ubiquitous 'Take Five', now a rather hackneyed survivor but, lemon fresh in 1963.

Easy Living frames a more introspective Desmond. With another musical thinker Jim Hall on guitar, these were the most fruitful sides Desmond made away from Brubeck. Recruiting Percy Heath (b) and Connie Kay (d) from the MJQ, the foursome producing thoughtful chamber jazz. The empathetic Hall (he and Desmond even looked alike) seemed to find other facets in Desmond. Two blues and eight superior standards are milked of all their melodic and harmonic possibilities with performances which invite comparison with the very best. Though the pair never once appeared together in concert, the product of their lengthy collaboration has been collated on 4-CDs *The Complete Recordings Of The Paul Desmond Quartet With Jim Hall* (Mosaic MD4 120). In the final analysis, apart from his last tragic session with Chet Baker everything Desmond did exuded class. JM

GERRY MULLIGAN-PAUL DESMOND QUARTET
(Verve 519 850 2)

DIRTY DOZEN BRASS BAND

MY FEET CAN'T FAIL ME NOW
(Concord CCD 3005) [L]

The Dirty Dozen Brass Band specialises in an area of jazz activity where the emphasis remains firmly on the feet. Their very special brand of dance music, taken from the syncopated, brass-bass marching band tradition of New Orleans, is a raucous, hand-clapping, foot-stomping affair that mixes traditional jazz, R&B, gospel and funk into something full of humour and life prompting the likes of Dr. John and Elvis Costello to join in. Formed in the '70s, the Dirty Dozen remain the masters of a style that has led to something of a youth trend in their home city, and has spawned a number of rivals, including the popular Rebirth Brass Band. *My Feet Can't Fail Me Now* is a live date from 1984, and represents what has so far proved to be the band's best period. LC

JOHNNY DODDS

JOHNNY DODDS 1926-1928
(JSP CD 319)

BLUE CLARINET STOMP
(RCA/Bluebird ND 82293)

Louis Armstrong was not alone in developing a solo style for his instrument. Alongside him in King Oliver's Creole Jazz Band, a similar task was being undertaken by clarinettist Johnny Dodds, who brought such diversity to his instrument's traditionally contrapuntal role that only he himself was able to better it. The resulting solo style was a pungent, earthy, serpentine 'black magic' concept of the blues. Very few revivalist or 'trad' clarinettists were able to capture its essence; most found it rather easier to follow the more consonant styles of Jimmie Noone or Omer Simeon. It is for this blues playing that he is most highly and widely regarded, as in major classics like 'Perdido Street Blues'. These performances represent an emotional involvement unusual in the music at this time, and make profound contrast with the more simply-based clarinet style of George Lewis. At the same time, despite apparently looking backwards into the jazz tradition, Dodds was among the first jazz musicians to make albeit small strides harmonically. But he also remembered the duty to entertain, frequently showing the 'good time musician' side, playing jazz purely for dancing in performances strong on beat and joy. CS

JOHNNY DODDS & JIMMY BLYTHE
(Timeless CBC 1-015)

ERIC DOLPHY

FAR CRY
(New Jazz 8270/OJC CD 400)

OUT TO LUNCH
(Blue Note CDP 746522 2)

Dolphy's admiration for Ornette Coleman has often been noted, but where Coleman's radicalism seems intuitive, Dolphy's is carefully worked out. The chortling alto sax, gobbling bass clarinet, twittering flute, skewed phrasing, microtonal pitching, intervallic gymnastics and harmonic extensions heard on the 1960 *Far Cry* hardly spell 'mainstream', but they do reveal a sound awareness of the rudiments. Despite their originality, Dolphy's late fifties innovations grew organically from Parker and remain of a piece with the tonal tradition more plainly represented here by 'It's Magic' and the celebrated jazz-noir solo 'Tenderly'.
Dolphy's appetite for new musical horizons (and his association with John Coltrane) soon obscured his debt to Parker, but the umbilical connection with tradition endured. While his 1964 masterpiece *Out To Lunch* superficially sounds as free as Ornette Coleman's improvised sessions, the freedom is anchored in a sure sense of form and arrangement, and acquires extra impact from the contrast. Supported by Freddie Hubbard (tpt), Bobby Hutcherson (vib), Richard Davis (b) and Tony Williams (d), the spareness and precision recall Webern at his most uncompromising, but the pulse is swinging, the accent is on improvisation and Dolphy's virtuosity is at its height on his Monk-tribute 'Hat and Beard', 'Something Sweet, Something Tender', 'Gazelloni' and the title track. MG

OUTWARD BOUND
(New Jazz 8236/OJC CD 022)

OUT THERE
(New Jazz 8252/OJC CD 023)

VINTAGE DOLPHY
(Enja 5045-24)

OTHER ASPECTS
(Blue Note B21 Y 48041 2)

EUROPEAN IMPRESSIONS
(Bandstand BD 1514) [L]

LOU DONALDSON

QUARTET/QUINTET/SEXTET
(Blue Note CDP 7 81537 2)

BLUES WALK
(Blue Note CDP 7 46525 2)

ALLIGATOR BOOGALOO
(Blue Note CDP 7 84263 2)

A NIGHT AT BIRDLAND
(Blue Note CDP 7 46519 & 7 46520)

Lou Donaldson sits fair and square in a linage of smokin' alto sax
popularisers that began with Tab Smith, Louis Jordan, Eddie
Vinson and Earl Bostic and carries on through to Cannonball
Adderley, David Sanborn and Everett Harp. A journeyman player
with a nose for newly-minted greenbacks, Lou Donaldson – just six
years Bird's junior – took the blues aspect of Parker's style and, as
one of the early architects of soul jazz first simplified, then popular-
ized it for mass commercial consumption. As if to prove the point,
Donaldson often included at least one Bird song on a date ('Dewey
Square', 'Confirmation', 'Cool Blues' etc). With close to one hun-
dred albums to his credit, Donaldson not only demonstrated his
ability to go with the flow, but sometimes direct it. In the process
he brought the talents of Clifford Brown, Horace Silver, Grant
Green and Big John Patton to the attention of Blue Note. In a more
straight ahead context his aggressive Parkerisms worked perfectly
alongside of Brown and Silver in a 1954 go-for-broke quintet propelled by drummer Art Blakey (*A Night At Birdland*). *Quartet/
Quintet/Sextet* was a variations on the same theme, whereas the addition of Ray Barretto's lopin' congas on *Blues Walk* injected even
more adrenalin. But it was in a Hammond 'n' Horn lounge bar context that Donaldson was happiest. When not working out with
Jimmy Smith, he put the likes of grits 'n' greens organists Baby
Face Willette, Big John Patton, Lonnie Smith among many to good
use. *Alligator Boogaloo*, with guitarist George Benson was
Donaldson's first to strike gold, remaining chart bound for an entire
year it brought home the fatback in more ways than one. RC

THE RIGHTEOUS REED/
THE BEST OF LOU DONALDSON
(Blue Note 8 30721 2)

KENNY DORHAM

ROUND ABOUT MIDNIGHT AT THE CAFE BOHEMIA
VOL. 1 & 2
(Blue Note CDP 7 46541 2/42 2)

QUIET KENNY
(New Jazz 8225/OJC CD 250)

UNA MAS
(Blue Note CDP 7 46515 2)

TRUMPET TOCCATA
(Blue Note CDP 84181 2)

The high regard with which fellow musicians held Tex-Bopper
McKinley Howard Dorham can be seen in the fact that Bird chose
him to replace Miles (1948-50), Art Blakey paired him with Hank

Mobley for the inaugural Jazz Messengers line-up (1956-58) and a distraught Max Roach felt only Dorham could fill the gap left by the death of Clifford Brown. Dorham's own career as a leader was accompanied with mixed fortunes. The May 1956 Cafe Bohemia set with tenorman J.R. Monterose is basically Dorham's short-lived Jazz Prophets with guitarist Kenny Burrell making it a six piece. Anyone who had been following Dorham's career couldn't have failed to appreciate how he had consistently worked on improving his tone as he moved from bop into the hard version. By the early sixties, Dorham may not have enjoyed the higher profile on some of his contemporaries, but he was far more adventurous than most. It was a pairing with new-kid-in-town, Joe Henderson (ts) that was to produce a remarkable string of five albums over an 18-month period for Blue Note. Commencing in April 1963 with *Una Mas*, it was followed two months later by Henderson label debut *Page One* (CDP 7 84140 2) which included Dorham's 'Blue Bossa'. Two more albums were cut under Henderson's leadership *Our Thing* (CDP 7 84152 2) and 1964's *In 'N' Out* (CDP 7 84651 2) before the two players cut their last session together in September under Dorham's name *Trompeta Toccata*. One other Blue Note date from this remarkably productive period teamed Dorham and Henderson with Eric Dolphy on Andrew Hill's sixties classic *Point Of Departure* (CDP 7 84167 2). Up until his death, in 1972, age 48, Dorham rarely equalled this creative high. RC

THE DORSEY BROTHERS

THE DORSEY BROTHERS: BEST OF THE BIG BANDS
(Columbia 471659)

JIMMY DORSEY: CONTRASTS
(MCA GRP 16262)

TOMMY DORSEY: THE LEGEND
(RCA PD 89810) 3-CD box

It was always Tommy really. An outstanding trombonist who could play anything from downright tasty tailgate to supersmooth sweet, it was obvious that he'd make it. His reed-playing younger brother Jimmy was more sensitive and shy and though technically superb, he played little that ever made a lasting impression. And he was the one left onstage when Tommy headed out of the Glen Island Casino in 1935, leaving behind a star-studded (Glenn Miller, Ray McKinley etc.) two-beat big band. The outfits that the twosome went on to head individually, reflected their differing personalities. Jimmy's was neat, polite and heavy on the commercial aspect, many of the hits resulting from duets between vocalists Bob Eberly and Helen O'Connell. Tommy's band was more exciting and though he recruited such singers as Frank Sinatra and Jo Stafford, there were always moments of sheer heat thanks to the inspired arrangements of Sy Oliver and the trumpet soars of Bunny Berigan, Ziggy Elman and Charlie Shavers, or the drum fusilades of Buddy Rich. Eventually, before swing ceased being the thing, the Dorsey Brothers got back together and even gained their own CBS-TV show. One day, an up and coming Elvis Presley was their guest. End of story. FD

TOMMY DORSEY: THE POST WAR ERA
(Bluebird 07863 66156)

YES INDEED!
(Bluebird ND 90449)

GEORGE DUKE

THREE ORIGINALS
(MPS 519 198)

Fusion keyboard pioneer George Duke began his career playing straight jazz in a house rhythm section that accompanied, in its time, Dizzy Gillespie, Dexter Gordon and Kenny Dorham. One of jazz's great eclectics, he rapidly became interested in a wide variety of styles; and found himself in demand from leading musicians across the popular music spectrum, from Sonny Rollins to Jean-Luc Ponty to Cannonball Adderley to Frank Zappa. Between 1970-75, Duke was an intergral part of Zappa's Mothers Of Invention. His own recordings peaked in invention in the '70s with a series of fusion records for the MPS label, before his music's edge became blunted by alternatively a bland cocktail sound or chart-aimed headbanging funk pyrotechnics with sometimes collaborator, bassist Stanley Clarke. *Three Originals* is a double CD set bringing together *Love The Blues, She Heard Me Cry, The Aura Will Prevail* and *Liberated Fantasies* – arguably Duke's finest outings from the mid-'70s. The music ranges from Headhunters-style jazz/funk, to tough R&B, to Zappa-influenced, humorous experimentalism, and features vocalist Flora Purim, percussionist Airto Moreira, guitarist Lee Ritenour, Santana/Crusaders drummer Leon 'Ndugu' Chancler and Johnny 'Guitar' Watson. Though nowadays Duke is best known for his production chores with singer Anita Baker and her altoist Everett Harp, his almost annual gig at the Montreux Jazz Festival affirms that he is just as likely to perform in a straight acoustic setting as reliving the past with Stanley Clarke. LC

BILLY ECKSTINE

EVERYTHING I HAVE IS YOURS – THE BEST OF THE MGM YEARS
(Verve 819 442 2)

For years he fought the battle of the baritones with Sinatra, each of them claiming their fill of poll wins with the mags that meant most. Not that there was much similarity between the voices, Eckstine's was vibrant, larger than life, somehow filling the songs and running over. A blockbuster at the box office, when Mr. B crooned romantic knick-knacks like 'Everything I Have Is Yours', to his countless female admirers there wasn't a dry seat in the house. Handsome as an open cheque, he began his career as band singer with Earl Hines, then, during the bop era, formed a dream band boasting Charlie Parker (as), Dizzy Gillespie, Miles Davis, Fats Navarro (tpt), Dexter Gordon, Lucky Thompson, Gene Ammons (ts), Art Blakey (d), and vocalist Sarah Vaughan, Billy himself occasionally playing valve trombone. Eventually, kitted out in an array of slick roll-collar shirts and suits, a hip fashion-plate he went solo, and cleaned up, recording for MGM not only with studio orchestras but also with Woody Herman, George Shearing, Bobby Tucker, Nelson Riddle, the Metronome All-Stars, Pete Rugolo and other worthies. Thankfully, most of the memorables turnup on the two CD MGM anthology. One day, Savoy and/or Spotlite might release a CD of that dream band. Meanwhile, this one drips class. FD

BASIE-ECKSTINE INCORPORATED
(Roulette RCD 59042)

NO COVER, NO MINIMUM
(Roulette CDP 7 98583)

TEDDY EDWARDS

TOGETHER AGAIN!
(Contemporary 7588/OJC CD 424)

TEDDY'S READY!
(Contemporary 7583/OJC CD 748)

Together Again! an on-form 1961 reunion which also involves Howard McGhee (tpt) and Phineas Newborn Jr (p) harks back to a decade earlier when Edwards and McGhee were an integral part of L.A.'s Central Avenue scene. If McGhee was local top bop trumpet man then Edwards was one-third of a tenor triumvirate that included Wardell Gray and Dexter Gordon. Mindful of such lofty reputations, they are further secured on 'You Stepped Out Of a Dream' and 'Misty'. As with so many players who remained on the coast, Edwards was beset with a succession of bad breaks that prevented him from realising his goal as a major league player. When Dial Records boss Ross Russell (for whom Edwards recorded) upped and moved to New York, Edwards stayed put only to see most local recording opportunities instantly dry-up. Infact, the foursome gathered for *Teddy's Ready!* - Joe Castro (p), LeRoy Vinnegar (b), Billy Higgins (d) worked and recorded under the name of whoever copped the gig. Recurring dental problems didn't help Edwards, neither did being dropped from the early version of The Lighthouse All-Stars when the likes of Jimmy Giuffre and Bob Cooper became available. Professionally, Edwards' biggest mistake was his decission not to go on the road with Max Roach and Clifford Brown (*In Concert* Vogue 655602): a position taken over first by Harold Land and then Sonny Rollins. Having hung in there for so long, Edwards has nevertheless become an integral part of the L.A. music scene, collaborating with Tom Waits and returning to the recording studio under the auspices of Verve. RC

ROY ELDRIDGE

HECKLER'S HOP
(Hep CD 1030)

AFTER YOU'VE GONE
(MCA GRP 16052)

ROY & DIZ
(Verve 521 647)

Roy Eldridge was 'Little Jazz' to the informed, just 'Jazz' to his intimates but very much 'Monster' Jazz to the world at large. A master of overstatement, Eldridge had a superb trumpet technique and saw absolutely no reason to disguise the fact. The bravura 1937 title track of *Heckler's Hop* might be classified as his calling card but, even in potentially restrained performances like 'Stardust' or 'Body And Soul', he hardly seems able to contain himself. The jazz chops had been built on the territory band's of Zach Whyte, Charlie Johnson and McKinney's Cotton Pickers but, by the late 30s, he had Louis Armstrong, Red Allen and Hot Lips Page looking over their shoulders. Good as his playing had been in that decade, he peaked in the 40s. *After You've Gone* shows his mastery in groups of all sizes and ushers his jazz to the threshhold of bebop. No marriage actually took place between Eldridge and bop but, from the 50s, they conducted an ongoing affair of some passion. His once disciple Gillespie was a kindred spirit and they frequently found themselves in each other's company, *Roy & Diz* being typical. It found neither conceding an inch to the style of the other but on titles like 'Trumpet Blues' producing a joyful celebration of the instrument's finest characteristics. Being unable to play his horn for the final couple years of his life must have been hell for Eldridge. BMcR

DUKE ELLINGTON

EARLY ELLINGTON
(MCA GRP 36402)

AT FARGO
(Vintage Jazz Classics VJC 1019/20)

THE BLANTON-WEBSTER BAND
(RCA/Bluebird 5659 2 RB)

DUKE ELLINGTON AT NEWPORT
(CBS 450986 2) [L]

SUCH SWEET THUNDER
(CBS 469140 2)

BLUES IN ORBIT
(CBS 460823 2)

MONEY JUNGLE
(Blue Note CDP 7 46398 2)

Sheer quantity at a multitude of levels defies any easy assessment of Duke Ellington's massive contribution to jazz – and music in general. Moreover, his band and his music, once developed, remained completely distinctive throughout their existence, as though Ellingtonia and jazz itself were separate, yet mutually dependent. Though born in Washington DC, almost all Ellington's musical growth occurred in New York, where jazz was developing at a different pace and in a different manner than in New Orleans or Chicago. From the start, the east coast had evolved its own brand of ragtime which, in turn, generated Harlem Stride (see James P Johnson and Fats Waller). Stride was a crucial element in Ellington's own piano style (which, like Count Basie's, was significantly influential) and thus much of his melodic writing. Equally crucial were the contributions of his first major trumpeter, Bubber Miley, in bringing the New Orleans influence directly to bear on Ellington's music. In simplest terms, the secret of Duke's success lay in the effective marriage of Stride, New Orleans (via Miley) and New York's sophisticated dance band style. In fact, Ellington reworked musical ingredients similar to those used by Don Redman with Fletcher Henderson, but came up with his own unique formula. Though it evolved, broadened, and deepened in sophistication, it henceforth remained essentially the same, so that there was always a recogniseable link between the former glories of 'East St Louis Toodle-Oo' or 'Black & Tan Fantasy' and latterday achievements like *Such Sweet Thunder* or *Far East Suite*.

The pivotal moment in Ellington's career came in 1927, when he took over the tenure at Harlem's Cotton Club. Its vivid floorshows imposed a direction on Ellington's earliest work, allowing it to expand into the larger-than-life music that remains his hallmark. And, despite Miley's important and often overlooked contribution, it was Ellington's urbanity, wit, sophisticated sense of form, taste and innate musicality which allowed his music to develop so brilliantly. Among the musical levels it permeated, while always retaining a unique character, were the exotica of so-called 'jungle music', the pop song, the miniature concerto, the extended work, impressionism and the jazz theme. Nor were these categories kept separate. Elements of each were likely to rub shoulders within any composition. Its unique flavour was maintained by Ellington's very special gift for writing for particular individuals in the band – as personnels changed, so too did the texture of the arrangements. Equally importantly, individual compositions made striking use of theme changes, rhythmic development, texture and unusual voicings.

Although the brocaded voluptuousness of the Ellington sound, its richness of texture, depth of melody and variety often defy description, the Duke himself often gave his compositions immensely evocative titles reflecting their character. Aside from those mentioned, the exotica include 'Creole Love Call' and 'The Mooche'. But daily life at the Cotton Club also ensured a ready supply of dance or stomp tunes – like 'Jubilee Stomp', 'The Creeper', 'Rockin' In Rhythm' or 'Ring Dem Bells'. While many would remain in the book, newer impressionistic pieces looked further forward – 'Mood Indigo', 'Misty Morning' and 'Awful Sad' reached out to 'Harlem Air Shaft' and Billy Strayhorn's 'Chelsea Bridge'.

But Ellington's muse was not long to be contained within the three-minute form imposed by 78rpm record sides. Preceded oddly by an extended treatment of 'Tiger Rag', also spread over two disc sides, the first genuinely extended composition was 'Creole Rhapsody', paving the way for such later triumphs as *Black, Brown & Beige* (premiered at Carnegie Hall in 1944), *Such Sweet Thunder* (1957) and *Far East Suite* (1964-7). The mechanics of the Ellington band remained functional, even traditional, however. Unlike Basie, with whom he shared the stride legacy, Ellington was not initially a rhythmic pioneer and it was almost a shock when his most important aggregation, that of 1940-42, threw up the bassist Jimmy Blanton, who was the key figure in his instrument's development from Walter Page to the men of Bebop ('Sepia Panorama', 'You Took Advantage Of Me', 'Jack The Bear').

Ellington neglected the tenor saxophone almost until the end of the 1930s, then hired Kansas City man Ben Webster, boosting the development of one of the most individual sounds in jazz ('Cottontail', 'Bojangles', 'Chelsea Bridge'). The unique Webster legatee Paul Gonsalves would carry the banner from 1951. Ellington also maintained an adventurous setting for Barney Bigard's New Orleans-based clarinet style ('Harlem Airshaft', 'Rumpus In Richmond') long after Swing mechanised the instrument. In Johnny Hodges he long had one of the most glorious alto styles to deploy ('The Mooche', 'Day Dream', 'Jeep's Blues', 'Never No Lament', In A Mellotone'), while Duke's longtime friend Harry Carney had only Basie's Jack Washington as a baritone rival ('Sophisticated Lady', 'Jumpin' Punkins', 'Perdido').

Bubber Miley ('Black & Tan Fantasy', 'Creole Love Call', 'East St Louis Toodle-Oo', 'The Mooche') was followed by the equally articulate Cootie Williams ('Double Check Stomp', 'Concerto For Cootie') but perhaps the most individual of all was Freddy Jenkins' successor Rex Stewart ('Dusk', 'Portrait Of Bert Williams', 'Morning Glory'). Above in the trombones, Joe 'Tricky Sam' Nanton made even more mysterious magic with the plunger ('Black & Tan Fantasy', 'Rockin' In Rhythm', 'Jack The Bear' 'Ko-Ko') while Lawrence Brown played the straight man ('Across The Track Blues', 'Me & You'). But, above all, the 1940s introduced Ellington's *alter ego*, Billy Strayhorn – 'Sweet Pea'. He grew rapidly from lyricist to the indispensible arranger, with pieces like 'Take The 'A' Train' and 'Raincheck' – later 'UMMG', 'Intimacy Of The Blues' and 'Smada' – establishing such empathy with Ellington that few could tell where one finished and the other began. In the first half of the 1950s, Ellington's star was in the wane, despite this rich legacy. The big band then on most fans' lips was neither his nor Basie's but Stan Kenton's. But, at the 1956 Newport Jazz Festival, Ellington was catapulted back into public recognition, not by his new suite (named for Newport), but ironically by a solo on an old one – Paul Gonsalves' 27 manic choruses on the 1937 'Diminuendo & Crescendo In Blue' (itself a five-year-old routine). It led to a renewed spurt in Ellington's own writing, ranging from the following year's important Shakespearean suite *Such Sweet Thunder*, to a host of shorter vehicles for individuals in the band. Many remained with him for most, if not all their lives but, though influential, few had impact on the more radical developments in jazz, with the exception of Paul Gonsalves, much admired by such as David Murray and Frank Lowe. Ellington himself re-established his piano as a seriously important step in jazz development, if belatedly, through a series of small band recordings in the 1960s, most notably the *Money Jungle* collaboration with Bop pioneer, drummer Max Roach and bass avant-gardist Charles Mingus. (There was also a collaboration with John Coltrane). Ellington died in 1974, but rests secure in having created out of jazz a new orchestral language which elevated the idiom to the status of an art form. But he went further, taking it to a level of maturity on a par with the likes of American composers Copland and Barber. CS

THE OKEH ELLINGTON
(Columbia 466964 2)

THE DUKE'S MEN VOL. 1 & 2
(Columbia 468618 2/472994 2)

THE GREAT ELLINGTON UNITS
(RCA/Bluebird ND-86751)

CARNEGIE HALL CONCERT, JANUARY 1943
(Prestige 2PCD 34004 2) [L]

WORLD FAMOUS ORCHESTRA
(Hindsight HBCD 501)

HAPPY-GO-LUCKY LOCAL
(Musicraft MVCD 52)

THE COSMIC SCENE
(Columbia 472083 2)

BACK TO BACK
(Verve 823637 2)

SIDE BY SIDE
(Verve 821578 2)

DUKE ELLINGTON MEETS JOHN COLTRANE
(MCA/Impulse MCAD 39103)

FAR EAST SUITE
(RCA/Bluebird ND-87640 2)

NEW ORLEANS SUITE
(Atlantic 781376 2)

THE ENGLISH CONCERTS
(Sequel NED CD 183)

THE PIANIST
(Fantasy 9462/OJC CD 717)

DON ELLIS

HOW TIME PASSES
(Candid 9004 CD)

Although trumpeter Don Ellis' search for new, musical territories occasionally outstripped his creative mechanisms, he was an interesting and challenging musician. He worked with several genuine experimentalists and did sterling service with George Russell (*Ezzthetics* Riverside 9375/OJC CD 070 2) and The Stratus Seekers (Riverside 9412/OJC CD 365).His musical aspirations were sometimes inexplicably associated with those of Ornette Coleman and Cecil Taylor but his clever use of the twelve tone row on Improvisational Suite No. 1 from *How Time Passes* has far more to do with the Gunther Schuller/John Lewis brand of third stream music. His first big band in 1965 made ambitious use of unusual time signatures. He introduced electronics, vocal groups or amplified string quartets and continued to widen the horizons of his music. He used a four valve trumpet to facilitate his use of quarter tones in his 12-pitch quarter tone scale and persuaded his trumpet section to follow suit. He did make commercial concessions and gained massive popularity as he moved into the rock/fusion area in the early seventies. At heart, however, there remained the spirit of Red Allen – his favourite trumpeter. BMcR

HERB ELLIS

NOTHING BUT THE BLUES
(Verve 521 674 2)

No matter the style or the instrument, from Charlie Christian, Jack Teagarden and Hot Lips Page through to Illinois Jacquet, Jimmy Giuffre and Ornette Coleman, Texan musicians have, in one way or another, all been touched with the blues. guitarist Herb Ellis is no exception. Best known as a mainstay of the Oscar Peterson Trio (in turn a JATP stalwart) and, much later, part of a festival-friendly three-hander with Barney Kessel and Charlie Byrd, *Nothing But The Blues* establishes that continual references to a distinctive Texas tradition are not without reason when Ellis is in the spotlight. The sole example of the mid-'50s albums he recorded for Norman Granz, Ellis bends notes to perfection on 'Pap's Blues' and others accompanied by a front line that has Roy Eldridge, but more so, Stan Getz in uncharacteristic greasy mode. In the absence of anything else from this period (*Thank You Charlie Christian*, *Midnight Roll* and *Meets Jimmy Giuffre*) it's also advisable to check out those Peterson albums where Ellis is featured (*Compact Jazz: Oscar Peterson Plays Jazz Standards* (Verve 833283) and *At Zardi's* (Pablo Live 2620118). An award-winning reunion by the trio (Ray Brown again on bass) *Live At The Blue Note* (Telarc CD 83304) and *Saturday Night At The Blue Note* (Telarc CD 83306) are by far his best current representation. RC

BOOKER ERVIN

COOKIN'
(Savoy SV 0150)

As befits a Texas tenor saxophonist, Booker Ervin was comfortable with the blues. He was, however, a player with much more to offer. His period with Charles Mingus from 1958 to 1962 showed him to be a powerful reader of his leader's message and an inventive soloist in his own right. As the title suggests, *Cookin'* is the full frontal Ervin, basking in the shade of Horace Parlan's highly supportive pianistics and presenting his solo credentials in a straight forward manner. Like *Cookin'*, *That's It* (Candid 9014) was made while he was still with Mingus. On it Mojo shows how he merged elements of Dexter Gordon and John Coltrane into a coherent, personal style. Poinciana generates its own underlying passions while Uranus parades a floating, almost gentle method of delivery. Ervin's father had played trombone with Texas giant Buddy Tate but Ervin's premature death at the age of forty robbed jazz of an important link in the Lone Star State's tenor lineage. BMcR

BILL EVANS

SUNDAY AT THE VILLAGE VANGUARD
(Riverside 9376/OJC CD 140) [L]

WALTZ FOR DEBBY
(Riverside 9399/OJC CD 210)

UNDERCURRENT
(Blue Note CDP 7 90538 2)

You create trends by going against existing ones. And this is precisely what Bill Evans achieved. Though he had gained notice on the fringes, it wasn't until he joined Miles Davis for *Kind Of Blue* that it became evident Evans was a quantum leaper. Whereas Hard-Bop pianomen were extremely percussive, Evans was a gentle Steinway stroker and it was this aura of organised calmness that attracted attention. In many ways, he followed the pursuit of beauty favoured by the likes of Stan Getz: lyrical to a fault, but never remotely sentimental. It wasn't just as a pianist that Evans made his reputation. In collaboration with Scott La Faro and Paul Motian, he redefined the roles of the bass player and drummer within the framework of a piano-led trio: La Faro simultaneously interweaving a parallel improvisational line to that played by Evans while Paul Motian did much more than simply keep time. *Portrait In Jazz* (Riverside 1162/OJC CD 088) and *Explorations* (Riverside 9351/OJC CD 037) initially layed out the new rules, but *Sunday At The Village Vanguard* and *Waltz For Debby* (both recorded the same evening) represent the trio at their best.

Tragically, just over a week later, La Faro died in an auto smash. Though deeply affected by this tragedy, Evans later regained his composure and recorded much great music, but never again quite equalled the chemistry of what took place that Sunday in New York City. Equal to his lyrical genius was his sheer mastery of the piano. Where other bludgeon the listener with an overpowering technical brilliance, Evans refrained from flaunting his capabilities. Not for him flying sparks, Evans utilised his prowess to create highly literate and frequently intoxicating variations on romantic and introspective themes. Perhaps this is why he was often likened to Debussy. In most cases, listening to Bill Evans is very much a one-on-one experience as he approaches each selection with the same lightness of touch that one would expect from a Sinatra or Bennett (infact, the first of two collaborations with Bennett is as good as they come with 'The Touch Of Your Lips' a definitive reading.) A prolific recording artist, Evans was thus forever mindful of the lyric when approaching the Great American Songbook. Outside of the States, he insisted that Paris, Tokyo and Buenos Aires were the places he liked to perform best. Recorded but one year prior to his wasteful death at the age of 49, *Live In Buenos Aires*

(West Wind 2061) plus further club sessions from Keystone Korner (on Timeless) and Ronnie Scott's (on Dreyfus) are so full of vitality that there was no suggestion of impending doom. It's engraved on stone tablets that Marc Johnson (b) and Joe LaBarbera (d) made this final line-up the most rewarding Evans had led since the LaFaro/Motian. As with so much of his work, he constantly revised his own compositions 'Laurie', 'Letter To Evan', 'Waltz For Debby' and 'Turn Out The Stars', off-setting them with material as diverse as a heartfelt 'I Love You Porgy' to a rippling 'Theme From M.A.S.H.' If Bud Powell influenced a previous generation of pianists, Bill Evans proved to be the main inspirational source for Keith Jarrett, Chick Corea, Herbie Hancock, Joe Zawinul, Michel Petrucciani and practically everyone else since. Piano playing just doesn't come any better than this. RC

AT THE VILLAGE VANGUARD
(Riverside 60 017) [L]

THE TONY BENNETT/BILL EVANS ALBUM
(Fantasy 9489/OJC CD 439)

THE COMPLETE RIVERSIDE RECORDINGS
(Riverside 12 RCD 018) 12-CD Box

GIL EVANS

JAZZ MASTERS 23
(Verve 521 860 2)

PLAYS THE MUSIC OF JIMI HENDRIX
(RCA Bluebird ND88409)

GIL EVANS/LAURENT CUGNY
(EmArCy 838 794 2)

Although the individuality of Gil Evans' arranging style – the deployment of conventional and unconventional instruments, the imaginative chord voicing, his acute sensitivity to dynamics and stylistic eclecticism – was evident in the late forties, he didn't record as a leader until the late fifties. His first such recordings maintained the closely written style of what is still his best-known work, the orchestral settings for Miles Davis (*Miles Ahead, Porgy And Bess, Sketches Of Spain*), but in the early sixties his work became more spontaneous, as is demonstrated by *Jazz Masters 23* which collects highlights from the 1964 *The Individualism Of Gil Evans* and three luminous arrangements for guitarist Kenny Burrell from the 1964 *Guitar Forms*. Later in the decade, like Davis, Evans fell under the spell of the jazz-friendly Jimi Hendrix, and several jazzed-up Hendrix numbers entered the Evans book. The 1974 *Music of Jimi Hendrix* is illuminated by two bowling swing versions of 'Up From The Skies' and the penetrating alto sound of David Sanborn on 'Angel' and the late Evans anthem 'Little Wing'. Evans drew on top drawer New York players for various ensembles through the eighties, but in presenting some of the finest readings of new and old Evans arrangements, one of his last engagements, with the Paris-based Laurent Cugny Orchestra, provided a fitting summation of his career. MG

OUT OF THE COOL
(MCA MCA CD 9653)

JON FADDIS

LEGACY
(Concord CJ 291)

DIZZY GILLESPIE JAM/MONTREUX '77
(Pablo 2308 211/OJC CD 381)

Jon Faddis is by far the most awesome of all the high note trumpet specialists. His tone at the top of his range is fully rounded, his note production is clean and his intonation accurate. The late Dizzy Gillespie was a life-long inspiration and, in the seventies, Faddis made distinguished contributions to the bands of Lionel Hampton, Thad Jones-Mel Lewis, Gil Evans and Charles Mingus. His instrumental facility also made him a popular figure in the studios and since the memorable *Dizzy Gillespie Jam/Montreux '77*, Faddis has become increasingly involved with the international jazz festival circuit. This frequently meant working with his idol Gillespie and, in the earlier days, distinguishing between the two players was not always easy. The emergence of his own musical personality has been gradual but it has been positive, and the 1985 Concord release portrays his gentle lyricism ('A Child Is Born'), his traditional awareness ('West End Blues') and his bebop bravado. Sparkling in attack, logical in his solo construction and a master of controlled excitement, Faddis always brings an air of expectancy to a concert audience. BMcR

TAL FARLOW

A SIGN OF THE TIMES
(Concord CCD 4026)

Tal Farlow was one of several white musicians who dominated the guitar in the 1950s [see also Jim Hall, Barney Kessel etc,] but, unlike the great majority of modern jazz players, he did not ignore the lessons of Django Reinhardt. Aside from Christian and Reinhardt, Farlow also absorbed the styles of pianist Art Tatum and altoist Charlie Parker. And, despite being self-taught, he quickly became admired for an adventurous sense of harmony, and a blindingly virtuosic technique which earned him the nickname 'The Octopus' when it was exercised on the inordinately fast pieces he called 'skimmers'. This brought him to the notice of vibist Red Norvo, with whose influential trio Farlow made his reputation in 1950-53 alongside bassist Charles Mingus. Group interplay was very important and Farlow's work added textural variety by including unusual harmonics and bongo effects. A sign painter by trade, Farlow expressed his distaste for touring by dropping out of the scene at the end of the 1950s, re-emerging from his fastness in rural New Jersey only in 1968 and 1976, when he recorded the *op cit*, revealing none of his powers to have waned. Unfortunately, at the time of writing, none of Farlow's influential Verve recordings have been reissued on CD outside of Japan. CS

CHROMATIC PALETTE
(Concord CCD 4154)

RED NORVO: MOVE
(Savoy SV 0168)

RED NORVO TRIO VOL. 2
(Vintage Jazz Classics VJC 1008)

ART FARMER

THE ART FARMER QUINTET WITH GIGI GRYCE
(Prestige 7017/OJC CD 241)

MODERN ART
(Blue Note CDP 7 84459 2)

LIVE AT THE HALF NOTE
(Atlantic 90666) [L]

BLAME IN ON MY YOUTH
(Contemporary CCD 14042)

Art Farmer was one of many hard bop trumpeters who, in the mid-
'50s, jostled for East-Coast record dates. However, from his early
partnership with Gigi Gryce (as), Farmer seemed more ambitious
than most. Eager to expand his musical experience, he served time
with Wardell Gray, Lionel Hampton (participating in Clifford
Brown's 1953 Paris sessions), Quincy Jones, Charles Mingus,
Horace Silver and Gerry Mulligan (1958-59). *Modern Art* (a 1958
date) which pairs Farmer with tenorman Benny Golson (and also
features Bill Evans) proved a promising dry-run for the Jazztet the
pair would launch the following year. As with Rollins, Desmond,
Giuffre and Evans etc, Farmer discovered an ideal foil in guitarist
Jim Hall and together they co-led a foursome that brought out the
best in both musicians (1962-64) and of their recorded legacy *Live
At The Half Note* is the most realised. At around this period, Farmer
dropped the trumpet infavour of the more luxurious sounding
flugelhorn. For someone who has retained a consistent recording
career (Inner City, Enja, Soul Note, Concord, Denon), his attributes are surprisingly overlooked. A case in point being a string of
late'80s dates for the resurrected Contemporary label. If *Blame It
On My Youth* is of 24 carat classic dimensions then the remaining
sessions are nothing short of brilliant. RC

VICTOR FELDMAN

SUITE SIXTEEN
(Contemporary 3541/OJC CD 1768)

Victor Feldman was Miles Davis' first choice when, in 1963, he
started hiring young guns for what became his second greatest
quintet. But the talented Londoner was so in demand on the lucra-
tive Hollywood session circuit, that he declined Miles' offer leaving
Herbie Hancock a clear run at the gig. However, Miles titled *Seven
Steps To Heaven* after one of Feldman's originals plus including
'Joshua'. The finest all-round jazz musician ever to come out of
Britain, Feldman (a child prodigy who, at seven, was billed as 'Kid
Krupa') had achieved everything the local scene had to offer and, in
1955, relocated Stateside, joined Woody Herman, and later, The
Lighthouse All-Stars. Thereafter, becoming a session supremo. As
good a drummer as he was a vibes player and a first division pianist,
not to mention his gift as a composer/arranger, Victor Feldman had
his own signature sound whatever the instrument. Impressive contributions to Shelly Manne's classic *At The Blackhawk* in 1959, led to
Feldman supplying high rolling piano work on Cannonball
Adderley's *The Lighthouse*, notably 'Sack O'Woe'. Before leaving for
the States, Feldman undertook marathon recording sessions for
Tempo (under Tony Hall's supervision) featuring London's jazz
elite: Jimmy Deuchar, Dizzy Reece (tpt), Ken Wray (tmb), Ronnie
Scott, Tubby Hayes, Derek Humble, Harry Klein (saxes),Tommy

Pollard (p), Tony Crombie, Phil Seaman (d) etc. Built around an extended Tony Crombie original of the same title and featuring Feldman on vibes, *Suite Sixteen* encapsulates some of the best moments while a quartet while also including tracks by a septet and a spirited big band, but equally important, is a vivid, if somewhat rare, snapshot from that era. RC

SHELLY MANNE & HIS MEN:
AT THE BLACKHAWK – VOL. 1-4
(Contemporary 7577- 80/OJC CD 656-59) [L]

VOL. 5
(Contemporary 7577 – 81/OJC CD 656-60) [L]

CANNONBALL ADDERLEY:
AT THE LIGHTHOUSE
(Landmark LCD 1305) [L]

MILES DAVIS: SEVEN STEPS TO HEAVEN
(Columbia 466970)

MAYNARD FERGUSON

THE BIRDLAND DREAMBAND
(Bluebird ND 86455)

MAYNARD '61
(Roulette CDP 7 93900)

A MESSAGE FROM NEWPORT
(Roulette CDP 7 9327) [L]

There's an awful lot of frantic Ferguson about, records on which the ex-Claude Raeburn, Kenton and Charlie Barnet trumpeter's prodigious talent is utilised purely for grandstanding, reaching for impossible notes and prancing shriek to shriek. Here though are three chapters that meet the expectations of those who admire both the powerhouse and play-pretty aspects of the Canuck's work with a big band. With a book overflowing with arrangements by Manny Albam, Bob Brookmeyer, Al Cohn, Jimmy Giuffre, Bill Holman, Johnny Mandel and Marty Paich among others, the 1956 *Birdland Dreamband* established Ferguson as a serious contendor with 'You Said It' just one of many adrenalin rushes. 'Blues For Kapp' on *Maynard '61* (a Paich arrangment) utilises dynamics in a manner befitting the best in Basie, while 'Go East Young Man' tumbles ever-forward in impressive fashion, spurred by the drumming of Rufus 'Speed' Jones. The *Newport* set, from 1958, also works well in terms of controlled excitement and has much in common with the swinging side of Kenton – predominantly on 'Fan It, Janet', during which the trombones adopt the tough-shod approach of Kentonian slide-men. Again though, there's a relaxed Basie feel to such cuts as 'And We Listened' that provide a perfect platform for the leader's pyrotechnics without the demand for ear-plugs exceeding normal demands. FD

RACHELLE FERRELL

DEBUT/PORTRAIT
(Blue Note/Somethin' Else TOCJ 5520)

Released on Blue Note in 1991, The Manhattan Project brought together Wayne Shorter (ts), Michel Petrucciani (p), Stanley Clarke (b), Lenny White (d) plus others in a supposed super-group context. The slightly modified video version of the event included an outstanding performance not present on the CD – singer Rachelle Ferrell's treatment of 'Autumn Leaves'. However, it did appear on her hard-to-get debut, and caused many d-js to put it on heavy rotation to signal that for once, here was a genuinely original talent as opposed to yet another marketing department hype. Ferrell's ability to revitalise over-used saloon bar standards such as 'Bye Bye Blackbird' and 'My Funny Valentine' – and, at the same time, avoid the obvious pitfalls which, in the past, have sunk promising careers on their maiden voyage, placed her in a position of strength. Blessed with a vocal range which, at it's top end (perhaps) only dogs can hear (!), Ferrell has avoided being admired purely as a technician. None of the false emotion or bogus histrionics which have become *de riguer* in the melodramatic world inhabited by such as Whitney Houston and Mariah Carey figure in her agenda. She has, on the basis of her initial showing, all the attributes to become the most accomplished singer of the decade.

However, it appears that Ferrell is being pulled in a number of opposite directions simultaneously. A second eponymously titled release (Capitol CDEST 2177) seems to have suffered from such restricted distribution to make one believe that, this, her dive into the pop mainstream, doesn't exist! At the time of writing, the world holds a collective breath! JF

ELLA FITZGERALD

75TH BIRTHDAY CELEBRATION
(MCA GRP 26192)

PURE ELLA
(MCA GRP 16362)

ELLA FITZGERALD 1957-1958
(Giants Of Jazz CD 53159) [L]

BEST OF THE SONGBOOKS
(Verve 519 804)

The most popular jazz vocalist of all-time, Ella's way of things has sometimes been trashed by those who adjudge her style as 'too pure', 'not earthy enough' or, amazingly, 'not jazz'. In reality, Ella has never been anything other than a jazz lady, right from her early days as band singer (and eventually leader) with the seminal Chick Webb Orchestra, through her countless tours with Norman Granz's Jazz At The Philharmonic and onto her installation as *the* curator of America's greatest songbooks. It's the purity of her voice that often causes problems with those who seek problems, a seeming naivity. Yet, on her best records, those made in the sole company of pianist Ellis Larkins (*Pure Ella* segues two of those albums with Larkins together), it's this very purity that wins through, linking popular music with jazz in a manner that few have ever managed to attain. The MCA 2-CD set documents all the early Ella moves, the period with Chick Webb, her bop-era scat masterpieces, and the great recording partnerships with Louis Armstrong, Louis Jordan and suchlike. *1957-1958* proves to be the ultimate in-concert shot, with the Oscar Peterson Trio, while *The Best Of The Songbooks* acts as a handy sampler to Ella's acquaintance with the works of the Gershwins, Cole Porter, Harold Arlen, Irving Berlin, Richard Rodgers, Duke Ellington and Johnny Mercer, a line maybe over-praised but still upper-echelon. FD

ELLA SWINGS LIGHTLY
(Verve 517 535 2)

THE INTIMATE ELLA
(Verve 839 838 2)

ELLA AND LOUIS – CHEEK TO CHEEK
(The Entertainers CD 0215)

THE WAR YEARS 1941-1947
(MCA GRP 26282) 2-CD

SINGS THE ELLINGTON SONGBOOK
(Verve 837 035 2) 2-CD

THE GEORGE AND IRA GERSHWIN SONGBOOK
(Verve 821 024 2) 3-CD

TOMMY FLANAGAN

GIANT STEPS: IN MEMORY OF JOHN COLTRANE
(Enja 4022 CD)

BEYOND THE BLUEBIRD
(Timeless SJP 350)

The danger of playing as effortlessly as Tommy Flanagan is that listeners suspect the perfunctory. Listening to his beguiling piano behind Ella Fitzgerald, it is easy to forget the sophistication of his work with trombonist J.J. Johnson or that he was in the boiler room when John Coltrane sailed into the dramatic *Giant Steps*. Perhaps appropriately, it is Flanagan's own 1982 trio album of the same name that serves as an ideal introduction to his music. Served by the immaculate bass of George Mraz and the propulsive drums of Al Foster, Flanagan parades his talents, never emasculating the material but touching it with a considerable craftsman's hand. The 1990 *Beyond The Bluebird* refers to the Detroit jazz room, renews his association with guitarist Kenny Burrell and, more significantly, re-affirms his commitment to bebop as the wellspring of his inspiration. For all his own immense talent, it is not unusual to see Flanagan in an audience, digging another pianist, just because he loves the instrument and the music. BMcR

BUD FREEMAN ✗

BUD FREEMAN
AND HIS SUMMA CUM LAUDE ORCHESTRA
(Affinity CD AFS 1008)

If Hawkins had 'Body And Soul' and the immediate connection with Lester came with 'Lester Leaps In', then one-time Austin High School Gang alumni Bud Freeman was known for 'The Eel', a wriggly, fiddly, edgy tenor sax workout that acted as a trademark tune for the rest of his life. His Summa Cum Laude Orchestra, with which he recorded throughout 1939-1940 featured many of those who knew Chicago jazz best and proved a precursor of those outfits that would take Eddie Condon (guitarist with the SCLO) to radio glory a few years later. A veteran, who'd worked his way through the ranks of bands headed by Red Nichols, Joe Venuti, Roger Wolfe Kahn, Ben Pollack, Ray Noble, Tommy Dorsey, Benny Goodman and various others who knew an outstanding musician when they heard one, Bud's been called the first great white jazz saxman. And his easy-swinging choruses on such sides as 'Satanic Blues', 'As Long As I Live' and 'Sunday' (sometimes roughly recorded here) confirm all that's been said. In later years, Freeman was a founder member of The World's Greatest Jazz Band. FD

CHICO FREEMAN

SPIRIT SENSITIVE
(India Navigation IN 1070)

THE PIED PIPER
(Black Hawk BKH 50801)

The reactionary listener's jibe that the free players cannot work with 'changes' has had a mixed response. Most of the accused have, at some time, produced their 'straight' album and, as if it mattered, some have revealed feet of clay. Son of Von, Chico Freeman inevitably had his basics sorted out at home. He played briefly with an R&B band but soon began ground work in the free aspect of his music with Muhal Richard Abrams and the AACM. He emerged to an international audience via the Seventies' New York 'Loft Movement', seemingly equipped for most contingencies. For that reason, it is instructive to compare the 1978 *Spirit Sensitive* with the 1984 *Pied Piper*. The former is Freeman's sop to the reactionaries; a near conventional reading of, in particular, 'A Child Is Born' and 'Autumn In New York' with only a trace of chromatic licence to liven them up. The latter is a more powerful album. Cecil McBee (b) and Elvin Jones (d) are tight on the reins but they allow Freeman the licence to unseat 'Morning Sunrise' and the title track. To some, these two albums might represent contrasting aspects of Freeman's music but it is only a matter of degree. The reality is that he has no need to satisfy the doubtors nor need to impress the 'freedom now' specialist. There are no feet of clay here. BMcR

BILL FRISELL

POWER TOOLS: STRANGE MEETING
(Antilles ANCD 8715)

HAVE A LITTLE FAITH
(Elektra Nonesuch 79301)

A guitarist of stunning individuality and creativity, Bill Frisell had developed a unique sound (involving long electronic sustain and gentle tonal distortion) and has incorporated it into a huge array of different musics. As a sideman, he has worked with Norwegian, folk-influenced saxophonist Jan Garbarek, New York-based noise terrorist John Zorn, contemporary jazz pianist Paul Bley and quirky, iconoclastic drummer Paul Motian. *Strange Meeting* is a fine example of Frisell's noisier and more extrovert sound, as he teams up with bassist Melvin Gibbs and drummer Ronald Shannon Jackson in the Power Tools trio. Fine, expansive compositions form the basis for explosive, free improvisation. *Have A Little Faith* features Frisell's current trio with bassist Kermit Driscoll and drummer Joey Baron (as well as special guest Don Byron on clarinet) – one of the most original and finely-integrated small groups in contemporary jazz. The work is a tribute to American composers from all eras and traditions, including Aaron Copland, whose 'Billy The Kid' pieces are reworked into delicate, small group masterpieces, Muddy Waters, Sonny Rollins and even Madonna. LC

SLIM GAILLARD

LAUGHING IN RHYTHM –
THE BEST OF THE VERVE YEARS
(Verve 521 651)

Jazz's Clown Prince, Bulee 'Slim' Gaillard invented his own language (vout) and then sang, strummed guitar, plonked piano and
generally tap-danced his way to the bank via an array of the nuttiest
songs ever to appear outside a Spike Jones movie. And if his back-
slang voutereenie phrases ever got boring (to Slim not his fans)
then he'd switch to singing in Arabic or maybe spam Spanish. A
brilliant multi-instrumentalist who played alongside Dizzy
Gillespie and Charlie Parker, Slim turned the world into just one
big "oroonie"and, in the process, got himself canonized in Jack
Kerouac's Beat odyssey *On The Road*. The title of the album is
something of a misnomer because several of the tracks stem from
Slim's '40s sojourn with MGM, before Norman Granz ever got
around to launching Clef and Verve. But any disc that contains the
four part 'Opera In Vout', a masterpiece aimed at wrecking any
pure thoughts concerning such jazz hits as 'One O'Clock Jump',
'Big Noise From Winnetka', 'A Smooth One' and 'Hamp's Boogie'
while reminding non-believers of the wonders that comprises 'Hit
That Jive Jack', 'Cement Mixer' and 'Flat Foot Floogie', has to be
one of life's essentials. Definitely the surreal thing. FD

JAN GARBAREK

EVENTYR
(ECM 1200 CD 829 384)

TWELVE MOONS
(ECM 1500 CD 519 500)

OFFICIUM
(ECM 1525 CD 445 369)

The best known of a group of Eurocentric jazz musicians who have
come to characterise the subtle aesthetics of Manfred Eicher's
highly successful independent ECM label, Jan Garbarek brings a
hard, icy and unsentimental sound to the saxophone. In performance, he plays a sparse, angular music that has more to do with his
native Norway's folk tradition than the blues. *Eventyr* is a compelling picture of Garbarek's bleak but beautiful vision. This trio
session from 1980 finds him in the distinguished company of fusion
guitarist John Abercrombie and the Brazilian percussionist Nana
Vasconcelos. From 1993, *Twelve Moons* is the most satisfying of a
number of records looking at the Scandinavian tradition. As well as
keyboardist Rainer Brüninghaus, bassist Eberhard Weber and percussionist Marilyn Mazur, it features celebrated folk singer Mari
Boine, and some of the strongest compositions Garbarek has
recorded so far. Demonstrating Garbarek's superb ability to blend
into a variety of unlikely contexts without ever jeopardising his
own sound, *Officium* (1994) finds him working with the Hilliard
Ensemble on a collection of music loosely referred to as Gregorian
chant. Sometimes the saxophonist uses his gentle tenor tone to
blend as one of the voices, at other times his piping soprano
embellishes the music with contemporary harmonic twists and
turns. LC

I TOOK UP THE RUNES
(ECM 1419 CD 843 850)

RED GARLAND

RED IN BLUESVILLE
(Prestige 7157/OJC CD 295)

SOUL JUNCTION
(Prestige 7181/OJC CD 481)

This book will cite many players whose astylistic abilities have made them welcome in various jazz departments. At times, for Red Garland, this situation came within the same performance. The needs of Miles Davis and John Coltrane could hardly have been more different but Red Garland's piano on *Relaxin' With Miles* (Prestige 7129/OJC CD 190) or *Steamin'* (Prestige 7200/OJC CD 391) was masterful in its problem solving. The reason is not difficult to find. As his 1959 trio *Red In Bluesville* shows, be it 'See See Rider' or 'M Squad Theme', Garland used the full range of the piano in a poised and yet percussive way. Certainly his improvisations bore a natural logic and this was consistent with his talent for satisfying his colleagues' musical requirements. There is little doubt that he inspired confidence, even in major players. There is even a didactic quality on *Soul Junction* that seems to keep Coltrane on the straight and involved, as well as bringing out the best in a young and not fully matured trumpet player, Donald Byrd. He dropped out of music around 1970 but was a sick man when he made a sadly unconvincing comeback in 1983, one year before he died. BMcR

ERROLL GARNER

CONCERT BY THE SEA
(Columbia 451042) [L]

A black elf who placed the Manhattan telephone directory on his piano stool before clambering on it, Garner was all at once funny and romantic. A pianist with a style all his own, a tumbling, almost behind the beat way of things, he often hummed and yammered along as he meandered through the tunes that filled his head, frequently turning his intros into a "what's he gonna play next ?" exercise. This, his biggest-selling album and one that ranges from the bop of 'Red Top' to the bounce of 'How Could You Do A Thing Like That To Me?', a one-time Sinatra special, delivers most of the things you need to hear, except that he doesn't play 'Misty' for you. You'll find that on *Compact Jazz: Erroll Garner* (Mercury 830695). Also worthy of investigation is a treasure trove of previously unreleased EmArCy material available under the title, The Erroll Garner Collection: *Vol. 1* (832 994), *Vol. 2* (834 935), *Vol. 3* (842 419) and *Vol. 4 & 5* (511 821). FD

KENNY GARRETT

BLACK HOPE
(Warner Bros 9 45017 2)

It is probably true to say that, in the last year of Miles Davis' life, it was the young altoist Kenny Garrett who carried the main responsibility in the trumpeter's group. A product of the Detroit jazz training ground, Garrett played with the big bands of Mercer Ellington and Mel Lewis and was, for a brief time, a Jazz Messenger. His first album, *Introducing Kenny Garrett* (Criss Cross 1014) provided a useful introduction to his blues based style and had him matching the educated trumpet of Woody Shaw. He was introduced to Davis by saxophonist Gary Thomas and played with the trumpeter until the end, four years later. While with Davis, Garrett's own albums made a considerable impact. He wanted an 'African' sound for *African Exchange Student* (Atlantic 82156 2) and had Elvin Jones in the drum chair to heighten the effect he needed. *Black Hope* presents his more cosmopolitan face. It welcomes the rivalry of Joe Henderson (ts) on, in particular 'Bye Bye Blackbird' and has the leader in various musical guises, from hard bop quartet on 'Jackie And The Bean Stalk', Milesish funk on '2 Step' and 'Bone Bop' and culminating with the most delicious of alto soliloquys on 'Last Sax'. Still in his early thirties, Garrett represents the open minded attitude of today's young tigers. He has paid massive dues and has emerged as a very creative, finished product. B McR

STAN GETZ

THE ROOST QUARTETS 1950-1951
(Roulette CDP 7 96052 2)

AT STORYVILLE VOL. 1 & 2
(Roulette CDP 7 94507 2)

THE COMPLETE RECORDINGS OF
THE STAN GETZ QUARTET WITH JIMMY RANEY
(Mosaic MD3 131) 3-CD

AT THE SHRINE
(Verve 513 753-2) [L]

WITH J.J. JOHNSON LIVE AT THE OPERA HOUSE
(Verve 831272) [L]

FOCUS
(Verve 821982)

GETZ/GILBERTO
(Verve 810048 2)

October '51: Billie Holiday and Stan Getz shared the bill at Boston's Storyville Club. Lady Day was 36 and hitting the skids, while at 24, fresh-faced Stan Getz was set to establish himself as tenor Top Gun. As a member of Woody Herman's 'Four Brothers' sax team, Getz's solo on 'Early Autumn' in 1948 captured the public's attention prompting him to turn solo the following year. For Storyville Getz fronted such proto-boppers as Al Haig (p) and the great Tiny Kahn (d), to go for the burn. His exquisite tone and flexible improvisations may have earned him the Captain Cool tag, but 'Parker 51', 'Mosquito Knees' and 'Rubberneck' proved such assumptions to be deceptive. Henceforth Stanley The Steamer would be cooler than December, but hotter than July. For many, these recordings represent his finest hour.

When dealing with such a consistent body of work recorded over a 40-year period, it becomes a problem to select one album in preference to another. For many it inevitably becomes a question of collecting the lot! However, *Highlights* (Verve 841 445) serves as a perfect introduction to his lengthy association on Verve under the supervision of Norman Granz and, later, Creed Taylor.

Though events a year in the future would forever transform Stan Getz's fortunes, the 1961 *Focus*, a one-off collaboration with composer/arranger Eddie Sauter remains the most inspired exploration in a fusion of pop jazz and contemporary classical music. No party is forced to compromise while the inventiveness of 'I'm Late', is never deminished. A chance encounter with guitarist Charlie Byrd resulted in the Bossa Nova and the top ten hit 'Desafinado'; a jazz-meets-brazilian samba phenomenemon which proved to be last great worldwide musical trend before Beatlemania and even then, it continued to florish right up until the mid-'60s. Though nearly every major recording artist clambered aboard the bandwagon, few came close to replicating the sheer sensitivity Getz instilled into producing such 'beautiful' sounding music.

The Girl From Ipanema/The Bossa Nova Years (Verve 823611 2) four-CD set brings together most all the material with Luiz Bonfa, Laurindo Almeida, Antonio Carlos Jobim, Joao and Astrud Gilberto plus big band recordings. So high-profile was his image that it seemed only natural that Getz would explore the realms of fusion, so he commissioned Chick Corea to custom-write an appropriate repetoire. Captain Marvel (Columbia 468412) was the result and remains a referral course for today's fusionists.

Recorded at Ronnie Scott's by George Martin in 1971, *Dynasty* has Getz bringing fresh colourisation to the ubiquitous tenor/organ/guitar/drums format with devastating originality, while ten years later *The Dolphin* and *Spring In Here* document a straight-ahead return to form. Eminating from a near perfect 1981 San Francisco club date, Getz personalises 'How About You' and 'Spring Is Here' with such sensitivity to where it's like hearing them for the first time. Getz has always exhibited finite taste in pianists and his choice of Kenny Barron for the last years of his life maintained his score. Time was not on his side, but courage certainly was when Getz returned to Copenhagen with only Barron to record *People Time*, an emotive postscript to his career that would be terminated three months later by cancer.

DYNASTY
(Verve 839117 2)

THE DOLPHIN
(Concord CCD 4158)

SPRING IS HERE
(Concord CCD 4500)

ANNIVERSARY
(EmArCy 838769 2)

SERENITY
(EmArCy 838770 2)

PEOPLE TIME 1991
(EmArCy 510134 2)

STAN GETZ AT LARGE VOL. 1 & 2
(Jazz Unlimited JUCD 2001/2)

AND THE OSCAR PETERSON TRIO
(Verve 827 826 2)

WITH BILL EVANS/BUT BEAUTIFUL
(Jazz Door 1208)

PURE GETZ
(Concord CCD 4188)

WITH CHET BAKER/TOGETHER FOR THE FIRST TIME
(Fresh Sound FSR CD 1022)

TERRY GIBBS DREAM BAND

DREAM BAND VOL. 1
(Contemporary CCD 7647) [L]

THE SUNDOWN SESSIONS VOL. 2
(Contemporary CCD 7652) [L]

FLYING HOME VOL. 3
(Contemporay CCD 7654) [L]

MAIN STEM VOL. 4
(Contemporary CCD 7656) [L]

Nobody organises a big band with the thought of ever making serious money. Certainly not top vibesman Terry Gibbs, who almost bankrupted himself in the process of having the time of his life! Despite averaging out at $14 a man, this didn't prevent Gibbs from stocking his now legendary, riotous Dream Band with L.A.'s finest: stellar players from the bands of Stan Kenton, Woody Herman and the Lighthouse All-Stars like Conte Candoli (tpt) Frank Rosolino (tmb) Bill Holman, Richie Kamuca (ts) Mel Lewis (d) and Lenny Bruce's mad-cap alto-blowin' sidekick Joe Maini. This was a strictly-for-kicks gig and, almost to a man, they insisted that during its two year existance (1959-61) the Dream Band was one of the greatest-ever aggregations on 34 legs!
Steeped in the Lionel Hampton endless-party tradition, quite often their vocal encouragement to one another's playing is almost as loud as the roar of the band itself as it blazes through 'Jumpin' At The Woodside', 'Flyin' Home', 'Billie Bounce' and much more. That Gibbs' Dream Band eventually failed, was purely a question of economics and not indicative of its musical worth. However, these five uncompromising bop-based albums (much of the content never previously released) go some way to supporting the Dream Band's enviable word-of-mouth reputation. Super-drummer Mel Lewis claimed his best work was with Gibbs before relocating in the Big Apple, to lead his very own equivilant at the Village Vanguard. California Cool? More like Hollywood Hot! RC

DIZZY GILLESPIE

SHAW 'NUFF
(Musicraft MVSCD 53)

DIZ AND GETZ
(Verve 833 559 2)

GROOVIN' HIGH
(Bandstand BDCD 1513) [L]

AT NEWPORT '57
(Verve 513754 2) [L]

GILLESPIANA/CARNEGIE HALL CONCERT
(Verve 519 809 2) [L]

DIZZY'S DIAMONDS
(Verve 513 875 2)

Dizzy Gillespie was a fine jazz singer, useful percussionist, creative composer and brilliant band leader. He played passable composer's piano but, above all else, was one of the greatest trumpeters in jazz history. His personal history goes back to the bands of Teddy Hill,

Cab Calloway and Lucky Millinder but his prime spot was as trumpet spokesman for bebop. Without Gillespie, there would have been no Miles Davis, Clifford Brown or Don Cherry. *Shaw 'Nuff* covers both big band and combo performances and it lays the ground rules. The chord sequences were the backbone of the style and Gillespie demonstrates how new tunes were constructed on them. Gillespie had few peers but his recordings with Stan Getz, improvisational architect of the tenor, tell us a great deal. Getz's beautiful ministration to the gently contoured 'I Let A Song' and 'It's The Talk Of The Town' are matched but, on the up tempo 'It Don't Mean A Thing' and 'Impromptu', Gillespie thinks better at speed and tends to overwhelm his colleague.

Gillespie took part on several State sponsored tours which, in the main, are poorly documented. The two live sessions on *Groovin' High* provide a fine sampling of one touring band's music, with masterful Gillespie trumpet on 'Cool Breeze', 'Dizzy's Blues' and 'A Night In Tunisia'. All three selections are reprised on *At Newport '57*, by an up-front big band that also includes Lee Morgan (tpt), Melba Liston (tmb), Ernie Henry (as), Benny Golson (ts) and Wynton Kelly (p), plus 'Manteca', 'I Remember Clifford' and selections from Mary Lou Williams' 'Zodiac Suite' which also features the composer on piano. One of his most rewarding, musical partnerships was with Lalo Schifrin. Gillespie used him as a pianist but, more significantly, as a writer and *Gillespiana* represents the musical high point of their association. It was inevitably written with the leader in mind, with dazzling, descending arpeggios, bebop double time dashes but, most especially, with devices to complement the dedicatee.

There were many other fruitful collaborations. *Roy & Diz* with Eldridge (t), *The Big Four* with Joe Pass (g) and *Max & Dizzy*, Paris 1989 with Max Roach (d) were among the most successful but, for an effective precis of his fine Verve output, *Dizzy's Diamonds* rates highly. Devoted to big band, combo, special guests and Latin over its 3 CD's it shows Gillespie to be musically well dressed, whatever the hat. It is fitting that his last big band should be called United Nations Orchestra. Gillespie was a true international. BMcR

ROY & DIZ
(Verve 521 647 2)

DIZZY'S BIG FOUR
(Pablo 2310 719/OJCCD 443)

MAX & DIZZY
(A & M 6404 2)

JIMMY GIUFFRE

JIMMY GIUFFRE 3, 1961
(Soul Note 121158 2)

It's a measure of the modernism of the long unavailable music on *Jimmy Giuffre 3, 1961* that it sounds like ECM might have issued it yesterday for the first time. It was certainly as harmonically adventurous as anything Coltrane was then attempting and as abstract as anything on the freer edge of the avant-garde. Yet it created this impression without being raucous or jettisoning notions of form. Indeed, Giuffre's concern with motivic unity is one of the striking aspects of his playing and composition here, and the dynamic, far from being perpetually loud and full, is subdued, spare, ascetic, but immensely lyrical. Steve Swallow's alert and sharply responsive bass and Paul Bley's understated piano are the perfect complement to the leader's warm, woody clarinet. *Liquid Dancers*, though recorded 30 years later, is clearly from the same pen. It shows how well Giuffre's concept transfers to what is nominally a fusion setting, and here the same scrupulousness and melancholia of mood receive extra rhythmic impetus and ensemble colour, with Giuffre playing tenor, soprano and bass flute as well as clarinet. MG

DIARY OF A TRIO: SATURDAY/SUNDAY
(Owl 059/060)

THE JIMMY GIUFFRE 3
(Atlantic 90981)

HOLLYWOOD & NEWPORT 1957-58
(Fresh Sound FSR 1026)

BENNY GOODMAN

THE BIRTH OF SWING 1935-36
(Bluebird ND90601) 3 CD set

THE HARRY JAMES YEARS – VOL. 1
(Bluebird 66155 2)

LIVE AT CARNEGIE HALL
(Columbia 450983 2) [L]

THE COMPLETE SMALL COMBINATIONS 1935-37
(RCA ND 89753)

THE GOODMAN TRIO, QUARTET AND QUINTET
(Bluebird ND 82273)

The King of Swing, the King of The Clarinet, Goodman was indeed royalty. But it was a hard climb. For years, Benny shuffled around his native Chicago and New York, acquiring a reputation as an ace session face, sometimes leading bands that lasted as long as a recording session. But in 1934 he built a beauty, one that found fame through appearances on the *Let's Dance* radio show, the kids that heard, piling into L.A.'s Palomar to acclaim that Swing was the thing and Goodman was the potentate most likely to wing it to world domination.

The Bluebird and RCA releases document the glory years, when Fletcher Henderson's arrangements (plus those of Edgar Sampson and Jimmy Munday) would provide a basis for virtuoso performances by Goodman, trumpeters Bunny Berigan and Ziggy Elman, plus flash'n'crash drummer Gene Krupa, a role model for Keith Moon and a zillion rock drummers yet to come. Boosted by such riff-things as 'Christopher Columbus', 'Bugle Call Rag' and 'Riffin' At The Ritz", the band swung mightily, an added powerhouse dimension being attained when Harry James joined the trumpet section. Between them, James and Krupa turned 'Sing, Sing, Sing' into a showpiece guaranteed to shake rafters, even at Carnegie Hall, which the band turned into jazz Valhalla one memorable day in 1938, presenting the whole history of the genre, with help from members of the Basie and Ellington orchestras. If his ebullient sidemen often grabbed the attention with the big band, Goodman dominated the small group offerings, hailed as historic not only from a musical standpoint but also from the manner in which black musicians (Lionel Hampton and Teddy Wilson) stage-shared with Goodman and Krupa. Though his bands of the '40s lacked the pzazz of his '30s crews, Goodman's popularity was maintained by

such instrumental hits as 'Mission To Moscow' and pianist
Powell's 'My Guy's Come Back', another boost being the appeal of
teen vocalist Peggy Lee who turned 'Why Don't You Do Right ?'
into a jive-time anthem that still refuses to go away. But, the most
important member of the band to emerge during the Columbia
years was Oklahoma's Charlie Christian, who forgot that guitars
were supposed to be rhythm instruments and opted instead to
move outfront. Playing figures more suited to maybe a tenor sax, it
was a ploy that served Christian well when he began jamming at
Harlem's Minton's Playhouse and, along with Dizzy Gillespie,
Charlie Parker and Thelonious Monk, helped shape not only the
birth of bebop, but the shape of jazz for the next couple of decades.
Benny himself moved belatedly into the bop field (assisted by
trumpeters Red Rodney and Fats Navarro and tenorman Wardell
Gray), but the fashion for clarinets and even big bands was on the
wane, something of which he must have become aware as early as
1943, when an up and coming Frank Sinatra came in to guest at
Goodman Paramount Theatre gig and stayed to take over the
whole shooting match.
However,Benny continued on till the end of his days, performing
immaculately with both classical and jazz orchestras, never hitting a
bum note and always pulling his fill of punters. But it was in the
'30s and '40s that he did the things that mattered. Which is why
this recommended listing is so truncated. FD

SOLO FLIGHT
(Vintage Jazz Classics VJC 1021 2)

BEST OF THE BIG BANDS – BENNY GOODMAN
(CBS 466620 2)

CHARLIE CHRISTIAN –
THE GENIUS OF THE ELECTRIC GUITAR
(Columbia 480612 2)

THE COMPLETE CAPITOL
SMALL GROUP RECORDINGS 1944-55
(Mosaic MD4 148) 4-CD box

DEXTER GORDON

DOIN' ALRIGHT
(Blue Note CDP 784077 2)

OUR MAN IN PARIS
(Blue Note CDP 746394 2)

NIGHTS AT THE KEYSTONE VOL. 1, 2 & 3
(Blue Note CDP 794848-2/794849-2/794850 2)

Latecomers probably think of tenor-player Gordon in terms of
Dale Turner, the ageing end-of-the-road character he portrayed in
the film *Round Midnight*. But to those who queued earlier, Long
Tall Dexter was the epitome of hip, the horn-clutching beau in the
sharp chapeau, set amid a cigarette-smoke swirl, and captured for
all-time by the lens of Herman Leonard for a poster that practically
guarantees to pervade the homes of all purchasers with the true
smell of jazz.
For Dexter the jump-start was the Lionel Hampton Band of the
early '40s, playing alongside Illinois Jacquet on the very session
that produced the flagwaving 'Flying Home'. By 1944 he was part
of Billy Eckstine's blues'n'bop big band, he and Gene Ammons

fashioning one of the first tenor battles on 'Blowin' The Blues Away', creating a crowd-pleasing genre that would later result in such barnstorming duets as 'The Chase' and 'Steeplechase' with Wardell Gray and 'The Duel' with Teddy Edwards. Two terms of imprisonment following drug busts marred the '50s though the decade closed more happily when Dex was requested to compose a score, play and act in the LA production of Jack Gelber' play *The Connection*. Three of the tracks 'Soul Sister', 'I Want More' and 'Ernie's Tune' are to be found on *Dexter Calling* (Blue Note CDP 746544 2). The lean years over, Dexter signed with Blue Note in 1961 and immediately moved into high-quality overdrive, fashioning such essentials as *Doin' Alright*, with an up-and-coming Freddie Hubbard providing youthful fire to Gordon's thoughtful, relaxed but ever-probing lines, plus such other not-to-be-misseds as *Go!* (CDP 746094 2) with it's breath-taking reading of 'Guess I'll Hang My Tears Out To Dry', *A Swingin' Affair* (CDP 784133 2) *One Flight Up* (CDP 784176 2) with a monumental modal 18-minute 'Tanya' offering superb examples of his big-toned cavernous sound and *Our Man In Paris*, the last named being a return to bebop heyday with the aid of such influential Bird buddies as Kenny Clarke (d) and Bud Powell (p). A lengthy sojourn in Europe resulted in a flow of recordings for Steeplechase and Black Lion, most of these possessing various highpoints – *Body And Soul* (Black Lion BLCD 760133) and *'Round Midnight* (Steeplechase SCCD 31290) being among the most creative -though, on the whole, they lack the cohesiveness and downright feel of the Blue Note period.

Reborn in the USA during 1976, following SRO gigs at the Storyville and Village Vanguard clubs, Dexter pacted to a US major for the first time in his life, one result being *Homecoming* (US Columbia 4664412), an invigorating live at the Vanguard set, recorded in the company of trumpeter Woody Shaw, though these sessions are easily matched by those that fill the *Nights At The Keystone* releases of 1978/79, all of which spotlight not only Gordon's ever-swinging, often humorous (the opening 'It's You Or No One' begins in a manner that would do credit to 'Hoots Mon!'), but also the remarkable keyboard-playing of George Cables. Virtually in retirement during the early '80s, but making spasmodic recordings to keep the chops in trim, Dexter faced yet another comeback in 1986 after starring in Bertrand Tavernier's *Round Midnight* and garnering himself an Oscar nomination. Music from the soundtrack appears on *The Other Side Of Midnight* (Blue Note CDP 746397 2) and provides, at the very least, an atmospheric way to say goodbye. FD

STEPHANE GRAPPELLI

SPECIAL 1947-61
(EMI CDP 794481 2)

Grappelli's old sparring partner Django Reinhardt once said of him "Because Stephane does not accept that there are limitations in music he is able to do anything". And certainly like Coleman Hawkins and Benny Goodman, Stephane has been able to circumvent fashions in jazz by simply ignoring them. Although the historic Hot Club of France recordings with Django are rightly regarded as classics, the violinist's work has consistently improved since then. More than anyone else he has done more for the acceptance of the violin as a legitimate jazz tool even though Joe Venuti and Stuff Smith (both jokers at heart), had stated claims for the instruments. Still it was Grappelli's insistent swing and dedication to the melody that saw off the cavilling critics. *Special* features tracks from 1947 to

1961 and is as fine a compilation as you would require. The early tracks feature an all-French line-up excluding Django and the choice of French tunes lends an evocative Gallic flavour. Grappelli seems determined to prove himself a formidable presence away from Django and largely comes on like an angry bee. 'Lady Be Good' leaps off the disc. It is difficult to imagine anyone else being so creative at such breakneck tempos. Through the 60's Grappelli recorded profusely with many combinations. His career stepped up a division in the 70's largely due to albums such as *Tivoli Gardens, Copenhagen, Denmark* (Pablo 2308 220/OJC 441) where he is perfectly matched with Joe Pass (gtr) and Niels-Henning Orsted-Pedersen (b) plus the campaigning efforts of British guitarist Diz Disley whose sympathetic playing can be heard with fellow plectrumist Martin Taylor on *Live in San Fransisco* (Black Hawk BKN 51601) from 1982. Now, well into his eighties, with his tone a little roughened but as vigorous as ever, this master musician can be caught in concert on *Nuages - Live in Warsaw* (Happy Price A AOMP 93382). Here, his improvisations are like a form of exquisite embroidery. Although with Grappelli the formula is always the same, his driving, energetic flow of ideas and *joie de vivre* is the reason why he has remained so relevant and popular over 50 years. JM

WARDELL GRAY

THE CHASE
(Giants Of Jazz 53064)

MEMORIAL ALBUM VOL. 1
(Prestige 7008/OJC CCD 050)

MEMORIAL ALBUM VOL. 2
(Prestige 7009/OJC CCD 51)

Known respectively as Long Tall Dexter and The Thin Man, Dexter Gordon and Wardell Gray were the sharpest pair along L.A.'s Central Avenue where, in the summer of '47, bop was big box office. In the wake of their hit single, 'The Chase' and later, 'The Hunt' the tenor tournements they staged almost nightly at The Bird In The Basket restaurant or during Gene Norman's all-star 'Just Jazz' shows generated the longest queues. Even beat author Jack Kerouac took notice, name-checking 'The Hunt' in *On The Road* as being a particular favourite of Dean Moriarty. While Dexter translated Bird straight onto tenor, Wardell retained his swing sensibilities absorbing only those bop devices that served his needs; a unique mix that, between 1948 and 1951, saw the elegant player dividing his activities between the small groups of Benny Goodman and Count Basie (with whom he cut 'Little Pony') plus occasional work with Tadd Dameron alongside Fats Navarro.
Memorial gathers up the best of his Prestige period and contains 'Twisted' recorded in 1949, using Bird's rhythm section of Al Haig (p), Tommy Potter (b) and Roy Haynes (d). Jivey it may well be, but Wardell drops in enough bop reference points to make it acceptable on 52nd Street. Again, when shoulder-to-shoulder with Bird on the 1947 Dial session that produced 'Relaxing At Camarillo' he was just as contemporary as the leader. Adept in constructing the most logical solos it's Gray's records that inspired 'vocalese' diva Annie Ross to first kit out 'Twisted' with a set of off-kilter lyrics and later two more of his Prestige sides, 'Jackie' and 'Farmer's Market'. *Live At The Haig 1952* (Fresh Sound FSR CD 157) freeze-frames him slightly less than eloquent with Art Farmer

(tpt) and the Hampton Hawes trio in suitable modernist mode. Just three months after Bird's shock death in 1955, Wardell Gray's own demise, age 34, was an ignominious drug related affair. His body, the kneck broken, was discovered in the desert on the outskirts of Las Vegas, sparking off rumours of gangland retribution, bizarre sex games, a heroin hot-shot. With insufficient fans to create a cult following, Wardell has become an almost forgotten figure. RC

BENNY GREEN

THE PLACE TO BE
(Blue Note CDP 8 29268)

Pianist Benny Green has never forgotten the valuable lessons learned at the jazz equivilant of boot camp – The Jazz Messengers. His respect for the past and his predecessors has been prominent on every album he's made as a leader. It's also evident that Benny Green is acutely aware of what was is require to float and then sustain a successful jazz career in the 1990s; an ability to appeal to both American and Japanese record buyers as a springboard to the lucrative international festival roundabout. Basically, don't make wave. Or, if you have to, make them small ones! After a couple of releases on Criss Cross, it seemed only natural for Green to gravitate to his spiritual home – Blue Note. Trio dates *Linage* (CDP 7 93670), *Greens* (CDP 7 96485) and *Testifyin': Live At The Village Vanguard* (CDP 7 98171) singled him out from the pack, but a desire to overtly pay respect to Bud Powell and Horace Silver meant that little of Green's originality shone through, At this juncture, the suggestion that his supporting role on other artists sessions seemed more testing wasn't without foundation. *The Place To Be* resolves some outstanding problems. Christian McBride remains constant on bass, the redoutable Kenny Washington replaces Carl Allen on drums, while arranger Bob Belden colours a number of tracks with contemporary sounding charts played by six horns. TH

GRANT GREEN

GRANTSTAND
(Blue Note B21Y 46430 2)

BORN TO BE BLUE
(Blue Note CDP 84432)

During one week in January 1961, guitarist Grant Green and organist Baby Face Willette appeared on each others Blue Note debut – *Grant's First Stand* (TOCJ 4064) and *Face To Face* (TOCJ 4068) then, with their mentor, altoist Lou Donaldson out front cut *Here 'Tis* (TOCJ 4066). In doing so, they served notice of new changes in Blue Note's policy that met with resounding commercial success the following year. By then, Green, Willette (soon to be replaced by Big John Patton) and drummer Ben Dixon had become the label's much-employed house rhythm section. All had extensive R&B bar-band experience which gave their work a passionate edge. *Grantstand* (recorded in August 1961 and featuring Green in a head-to-head with organist Brother Jack McDuff and saxman Yusef Lateef) gives some indication as to the game-plan. The biggest obstacle confronting modern jazz guitarists had always been establishing an instantly recognisable signature. In too many instances, the electrics got in the way of the ideas reducing the instrument's natural sound to muffled dust-on-the-needle dimensions. No such problems hampered Green, the guitar's most accomplished improviser since Wes Montgomery. A devotee of Charlies Christian and Parker, he adopted the single string lines of the former, the hornlike constructions of the latter and a sweet-and-sour tone all of his own making. Whereas, such recordings were focused upon hittin' a groove (a genre he would return to in the '70s), a series of straight ahead sessions Green convened with pianist Sonny Clark of which *Born To Be Blue* is a taster for the Mosaic's more expansive 4-CD evaluation *The Complete Blue Note Recordings Of Grant Green with Sonny Clark* (Mosaic MD4 133).   RC

JOHNNY GRIFFIN

INTRODUCING
(Blue Note CDP 7 46536 2)

WES MONTGOMERY: FULL HOUSE
(Riverside 9434/OJC CD 106) [L]

Johnny Griffin blew in from the Windy City, in 1956, and with his Blue Note debut, *Introducing* (aka *Chicago Calling*) put fellow tenormen on notice that he was taking scalps! Extensive road work with the kamikazi R&B band of trumpeter Joe Morris and Lionel Hampton's sweat-soaked Flying (Home) Circus, built up Griffin's stamina to where he was in a position to take on all-comers. And did! Relentless to a fault, on the five minute sprint that is 'It's Alright With Me' he comes close to running Wynton Kelly (p), Curley Russell (b) and Max Roach (d) ragged. That's not Max yelling encouragement but a plea for mercy! As with any good musician he borrowed freely from the best sources (Hawkins, Jacquet, Rollins), but what came out carried his own individual stamp. Aside from his quick-draw skills, it has was Griffin's sheer cockiness ,wry sense of humour and overall exhuberance that made him irresistable. Such fiestiness so impressed Art Blakey that he inaugurated Griffin as a Jazz Messenger in time for their summit meeting with Thelonious Monk.

In turn, Griffin enrolled in Monk's College Of Knowledge following Rollins and Coltrane as front man onto the stage of The Five Spot. An assignment which in no way cramped Griffin's style. The resulting evidence *Thelonious In Action* and *Misterioso* corrobrates, it was business as usual. Other rewarding encounters included a lengthy run as one half of a two tenor tag team with Eddie 'Lockjaw' Davis which had Griffin snapping like a demented terrier at his partner's heels (*Lookin' At Monk*).

Full House is the result a near-perfect 'live' off-the-cuff date from June '62 with guitarist Wes Montgomery and the Miles Davis rhythm section. The juxtaposition on 'Cariba' and the title track of Montgomery's unique melodic double octave runs to Griffin's familiar though seductive attack made for strong medicine. The mid-'60s saw Griffin move to Europe – his base of operations ever since. And while recording prolifically, never again quite found himself as confrontational as when pitching in with Lockjaw, Monk or Blakey. JF

THELONIOUS IN ACTION
(Riverside 1190/OJC CD 103) [L]

MISTERIOSO
(Riverside 1133/OJC CD 206) [L]

LARS GULLIN

VOL. 1 1955-56 WITH CHET BAKER [L]
(Dragon DRCD 224)

VOL. 2 1953
(Dragon DRCD 234)

Never mind the can-white-men-sing-the-blues argument. Back in the early '50s, the big debate was, can Swedes play Bebop? Outside of the US, a group of Stockholm based torch-bearers lead by Arne Domnerus (as), Bengt Hallberg (p) and a highly inventive baritone sax player Lars Gullin, were not only amongst the first to decipher music's new language but to do so with such authority as to have their records released in both the US (Blue Note, Contemporary etc,) and the UK (Esquire).The inspiration for the wayward sax-man in the cult movie, *Sven Klang's Quintet*, Lars Gullin's name may well be mentioned in the same breath as Serge Chaloff and Gerry Mulligan, but he had such a distinctive sound so very much his own that there was no mistaking his work. The same criteria applied to his compositional efforts which were often based on Scandinavian folk melodies. Though closer in temperment and agility to Lee Konitz (present on Vol. 2 together with a contingent of Kentonites) than any other player, Gullin, as the airshots with the Chet Baker Quartet (featuring doomed pianist Richard Twardzik) reveal, would later reach a state of grace equal to that of Serge Chaloff. A major league player from the outset, these represent the first two installments in Dragon's vocational vinyl-to-CD transfer of the great man's work which promises all the mid-'50s sides Gullin recorded with a quartet that included guitarist Rolf Berg. RC

BOBBY HACKETT

COAST CONCERT/JAZZ ULTIMATE
(Dormouse International DMI CDX 02)

Bix didn't die, he just lived on in the trumpet/cornet playing of Bobby Hackett. His playing was beautiful. No other word for it. There was a crystalline quality about his work. His tone was perfection itself. And his solos were immaculate, each note exactly where it ought to be, no more, no less. Thing was, Bobby could play in any setting. Basically a guitarist with a drinking problem when he worked with Glenn Miller, one day he upped and played a cornet solo on 'String Of Pearls'. Yes, *that* cornet solo. After which, nobody ever attempted to play it differently and the solo became virtually a part of the written arrangement. A regular at Eddie Condon's in a pure jazz capacity, he switched yet again during the '50s and made a series of gorgeous mood albums with a string orchestra theoretically headed by comedian/actor Jackie Gleason. There were more jazz recordings along with regular helpings of back-up work with such singers as Tony Bennett ('The Very Thought Of You') and Lee Wiley. And though compounded by insomnia the alcohol gradually took its toll, on record Hackett continued to supply solos that were so artistic they should be framed and hung in some gallery alongside the best of Monet. *Coast Concert*, half of which is by Hackett and half by a Jack Teagarden Quintet, is representative of late '50s mainstream jazz, but true romantics might well bend an ear to Jackie Gleason's doubleplay *Music To Make You Misty/Night Winds* (Capitol CDP 7 92088 2) the first half of which features Hackett playing sheer melody. And if ain't jazz, then it damn well ought to be. FD

CHARLIE HADEN

CLOSENESS DUETS
(CDA 0808)

FOLK SONGS
(ECM 1170)

LIBERATION MUSIC ORCHESTRA
(Impulse MCAD 39125)

Charlie Haden is an excellent bassist, a fine composer, imaginative band leader and, unquestionably, a political animal. If he had done nothing but play superbly with Ornette Coleman (*Beauty Is A Rare Thing* – Rhino/Atlantic R2 71410), his position in jazz would have been secure. Ironically, the same could be said of his work with Archie Shepp, Keith Jarrett, The Jazz Composer's Orchestra and Old And New Dreams. He was simply the first bassist to fully appreciate the rhythmic needs of the free form combo.

He has a full, warm tone, a relaxed dexterity and he colours all he plays with a touch of vibrato. Only the 1976 edition of his superb *Duets* has been released but it shows how superbly he responds to Jarrett, Coleman, Alice Coltrane (p) and Paul Motian (d) in the confined space of a duo. Almost contemporary with them, *Folk Songs* exhibits somewhat different merits with saxophonist Jan Garbarek and Egberto Gismonti on guitar and piano but with Haden voluntarily accepting an auxiliary role. His debut as leader could not have been better. The 1969 *Liberation Music Orchestra* exploited the international aspects of his music as well as his politcal awareness. It linked the battle cries of the Spanish Civil War with the anguished side of the American avant garde. Carla Bley did most of the arranging but all involved contributed to the marvellously evocative music and in 'Song For Che', Haden provided its crowning glory. Haden co-formed the Coleman style Old And New Dreams in 1976 and, in the eighties, recorded with a new LMO formed by teaming Carla Bley's band with O & ND. (*Ballad Of The Fallen* ECM 1248). Haden's fascination with *film noir* era Hollywood movies found its outlet in his pollwinning Quartet West with saxophonist Ernie Watts, pianist Alan Broadbent and drummer Larance Marable. A regular attraction in the 90s, it upholds Ornette Coleman's statement that 'Charlie's music brings one stranger to another and they laugh, cry and help each other stay happy'. BMcR

HAUNTED HEART
(Verve 513 078 2)

ALWAYS SAY GOODBYE
(Verve 521 501 2)

JIM HALL

JAZZ GUITAR
(Pacific Jazz 7 46851 2)

WITH BILL EVANS: UNDERCURRENT
(Blue Note CDP 7 90538 2)

Often more pursasive in tamdem with such individualists as Bill Evans, Jimmy Giuffre, Sonny Rollins, Paul Desmond, Art Farmer and Michel Petrucciani, Jim Hall gained instant recognition by virtue of his guitar work in the commercially successful chamber-jazz environs of Chico Hamilton's Quintet (1955-56) and later with

Jimmy Giuffre's folksy The-Train-And-The-River era trio (56-59). A more supportive role working in Ella Fitzgerald's rhythm section (1960-61) was followed by brief associations with Lee Konitz and 'Bridge'-period Sonny Rollins before involving himself in an inspired collaboration with Art Farmer (1962-64). Initially Hall's style may have been an extension of Charlie Christian's, but one could also detect traces of Django Reinhardt. However, it was his ability to enhance proceedings with a highly-personalised azure tinge that gave Hall a personal signature which he used to great effect on Bill Evans' *Undercurrent*. An often dream-like 1962 summit meeting with the impressionistic jazz pianist, it presented Hall at a creative peak. Though he records regularly (Concord, Limelight), Hall's last great encounter was Michel Petrucciani's *Power of Three*. Recorded live at the 1986 Montreux Jazz Festival, what was originally intended as a duo between Petrucciani and Hall took on an added bonus dimension with the introduction of tenor saxophonist Wayne Shorter which produced the memorable 'Bimini'. RC

ALL ACROSS THE CITY
(Concord CCD 4384)

LIVE AT TOWN HALL
(Limelight 820843) [L]

POWER OF THREE
(Blue Note CDP 7 46427 2) [L]

SCOTT HAMILTON

IN CONCERT
(Concord CCD 4233) [L]

THE SECOND SET
(Concord CCD 4254) [L]

GENE HARRIS-SCOTT HAMILTON QUINTET: AT LAST
(Concord CCD 4434)

There's nothing wrong with being old fashioned if you sound like Scott Hamilton. Unlike others of his generation, Hamilton goes back to the 1930s and 1940s for his source, ignoring the middlemen. His heroes are Coleman Hawkins, Ben Webster, Lester Young and other charismatic big-toned tenors of the pre-Bop era. Hailed by many as the 'Mainstream Messiah', *In Concert* and *The Second Set* both stem from one concert taped in Tokyo (1983), during which the Young Fogey of the tenor roots through tried and tested standards ('All The Things You Are', 'One O'Clock Jump' etc) in his non-partisan way backed by his New England compatriots with John Bunch, an automatic choice on piano. Hamilton appears to favour medium tempos, swooping in with long slurred phrases interspersed with jumping clusters and imbuing them with so much inventive melody that the improvisations sound like sketches for future ballads. 'Stardust' is a perfect example of his ruminative style. His absorption of new trends adds an updated perspective to his Swing-based stance. Similarly on *At Last* pianist Gene Harris pushes the set along eliciting from Hamilton a blistering 'After You've Gone', a shimmering 'Blues For Gene' and a full-bodied 'I Fall In Love Too Easily' with the saxman, again, in his expected ballad form. JM

LIONEL HAMPTON

LIONEL HAMPTON AND HIS ORCHESTRA
(Giants Of Jazz CD 53115)

CHICAGO JAZZ CONCERT
(Columbia 21107) [L]

Vibraphonist/drummer/pianist, Hampton's whole resume, from his days as a sideman in the late '20s and '30s, through to a his era as leader of a dynamic big band during the '40s and '50s, is laid out on Danish-based Official's *Most Important Recordings* (83059) . But the GOJ offering contains all you really need to know about the frantic antics of that memorable big band, the endless two-fingered piano boogies, the torrid tenor rides that comprised 'Flying Home' (with Illinois Jacquet) and 'Flying Home No. 2' (with Arnett Cobb), the zany pop chant of 'Hey! Ba-Ba-Re-Bop' and the bop-meets-R&B integration that is 'Red Top'. In much the same spirit, the 1954 *Chicago Jazz Concert* allows you to feel the hot breath of the beast from a front row vantage point. Nothing's tidy or hung up in the right place. But that's the fun of things. It's a free-spirit world of steam-heat trumpets, tenors that go walkabout, a rhythm section born in a Harlem juke-joint and a genius of the vibes who can out-swing anyone no matter their instrument. Go, Hamp, go! FD

1946-47 – MIDNIGHT SUN
(MCA GRP 16252)

HOT MALLETS – VOL. 1
(Bluebird ND86458)

THE JUMPIN' JIVE 1937-39 – VOL. 2
(Bluebird ND82433)

HAMP & GETZ
(Verve 831 672 2)

HERBIE HANCOCK

MAIDEN VOYAGE
(Blue Note CDP 7 46339 2)

CANTALOUPE ISLAND
(Blue Note CDP 7 8 29331 2)

MWANDISHI –
THE COMPLETE WARNER BROS RECORDINGS
(Warner Archives 9362 45732 2) 2-CD

HEAD HUNTERS
(Columbia 65928)

QUARTET
(Columbia 46642)

You want, Herbie's got it. That's the way of things and always has been. Movie soundtracks? Check out *Blow-Up* or maybe *Death Wish*. Support jobs? That's Herbie behind Miles on everything from *Miles Smiles* to *Bitches Brew* and backing Dexter Gordon on *Takin' Off* and the *Round Midnight* soundtrack. A kid who grew up adoring the keyboard playing of George Shearing, then forgetting everything he learned in an attempt to fashion his own style, Herbie's a piano-man for all reasons. Scratch a '60s pop fan and maybe he'll tell you that double-H wrote 'Watermelon Man' the chunk of latin funk that graced his debut set *Takin' Off* and inspired a chart hit by Mongo Santamaria. Think electronic dance and maybe someone will remember that Herbie shaped 'Rockit', an invitation to raves yet to come. He can be as commecial as a detergent ad or so introspective that an audience can be induced into sonambulism after just a couple of on-stage ballads. Perhaps he's at his best when touching the rails on both sides, dreaming up tunes to whistle at jazz cafes yet using these easy-to-loves as a basis for experiments to keep 'em alive, intriguing, probing, open for business. Virtually every aspect of the *ouevre* is open for inspection via the listed albums, *Maiden Voyage* (1964) proving ideal starter for one. The *Cantaloupe Island* compilation is a *Best Of* that includes 'Watermelon Man' and the title track, a Hancock composition that not only hit platinum when rapped-up recently by US3 but also continues to decorate a better class of TV commercials rather than test cards. The Warner double-CD, which links 'Fat Albert Rotunda', a funky-butt special for the in-crowd, with 'Mwandishi' (basically a suite pieced together by Herbie, clarinet-player and flautist Benny Maupin,along with trombonist Julian Priester) can be filed under 'Ambient African', demonstrating just how diverse a musician Hancock can be, all within the space of one brief recording contract. The synth-full *Headhunters* (1973), is the *bona fide* fast fusion classic, Herbie's own *Bitches Brew* or thereabouts, with a track title 'Sly' providing a probable nod in the direction of another funk influential. *Quartet* (1982) brings everything back to home base, as Hancock switches off the current and swops choruses with Wynton Marsalis, as his former Miles Davis Quintet rhythm pals, Ron Carter and Tony Williams provide a bass pad for which to launch tuneful assaults on such standards as 'I Fall In Love Too Easily', 'Well You Needn't' and 'Round Midnight', the last named perhaps acting as a reminder that Hancock grabbed an Oscar for his score to the Tavernier movie. We'll he would, wouldn't he!   FD

ROY HARGROVE

APPROACHING STANDARDS
(Novus 63178 2)

MEETS THE TENORS OF OUR TIMES
(Verve 523019 2)

A Wynton Marsalis discovery, Texan Roy Hargrove refuses to follow the narrow stylistic path favoured by the current intake of trumpet players, preferring instead to blow away any restrictive barriers. Not only has Hargrove taken on board the more obvious characteristics of Fats Navarro, Clifford Brown and Lee Morgan but also the earlier up-front work of Doc Cheetam and Roy Eldridge. Fleet at fast tempos and with a bold tone you can spot a mile away, Hargrove is particularly convincing when handling ballads. With 'The Things We Did Last Summer' amounting to a impressive progress report of his abilities, *Approaching Standards* effectively showcases this side of his character, being a selection of tracks lifted from the albums he recorded for Novus. His much-publicised signing to Verve wasn't matched by his label debut. In reality, *The Tenors Of Our Time* didn't quite live up to the marketing campaign. The 'wish-list' of tenor partners may have looked like a dream-ticket but there seemed little room to manoeuvre for Joe Henderson, Johnny Griffin, Branford Marsalis, Stanley Turrentine and Joshua Redman, plus Hargrove's own hornman Ron Blake. Infact, Hargrove almost becomes a 'bit player' on his own album

Perhaps, the guest list should have been restricted to no more than a couple of well-wishers. As it is, there's no sign of flag-waving, with the mood kept mostly to mid-tempo. It's as though nobody wanted to break ranks and run with it and as a result nobody really shines. **TH**

BILL HARRIS

BILL HARRIS AND FRIENDS
(Fantasy 3263/OJC CD 083)

Aside from a few detours, such as a four year stint with JATP (1950-54), Bill Harris spent the most productive years of his career as star trombonist with Woody Herman (1944-59). Perhaps, it's the nature of the instrument, but Harris like a number of great trombonists (Jack Teagarden, Frank Rosolino) exhibited a robust, slightly off-kilter humour in his work. A swing-into-bop extrovert, Harris greatly favoured the former while offering a cursory nod to the latter. Recorded in 1957, with tenor legend Ben Webster sharing the front line and Jimmy Rowles (p), Red Mitchell (b) and Stan Levey (d) the epitome of taste and ingenuity, such familiar material as 'It Might As Well Be Spring' and 'Where Are You' are all the better from the attention afforded them by all five participants. And, that goes for an impishly wicked reworking of 'Just One More Chance'. A reappraisal of his artistry is long overdue. **RC**

DONALD HARRISON

FULL CIRCLE
(Bellaphon 660 55 003)

To be born in New Orleans, to study under Ellis Marsalis, to hone up at Boston's Berklee School Of Music and to be a fully fledged Jazz Messenger as twenty two are not bad recommendations for a career in jazz. Alto saxophonist Donald 'Duck' Harrison has taken full advantage of his early career resume. His spell with Art Blakey placed him with trumpeter Terence Blanchard and tenor saxophonist Jean Toussaint and *New York Scene* (Concord CCD 4256) shows that line-up is amongst the best editions of the band. *Full Circle* finds him amongst peers Cyrus Chestnut (p) and Carl Allen (d) and demonstrates the full range of his approach. There is a hint of greater, melodic freedom on 'The Force' but, in the main, it shows Harrison's place in the Charlie Parker lineage – a 'bird' with an ear for Eric Dolphy rhetoric. Comfortable with a Jon Faddis Quintet, he refuses to ignore the folk elements of the past and parts of *Indian Blues* (Concord CCD 79514) are a real Crescent City frolic. Harrison is already established as a festival tour major and, heard live, convinces with his big tone, improvisational confidence and his presence in general. **BMcR**

STAN HASSLEGARD & BENNY GOODMAN

AT CLICK 1948
(Dragon DRCD 183)

Some dreams *do* come true. When Swedish clarinettist Stan Hasslegard journeyed to the States it was with the intention of hearing his idol Benny Goodman in person. This, he achieved. But, more importantly, Benny got to hear young Stan play. A man not easily impressed, The King of Swing immediately invited the

Swingin' Swede to share the frontline with tenorman Wardell Gray and himself in a new Septet. Benny's movtives may not altogether have been philanthropical. Hasslegard was on a bop kick and Goodman (aware of the winds of change) was keen to investigate the *new* music's potential at close quarters. So what better than from an infatuated, but genuinely talented devotee – thus Bird's boppish 'Donna Lee' shows up in the same set as twice-around-the-block 'Bye Bye Blues'. At times, there's little to choose between the two players whilst any opportunity to catch the Thin Man on tenor should never be passed up. Though the transcription discs which preserved these radio shows (aired live from this now-legendary Philadelphia nightspot) have, in places, been damaged, their importance far exceeds such faults. Sadly, it was only a fatal auto accident, in 1950, that (arguably) prevented the undeniably talented Hasslegard from going the full distance. RC

HAMPTON HAWES

THE TRIO
(Contemporary 3505/OJC CD 316)

BLUES FOR BUD
(Black Lion BLCD 760126)

LIVE AT MEMORY LANE
(Fresh Sounds FSR CD 406) [L]

Hampton Hawes led a chequered career. At his best, a stunningly inventive and vibrant pianist, at his worst, less than happy with strings and a suspect programme selector. While with the Howard McGhee 1950-51 band he played with Charlie Parker and always claimed that his approach to his instrument avoided pianistic, middle men and came direct from the Bird. This is certainly true of the 1955 *Trio* performances, where the precision of his up tempo work ('I Got Rhythm') and the thoughtful development of his ballads ('These Foolish Things') speak as much for an outstanding jazzman as they do a gifted pianist. Because of a drug conviction, Hawes was off the jazz scene in the early sixties but, although his comeback was less than instant, the 1968 *Blues For Bud* showed him returned to full fire power. It emphasized the blues aspect of his playing and, with 'Sonora', added a fine song writing extra. His flirtation with electronic keyboards was mainly abortive but, on the acoustic instrument, he remained a strength in the groups he led. A 1970 club date *At Memory Lane* even had Joe Turner as guest singer and an odd personnel with Harry Edison (tpt), Sonny Criss (as) and Teddy Edwards (ts), Hawes supporting of each one of them as he showed the merit of eclecticism backed by sound technique and a creative mind. Furthermore, Hawes' autobiography *Raise Up Off Me* remains one of the best books about the jazz life. BMcR

COLEMAN HAWKINS

COLEMAN HAWKINS 1929-1934
(Classics 587)

COLEMAN HAWKINS 1939-1940
(Classics 634)

HAWK FLIES HIGH
(Riverside 233/OJC CD 027)

Coleman Hawkins never sounds less than the master tenor saxophonist. Instantly recognisable, he was the man that gave the instrument its mature voice. Initially seeking his own identity with Fletcher Henderson in the twenties, it was the trumpet of Louis Armstrong, rather than other saxophonists, that was the all pervading influence. From it he evolved an improvisational style that had power, grace and genuine rhythmic strength. The *1929-34 Classic* documents the first flowering, the busy bluster of 'Hello Lola', the rhapsodic romanticism of 'One Hour', as well as three remarkable tenor/piano duos. These factors alone would have made him most player's role model but the full throated beauty of his tone and his majesterial delivery made him the most copied saxophonist of his era. He exerted similar influence while working in Europe in the middle thirties yet, on returning to America, recorded the legendary 'Body And Soul' as if to set the seal on an astonishing decade. Always aware of trends, he embraced the bebop of the forties with open ears and showed on *Hollywood Stampede* that he could master the new mode and also provide it with suggestions of his own. One branch of the music saw a return to swing era virtues in the fifties. *Hawk Flies High* reveals Hawkins bringing his bebop resources to this mainstream cause and, on the *Flies High* session from 1957, playing a timeless blues like 'Juicy Fruit' alongside a tender ballad like 'Laura'. This blend of didactic fervour and emperical drive carried into the sixties. He was intrigued with the new wave and recorded effectively with Sonny Rollins in parts of *All The Things You Are*. Rumour had it that he died because he could not bear to grow old. Nothing he ever put on wax gave any support to such a theory. BMcR

HOLLYWOOD STAMPEDE
(Capitol CDP 7 93201 2)

ALL THE THINGS YOU ARE
(RCA Bluebird ND 82179)

TUBBY HAYES

WITH CLARK TERRY/THE NEW YORK SESSIONS
(Columbia 466363)

FOR MEMBERS ONLY
(Mastermix CD CHE 10) [L]

200% PROOF
(Mastermix CHE CD 105) [L]

Not for nothing was Tubby Hayes – who died, aged 38, in 1973 during open-heart surgery – affectionately known as 'The Little Giant'. Embraced by US heavyweight tenormen as an equal, Hayes proved his worth by not just being the only British horn-man to be regularly booked into leading US clubs but also to record Stateside with the likes of saxmen Roland Kirk, James Moody, (included on Kirk's *Rahsaan* Mercury 846630) and Clark Terry (tpt). A prodigious talent, Hayes first appeared on the local scene when just 15, and a year later joined Kenny Baker before quickly moving through the big bands of Ambrose, Vic Lewis and Jack Parnell. A contract with the Tempo label followed which allowed him to record varying sized combos and resulted in Hayes forming his own working octet (1955/56). Unquestionably, his most important role was in the now legendary Jazz Couriers (1957-59); an two tenor quintet which he co-led with Ronnie Scott with great success. So impressed was Art Blakey with his work in both The Couriers and on a Blue Note date by Dizzy Reece (tpt) *Blues In Trinity* ('Round Midnight'), that he once shortlisted the pair for a possible Jazz Messengers frontline. The '60s had Hayes dividing his time between running a small combo, a world-class Big Band (a showcase for his arranging) and recording prolifically for Fontana. Gifted with a phenomenal technique and a penchant for lengthy speed runs, Tubby's influences spanned Hank Mobley and Johnny Griffin as well as Coltrane and Rollins (the latter's 'Airegin' and 'Doxie' being included on the boisterous *The New York Sessions*). And while tenor may well have been his prime instrument Tubb's prowess on baritone sax, flute and vibraphone was in every way just as impressive. While the Clark Terry and Dizzy Reece sessions are the only available evidence of his studio work, *For Members Only* brings together three 1967 BBC broadcasts featuring Mike Pyne (p), Ron Matthewson (b) and Tony Levin (d) while *200% Proof* is a 1969 airshot dominated by Tubb's rip-roaring Big Band. Not much to show when considering his output, but more than sufficient to support his reputation. RC

JULIUS HEMPHILL

JULIUS HEMPHILL BIG BAND
(Elektra Musician 960831 2)

FAT MAN AND THE HARD BLUES
(Black Saint BSR 1201152)

Perhaps best known as the founder member of the popular and highly influential World Saxophone Quartet, Julius Hemphill is an intense, earthy alto saxophonist specialising in a combination of modern and demanding ensemble compositions and arrangements, and fractious, edgy improvisations. *Julius Hemphill Big Band* is a good opportunity to enjoy his compositional skills, brought to life by a superb contemporary jazz orchestra featuring trombonist Frank Lacy, guitarist Bill Frisell, drummer Ronnie Burrage, and two cleverly integrated French horn players. *Fat Man And Hard Blues* came three years later in '91, and consists of the unusual format of a saxophone (and flutes) sextet – an extension of his work with the WSQ. It is a courageous and inventive album, with just the right balance of composition and improvisation, and some superb individual playing from the leader. LC

FLETCHER HENDERSON

THE COMPLETE LOUIS ARMSTRONG
FLETCHER HENDERSON 1924-1925
(FRP F-38001/2/3) 3-CD set

FLETCHER HENDERSON 1925-1928
(BBC CD 720)

A STUDY IN FRUSTRATION
(Columbia 57596) 3-CD

The Henderson outfit of the early '20s, despite having a line-up that boasted the talents of Coleman Hawkins and Don Redman, could often sound dancehall dull. The arrival of Louis Armstrong helped light the blue touch-paper. But sometimes even that wasn't enough. Given such dire ditties as 'I Miss My Swiss (And My Swiss Miss Misses Me)' the band could only play what sounded like stock arrangements then sit back while Louis rode out the final choruses, much in the manner that Bix kicked the Paul Whiteman leviathan into spasmodic action. Thankfully, better material such as 'Sugar Foot Stomp' provided an opportunity for the musicians to reach out and eventually metamorphosise into the the finest 'hot' band in America. The BBC release, wonderfully mastered by Robert Parker, presents the band in

full stomping glory, with masterful Redman arrangements and various solo contributions from Fats Waller, Tommy Ladnier, Rex Stewart and others, the final transition to a high-order swing/dance band being documented by the giveaway (but good) Tring 25-tracker, which spans the 1937 period and explains (to some extent) why Benny Goodman signed the man known as 'Smack' as staff arranger and pianist. FD

FLETCHER HENDERSON 1931-1932
(Classics 546 CD)

FLETCHER HENDERSON 1932-1934
(Classic 535 CD)

JOE HENDERSON ✶

INNER URGE
(Blue Note CDP 7 84189 2)

Down Beat's 1993 Top Tenor award winner and Musician Of The Year, Joe Henderson had taken a long time to get the universal recognition he deserves. Of course, the cognoscenti had always known, and albums like *Our Thing* and *Inner Urge* had shown that, in the sixties Henderson was already a major talent. His solos seem almost pre-prepared, he never seems to be rushed out of his stride and never seems lost for an idea. His music is the perfect example of a strong, hard bop tenor with a superb tone that seems purpose built for such music.

Henderson's ground work with redoubtable pianists such as Horace Silver and Herbie Hancock prepared him for his own role as leader. *The State Of The Tenor*, recorded live at the Village Vanguard in 1985, showed him at ease with such a role and perhaps emphasized the fact that his playing fell well outside the all pervading influence of John Coltrane. On a programme that hand picks lesser-known works by Monk, Ellington, Mingus, Horace Silver and Bird, one hears in his playing the largess of Sonny Rollins, occasionally the chromatic licence of Ornette Coleman but as *Lush Life* displays, Henderson can channel his own highly personal style in many directions – even into the romantic world of Billy Strayhorn. BMcR

LUSH LIFE
(Verve 511 779 2)

OUR THING
(Blue Note CDP 7 84152 2)

THE STATE OF THE TENOR VOL. 1 & 2
(Blue Note CDP 8 28879 2) [L]

THE BLUE NOTE YEARS 1963-90
(Blue Note CDP 7 89287 2) 4-CD Box

THE MILESTONE YEARS 1967-76
(Milestone MCD 4413 2) 4-CD Box

WOODY HERMAN

THE V-DISC YEARS 1944-46 VOL. 1 & 2
(Hep CD 2/3435)

THE THUNDERING HERDS 1945-47
(Columbia 460825 2)

KEEPER OF THE FLAME
(Capitol CDP 7 98453 2)

LIVE FEATURING BILL HARRIS 1957 VOL. 1 & 2
(Status STCD 107 & STCD 110) [L]

For years, Herman's big bands played the blues. Then, sometime during a mid-'40s recording ban (what a way to start !) he pieced together one of the greatest ensembles ever to blow its way out of bebop alley. If the band that became known as The First Herd jumped like a scalded cat, fired by trumpeters Sonny Berman and Pete Candoli, tenor ace Flip Phillips, trombonist Bill Harris, a frantic rhythm section of Chubby Jackson (b) and Dave Tough (d), plus the arrangements of Ralph Burns and Neil Hefti, it was only surpassed musically by The Second Herd. It was The Second Herd whose three tenors-and-a baritone, sax line-up of Stan Getz, Zoot Sims, Herbie Steward (replaced by Al Cohn) and Serge Chaloff blowing on Jimmy Giuffre's 'Four Brothers' was the kind of thing miracles are made of. A distinctive signature sound that Herman retained for the rest of his career. Every aspect of those two bands are featured on the indispensable Hep, Columbia and Capitol releases: the sheer madness of 'Caldonia', 'Northwest Passage', 'Wild Root', 'Lemon Drop' and 'Blowin' Up A Storm'. It was with the Second Herd that Getz first made his reputation with 'Early Autumn' (the fourth-part of pianist Ralph Burns' atmospheric 'Summer Sequence') and featured on *Keeper Of The Flame*
The Third Herd kicked up considerable dust in the early-'50s, as did the 1957 line-up present on the Status releases. Taped 'live' in Omaha, it might have been short on big names save for Bill Harris, but as a self-contained working unit it was as good as they come. Likewise the 1965 edition caught in action in San Francisco (*Woody's Winners* (Columbia 468454 2)) with the Bill Chase-lead brass section in scene-stealin' mood and a never-to-be-forgotten refit of Horace Silver's 'Opus De Funk.' Though not as established a stylist as Swing Era clarinettists Benny Goodman or Artie Shaw, Herman was, nevertheless, able to progress his various Herds to accommodate major shifts in trends from bop ('Apple Honey') to boogaloo ('Watermelon Man') – quite a long haul from 'Woodchoppers' Ball'. Though, bad management, robbed Herman of all his money and eventually his own home, to the very end (1987), he retained his status as one of the all-time greatest (and most likable) band leaders. FD

VINCENT HERRING

FOLKLORE LIVE AT THE VILLAGE VANGUARD
(Limelight 522 430) [L]

NAT ADDERLEY: WORK SONG
(Sweet Basil 660 55 007 CD) [L]

The scenario ran along these lines: unknown alto sax player Vincent Herring approached Nat Adderley boldly claiming he could play anything recorded by the cornet player's late brother,

Cannonball Adderley. There was only one way to find out. Herring promptly put his money where his mouth was, and, to his astonishment was immediately hired by brother Nat, not because he was a Cannonball clone, but because Nat could hear beyond the obvious. Herring is just one of many who first bypassed Bird to use Cannonball's more simplistic soul jazz approach as an initial jumping off stage, before backtracking to the original source and the Parker legacy. While *We Remember Cannon* (In + Out 7012 CD) serves up the obvious, *Work Song* is a more inspired event with the addition of Sonny Fortune (as) and plenty of upfull moments on 'Hi-Fly' and 'Jive Samba'. *'Live at The Village Vanguard* drives home the point that as Herring has progressed from excitable sideman to a go-for-broke leader, he doesn't believe in doing things by half, throwing himself into the fray to demand undivided attention. This he gets. Cannonball's influence remains detectable but not a distraction, for Herring together with able-bodied trumpeter Scott Wendholt and pianist Cyrus Chestnut have come up with a fresh look at familiar routines with a reworking of Hank Mobley's 'This I Dig Of You' most praiseworthy. The earlier *Evidence* (Landmark LCD 1527 2) is an admirable Hard Bop excursion from 1990 with Wallace Roney (tpt) proving an ideal foil, while *Secret Love* (MusicMaster 65092), a 1992 quartet dates comes across as a thoughful endeavour in skillful programming. For once, Herring eases up on the gas and with Renee Rosnes (p) offers a personal re-evaluation of standards such as 'Skating In Central Park' and 'Chelsea Bridge'. RC

DAWNBIRD
(Landmark LCD 1522 2)

MELVIN RHYNE – TO CANNONBALL WITH LOVE
(Bellaphon KICJ 147)

ANDREW HILL

POINT OF DEPARTURE
(Blue Note CDP 7 84167 2)

VERONA RAG
(Soul Note 121110 2)

The more obvious alternatives to Ornette Coleman's freedom route in the early sixties were posted by Miles Davis, John Coltrane and Sun Ra. Less obvious, but no less potent was that suggested by pianist Andrew Hill. His major label debut album *Black Fire* came in 1963 and immediately established that his highly personal compositions, his off centre rhythmic emphasis and his confidence with new harmonic freedom made him an important figure. The superb *Point Of Departure* introduced horns (Kenny Dorham, Eric Dolphy and Joe Henderson) into the equation, upped the emotion-count ('Refuge' and 'New Monastery'), while still maintaining structural cohesion.

It presaged a flurry of recording activity and left a jazz world slightly open mouthed. A steady stream of impressive recordings continued through the seventies and eighties but did not always attract the attention they deserved. The solo *Verona Rag* presented the many sides of Hill the pianist, from the Bixian (piano) impressionism of 'Darn That Dream' to the James Scott via Jelly Roll Morton lift of the title track. The 1986 *Shades* shows that the Hill method updates very effectively. It progresses the trio adventure of *Black Fire* with its arabesque of rhythmic attitudes and introduces the tenor of Clifford Jordon to provide the bulwark against which the demanding intricacies of the trio can be judged. The style sounds equally effective and challenging today. BMcR

BLACK FIRE
(Blue Note BCT 84151 2)

SHADES
(Soul Note 121113 2)

JUDGMENT
(Blue Note B2 8 28981 2)

EARL HINES

PIANO MAN
(Giants of Jazz CD 53118)

LIVE AT THE VILLAGE VANGUARD
(CBS CD 462401) [L]

PLAYS GEORGE GERSHWIN
(MusicDisc 50052)

Earl 'Father' Hines is probably the most taken-for-granted of all jazz pianists. The Father of Modern piano, he was right in at the beginning and his influence was incalcuable to future generations. Both Art Tatum and Teddy Wilson were quick to acknowledge him as an inspiration. Perhaps his Playboy image worked against him. Photos tend to show him with cigar clenched between his teeth and sporting a wide manic grin. Hines was the innovator of the 'trumpet style' of piano playing – using a tremelo effect to suggest a trumpet vibrato tone, a direct, yet ornate, device not previously used.

Coupled to this, he was manically creative, switching tempos, flying off in all directions but resolving everything. There is no better introduction to Hines' pedigree than *Piano Man* (1928-55) which includes two monumental classics 'Weatherbird' a duo with Louis Armstrong and 'Blues in Thirds' with Sidney Bechet. Hines' desire to be a star band leader led him off in the wrong direction, for the Big Bands he led tended to be just backings for his pianistics and had very little identity of their own but several of the best tracks from his Grand Terrace Orchestra are worth a play. Indeed, Hines' long unfruitful stay at Chicago's Grand Terrace, was due more to Mafia pressure than to his own.

Taped in 1965, the *Village Vanguard* set is vintage Hines. Re-united with ex-sideman tenorist Budd Johnson, the two build up a storming set culminating in a blinding reworking of 'Tea For Two' and the definitive version of his signature tune 'Rosetta'. In a solo context,the Ducal tribute *Earl Hines Plays Duke Ellington* (New World NW 361/362) finds Hines literally re-inventing Ellington's repertoire with discretion and bringing to pieces such as 'Black And Tan Fantasy', 'Sophisticated Lady' and 'C Jam Blues' a whole new set of values. But, of the later Hines records, the best has to be the *Plays George Gershwin* recorded in Italy in the 70's, when his career was up and running again. Offered this superior material Hines makes this a brilliant addition to his formidable legacy for on 'Love Walked In' and 'They Can't Take That Away From Me' he leaves no possibility unexplored. JM

BLUES IN THIRDS
(Black Lion CLCD 760120)

ART HODES

SESSIONS AT BLUE NOTE
(Dormouse DMI CDX-04)

An immigrant from the Ukraine (long before the Ganelin Trio spotlighted Soviet jazz), Art Hodes was an original 'moldy fig', leading the internecine row between traditionalists and modernists, but with a humour lacking in many of the participants. And, although he played the part (especially in his magazine, *The Jazz Record*) his playing revealed unexpectedly open ears to evolving music. Thus the performances here by a Chicagoan-type line-up, reflecting Hodes' jazz beginning, exceed Dixieland. They are, like Hodes himself, forward-looking, anticipating the modified Swing of the next decade's Mainstream style – as you might expect from men like Sandy Williams (tmb), Vic Dickenson (tmb), Max Kaminsky (tpt) and Edmond Hall (clt). Part of this success is due to Hodes' fine rhythmic sense, which enables him to create complex patterns from the simplest materials. Against this sophistication, he never neglected the roots. Though a foreigner, he took naturally to the blues, in which he was without a better, as borne out by 'Slow 'Em Down Blues', 'KMH Drag' and 'Gut Bucket Blues'. For Hodes, blues are blues, whether played by Jelly Roll or Thelonious. CS

THE COMPLETE ART HODES BLUE NOTE SESSIONS
(Mosaic MD4 114)

BILLIE HOLIDAY

LADY DAY AND PREZ 1937-1941
(Giants Of Jazz CD 0218)

THE COMPLETE ORIGINAL AMERICAN DECCA RECORDINGS
(MCA GRP 26012) 2-CD

FIRST ISSUE: THE GREAT AMERICAN SONGBOOK
(Verve 523 003 2) 2-CD

LADY IN SATIN
(CBS 450883)

Lady Day was (and still is) the yardstick by which all other jazz singers are measured. Given even the most purile material, which she sometimes was in her early days, she could perform sheer alchemy. Thing was, Billie didn't scat and hardly deviated from the original melody. Not for her, extended workouts merely keeping the chord changes in mind. Truth is that, in terms of range and power, Billie didn't have much of a voice and always appeared to be languishing behind the beat. But amid that frail structure lay one of the great blues voices. Not of the Bessie Smith kind. Something smaller, something that grabbed hearts and opened tear-ducts. She half-whispered, half moaned in your ear and in doing so, personalised a lyric in such a way that it was difficult to imagine anyone else ever delivering those same thoughts again.

She started out with the Teddy Wilson band, helping to shape material that was often considered sub-standard and worked her way from the 'with vocal refrain' category to main name status, later records appearing as by 'Billie Holiday And Her Orchestra'. Everything recorded during this period 1933-1940 appears on various volumes of Sony's truthfully titled *Quintessential Billie Holiday* series, all of which deserve a good home. But for those seeking a budget alternative then *Lady Day And Prez* is remarkable value, featuring two dozen of the best tracks from the period when Billie and tenor man Lester Young appeared to be two halves of the same musician, Prez seemingly reading Day's mind and vice versa.

The Decca compilation, which spans the late '40s and early '50s, contains most of those songs that Diana Ross and an army of late, Hollywood-inspired admirers know best – 'God Bless The Child', 'Don't Explain', 'Good Morning Heartache' etc. and, as far as purists are concerned, mark the beginning of the end – a near sell-out to commercialism assisted by a failing voice. All complete nonsense. Whatever Billie lacked in purity, she compensated in sheer feeling as the *Songbook* amply illustrates. If her voice grew grittier it was the kind of grit that eventually produced pearls, and, backed by Norman Granz's JATP heroes: Charlie Shavers (tpt), Flip Phillips (ts), Oscar Peterson (p), Barney Kessel (g), along with various Basie-ites and other worthies Billie, given the kind of material she could only dream of in her debut days, fills ballads with raw emotion and uptempo songs with an irrestistable warmth.

Maybe that voice, that unique instrument, was shot at the end of her days, and maybe too, there were times when she wandered off-pitch. But nobody else could transfer hurt and pain into something that so utterly grabbed the listener. And listening to such records as *Songs For Distingue Lovers* and the string-beset *Lady In Satin* brings its uncomfortable moments. Even so, the latter is still a marvellous album, full of heartbreak, a life laid bare. For those who are glad to be unhappy, few other records will suffice. FD

SONGS FOR DISTINGUE LOVERS/LAST RECORDINGS
(Verve 840 814)

LADY IN AUTUMN
(Verve 849434)

JAZZ AT THE PHILHARMONIC
(Verve 521642) [L]

DAVE HOLLAND

CIRCLE – PARIS CONCERT
(ECM 843 163 2) [L]

CONFERENCE OF THE BIRDS
(ECM 1027 373 2)

A pioneer of the European, free movement with the Spontaneous Music Ensemble, Dave Holland worked with an astylistic array of British leaders before becoming an important cog in Miles Davis' revolutionary wheel in the late sixties. He lent his supple, rhythmic impetus and cleverly realised solos to the Circle cause with Chic Corea (p) and Anthony Braxton (as) through 1970/71 and the Paris concert was an important recording of its era. His work is never better documented than on his own *Conference Of The Birds*, where superior recording quality highlights his outstanding facility as well as his improvisational skills. He actually up-stages Sam Rivers (ts) and the redoubtable Braxton. His involvement with New York's M. Base in the eighties led to some fine recordings with other leaders from within the group but it was his superbly self indulgent partnership with Steve Coleman on *Extensions* that is the cream of the crop. BMcR

EXTENSIONS
(ECM 1410 841 778 2)

RICHARD 'GROOVE' HOLMES

WITH BEN WEBSTER/GROOVE
(Pacific Jazz CDP 7 94473 2)

WITH GENE AMMONS/GROOVIN' WITH JUG
(Pacific Jazz CDP 7 92930 2) [L]

Just because Muhammed Ali was, for what seemed like an eternity, undisputed heavyweight champion of the world, didn't mean the contendors were flakes. Quite the opposite – he was boxing the best. The same can be said of Jimmy Smith. He may have been the Hammond's hardest hitman, but the grits 'n' greens opposition fronted up by the likes of Brother Jack McDuff, Big John Patton and Richard 'Groove' Holmes could often be equally as rewarding. Not for these men the sonic booms, but the ability to cook on gospel's eternal flame. In the company of first Ben Webster and then Gene Ammons, the Groover was matched with prime cut tenormen, players of emotional depth and burning intensity. Especially so with Ammons whose career had frequently been placed on hold due to his chronic drug dependency. The date with Holmes started in the studio and was completed 'live' the very same evening on stage at L.A.'s Black Orchid club. Tensions run high, paving the way for the good groove reached on 'Hittin' The Jug'. For his label debut, which matched Holmes with Ben Webster's majestic tenor plus his piano-pumpin' patron Les McCann, trombonist Lawrence 'Tricky' Lofton also found a place on the team. But all eyes were on the two featured bill-toppers who collided with excellent results on the breathy 'Deep Purple' and the jazz-dance classic 'That Healin' Feelin''. Still active, in recent times Holmes has paired with fellow Hammond hero Jimmy Smith as an international jazz festival attraction, but on record he has yet to surpass these earlier efforts. RC

ELMO HOPE

TRIO & QUINTET
(Blue Note CDP 7 84438)

A close friend of Bud Powell and Thelonious Monk, it's said that some of the innovations credited to Powell were infact originally shown to him by Hope during their many practice sessions together. To make ends meet, Hope played piano alongside Johnny Griffin (ts) and Philly Joe Jones (d) in the Rhythm and Blues band of trumpeter Joe Morris (1948-49), before taping two 10-inch albums, in 1953, for Blue Note. It's these two albums that comprise the CD release. The ten tune trio set with Percy Heath (b) and Philly Joe includes 'Carvin' The Rock', a darkly, brooding, minor-key swinger Hope co-wrote with Sonny Rollins and which he first brought to a Clifford Brown-Lou Donaldson session. Moving to the West Coast in 1957, which Hope found creatively unhelpful, didn't altogether blunt his work. Infact, his contribution as both pianist and writer on Harold Land's near-classic *The Fox* (Contemporary 7619/OJC CD 343) proved outstanding and placed him in good stead for his return to New York where, in the company Blue Mitchell (tpt), Jimmy Heath, Frank Foster (ts), plus the Heath-Philly Joe rhythm team he cut *Homecoming* (Riverside 9381/OJC CD 1810) plus duets with piano-playing wife, Bertha. Elmo Hope died in 1967, age 43. Yet another victim of heroin, prison spells and associated problems which terminated what should have been a rewarding career. His playing, despite some superficial comparisons with that of Bud and Monk, is in fact totally original in an anguished, quirky and turbulent way that never really fulfilled itself. TH

ELMO HOPE TRIO
(Contemporary 7620/OJC CD 477)

FREDDIE HUBBARD

OPEN SESAME
(Blue Note CDP 7 84040 2)

BREAKIN' POINT
(Blue Note CDP 7 84172 2)

Whereas, in the current clime there appears to be only room for one major high-profile player per instrument at any given time, things were different back in 1959 when Freddie Hubbard arrived in New York from Indianapolis. Competition amongst trumpet players was particularly rife with the likes of Lee Morgan, Donald Byrd, Art Farmer, Bill Hardman, Booker Little, Blue Mitchell and Ted Curson, amongst others, vying for attention. Within a year, Hubbard demonstrated that he was the most adaptable of the Young Turks on his instrument. In July 1960, at the age of 22, he knocked out *Open Sesame* in partnership with star-crossed tenor-man Tina Brooks plus pianist McCoy Tyner. The extent of Hubbard's versality came at Yuletide when he and Eric Dolphy (as) squared off against Don Cherry (tpt) and Ornette Coleman (as) for the innovative double-quartet recording of *Free Jazz* (Atlantic 81347). Come February, he and Dolphy were part of the rootsy septet Oliver Nelson assembled for *Blues and The Abstract Truth* (Impulse! MCAD 5659). Soon, he had replaced Lee Morgan in The Jazz Messengers for a run of albums that include *Mosaic* (Blue Note CDP 7 46523 2) and *Ugetsu* (Riverside 9464/OJC CD 090) and earned Down Beat's New Star Award. February 1964, and Hubbard was again at Dolphy's side for the saxman's classic *Out To Lunch* (Blue Note CDP 7 4652 2), attending Coltrane for the taping of *Ascension* and *Ole* and then the aptly titled *Night Of The Cookers* (Blue Note CDP 28882) featuring Hubbard and Lee Morgan in an uncompromising head-to-head.

Fusion didn't pass un-noticed as the best-selling *Red Clay*,(CTI ZK 40809) revealed. Cut in 1970 with Joe Henderson (ts) and Herbie Hancock (p), it was far superior to the much less interesting *First Light* which. for all its short comings earned him a Grammy two years later. However, it didn't afford Hubbard the kind of lucrative crossover exclusive to Weather Report, Return To Forever or Miles Davis. Infact, by the mid-'70s, Hubbard took over the role that had once been Miles' when he reunited with Wayne Shorter (ts) Herbie Hancock, Ron Carter (b) and Tony Williams (d) in Yen-grabbing jazz supergroup, VSOP. In retrospect, Hubbard's achievements are quite astounding. With his instantly recognisable full brassy tone he added much to the trumpet's known vocabulary with a combination of his masterful dexterity and technical effects. As both the last of the Hard Bop stylists (his influence extending to Randy Brecker and Wynton Marsalis) and a willing participant in the experiments of Ornette Coleman and Eric Dolphy such qualities mark Freddie Hubbard as a player with few equals. RC

HERE TO STAY
(Blue Note CDP 7 84135 2)

ABDULLAH IBRAHIM

FATS, DUKE AND THE MONK
(Sackville SKCD 2 3048)

WATER FROM AN ANCIENT WELL
(Tiptoe 88812)

Abdullah Ibrahim personifies the concept of total music. He does not so much use the piano to deliver his music, as accept it as the core around which his composing, arranging and playing revolve. 'Composer's piano' is an insult but in Ibrahim's case it can be applied to the way in which his keyboard provides both structure and development. Despite its name, most of the *Fats, Duke And The Monk* album concentrates on his own works, merely alluding to the dignitaries of the title. It shows, however, just how effectively Ibrahim interprets the music of his homeland, South Africa, and does so within the jazz ethic. Throughout the eighties, he struck up a valuable musical partnership with saxophonist Carlos Ward. *Water From An Ancient Well* shows that it was the pianist's strong left hand, propulsive attack and high-life rhythms that cemented the partnership but the mere presence of Ward's wispy alto seemed to give the music a heady quality. BMcR

IRAKERE

THE LEGENDARY IRAKERE IN LONDON
(Ronnie Scott's Jazz House JHR CD 005) [L]

FELICIDAD
(Ronnie Scott's Jazz House JHR CD 014)

Pianist Chucho Valdes' rocket-fuelled Cuban jazz band are regular and very popular visitors to Soho's Ronnie Scott's club, so it is hardly surprising that they are one of the most featured groups on the club's recently launched record label. Featuring an intensely exciting concoction of Cuban salsa and energetic bebop, these live dates capture the enthusiasm (sometimes very close to hysteria) that the band induces amongst an audience. In terms of quality, there is little to choose between the two sessions. *The Legendary Irakere In London* was the result of a week at Ronnie Scott's in 1987; *Felicidad* came two years later, but the frenzied enthusiasm and consistent virtuosity are such that it could have been recorded on the following night. There was a time when Irakere's line-up included saxophone star Paquito D'Rivera and trumpet virtuoso Arturo Sandoval. A Stateside release being prepared by Columbia from this period is worth seeking out. LC

MILT JACKSON

MILT JACKSON
(Blue Note CDP 781509 2)

BAGS & TRANE
(Atlantic 7567 81348 2)

BROTHER JIM
(Pablo 2310-916)

For some observers Milt Jackson is one of the finest of all vibes players, not because of his playing in the Modern Jazz Quartet, but inspite of it. This is an extreme stance and one not supported by the evidence.Celtainly, ln the early years, Jackson found the MJQ a stimulating environment. His bop mastery shows on 'Vendome', his relaxed swing propels 'All The Things You Are', while the title track of *Django* (OJCCD 057) emphasises the structural logic of his solos.It was his work away from the group that rightly found the most unqualified support. *Milt Jackson*, an album from 1948 to 1952, documents the period superbly, not only with Thelonious Monk but also with a group that later did become the MJQ. Inevitably, his involvement with that group did restrict his other recording opportunities but, in the right company, he always produced peerless performances. The 1959 *Bags & Trane* surpassed all expectations wlth the two masters keeping the blues in mind and adopting a jam session atmosphere on the rollicking 'Three Little Words'. Jackson was a natural swinger, with or without the MJQ but albums like *Brother Jim* with saxophonist Jimmy Heath found him taking a more laissez faire atitude.Currently on the festival tour circuit, he is still delivering a firm message. When lt comes to vibes and the blues – do not mess with the Bag's man. BMcR

ILLINOIS JACQUET

FLYING HOME – THE BEST OF ILLINOIS JACQUET
(Verve 521 644 2)

JATP: THE FIRST CONCERT 1944
(Verve 521 646 2)

Twenty-five years after his death, Coltrane proves to be as much a source of frustration as he is an inspiration. As a result, his most fiesty disciples have placed a hold on technical ability and gone in search of the enigma of the instrument's heart-stopping big tone and the likes of Hawkins, Webster and Illinois Jacquet. The toughest of the Texas Tenors and the link between jazz and R&B ('No Sweat'), Jacquet earned a formidable reputation first with Lionel Hampton ('Flying Home') and then, as a hard-hitting Jazz At The Philharmonic heavyweight. However, once his brow was mopped dry, he could be everything from larconic ('Lean Baby') to downright romantic ('Talk Of The Town'). The suggestion that rock 'n' roll (or even for that matter the avant garde) was born in LA on July 2, 1944, at a fundraiser organised by Norman Granz in support of Mexican youths wrongly jailed following the 'Zoot Suit' riots, can be supported by 'Blues' on *The First Concert*. Suddenly, Illinois Jacquet squares off against fellow quickdraw tenor Jack McVea in a showdown of skill, excess and endurance which brings to its feet a beying audience who, by the sound of things would be equally at home ringside for a Tyson brawl. The screams and scrambles, the honks and hysteria, are not that far removed from the sounds of the free movement two decades in the future! RC

AHMAD JAMAL

LIVE AT THE ALHAMBRA
(Vogue 655002) [L]

CHICAGO REVISITED:
LIVE AT JOE SEGAL'S JAZZ SHOWCASE
(Telarc CD 83327) [L]

Miles Davis was perhaps a trifle generous to cite Ahmad Jamal as his favourite pianist, but nevertheless he not only showed his admiration by recording Jamal's 'New Rhumba' but also lifted the pianist's arrangements ('Billy Boy', 'But Not For Me' etc) for personal use. Jamal's timing, his judicious use of space and the arranging skills heard on *Live At The Alhambra* from 1961 are impressive but there remains a certain feeling of over complacency in some of his work.

He is certainly an original pianist and his deliciously out of kilter note placement is very much his own. His approach to solo building does occasionally give the impression of a man relying on last minute inspiration but this does not question his inventiveness. He first recorded as a leader with his Three Strings in 1951, while during the sixties, his albums (*Live At The Pershing*, *But Not For Me* etc) became chart fixtures, but he is better served by more recent work. *Chicago Revisited* from 1992 has him at his percussive best, jousting with the waltz time 'Dance To The Lady', treating 'Blue Gardenia' with kid gloves and swapping them for the boxing variety for a headlong 'Lullaby Of Birdland'. A prominent touring artist on the festival merry-go-round, Jamal is still a daunting presence in that field and, when the mood is right, a very substantial performer. BMcR

HARRY JAMES

EMBRACEABLE YOU
(Conifer Compact Selection TQ 133) [L]

Both loved, loathed and frequently envied (he married movie star pinup Betty Grable, whose legs were insured for a million dollars) trumpet ace Harry James could either play hot or sickly sweet. A mainman with the Benny Goodman band, he quit to form his own brassy outfit in 1938. His bands varied in style over the years – later line-ups of the '60s featuring almost Basie-like arrangements – but it was during the '40s that James really made the grade, topping trumpet polls, stacking up the hit singles and appearing in Hollywood musicals.

Few albums have ever really captured the true essence of the James band at its most potent but this live recording, cut in California during 1946, gets nearest to perfection, as the muted James swings authoritively on 'Moten Swing' then grandstands his open-horn way through 'Perdido' and other riff-ridden things before reverting to the sometimes string-laden supergoo. Star sidemen Juan Tizol (tmb) and Willie Smith (as) aid and abet. FD

COMPACT JAZZ
Verve 833 285)

THE CAPITOL YEARS
Capitol CDP 7 98952 2)

KEITH JARRETT

THE KÖLN CONCERT
ECM 1064/5) [L]

EXPECTATIONS
Columbia 467902 2)

VIENNA CONCERT
ECM 1481) [L]

BYE BYE BLACKBIRD
ECM 1467 513074 2)

Keith Jarrett came into sight as a Jazz Messenger, added most of the backbone to Charles Lloyd's 'flower power' group and assisted Miles Davis in his direction seeking in the early seventies. As a pianist, he is blessed with a daunting technique but it is one that he does not always put to the best service. In solo performances like the 1975 *Köln Concerts* we get the cut glass articulation, the near classical presence and the conscious drama. There is no doubting the instrumental virtuosity but it comes from a jazz dilettante. In the continued absence of CD issues for *Death Of The Flower* and *Back Hand* from 1974, the 1972 *Expectations* gives the most graphic example of Jarrett's work with one horn (Dewey Redman) and a percussion augmented quintet. In this case, the lily is gilded in places by the presence of a rock guitarist and a string section, although the main body of the album is of good, Jarrett tunes treated with sympathy by Redman and the composer alike. Jarrett continues to 'stay out of the kitchen' and ply his trade in the 'heat' free area of the concert hall. It is usually solo, as in 1991 *Vienna*, and he does it superbly well. He demands a perfect instrument, plays it perfectly but rarely ruffles any jazz sensibilities. To prove he can get more involved, the 1991 *Bye Bye Blackbird* pays tribute to Miles Davis. With Gary Peacock (b) and Jack De Johnette (d), Jarrett does get under the music's skin. The hypnotic 'For Miles' is a touch overlong but the remainder of the date, mainly standards, confirm that when Jarrett avoids window dressing, he still has very much to say. BMcR

BUNK JOHNSON

BUNK JOHNSON 1944
(American Music AMCD 3)

Bunk Johnson was born a year after Buddy Bolden in 1889, the first larger-than-life figure in jazz history, and the man who is credited with taking the first steps in the shaping of jazz when, in 1894, he improvised a blues in public ('Make Me A Pallet On The Floor'). But, just as no recorded evidence exists of Bolden, none exists of Johnson's playing before enthusiasts dragged him from the Louisiana ricefields in 1942, weak of lip and more than a decade out of practice. But, if Johnson's straight, undecorated trumpet style suggests something untouched by the previous two decades of progress in jazz, the work of his fellows was not, so the overall impact of the music affords only a fragmented glimpse of the 'Days beyond recall' revivalists were trying to recapture. As *Bunk Johnson 1944* with a personnel that includes Jim Robinson (tmb), George Lewis (clt), Baby Dodds (d) illustrates, the result was ensemble jazz of uncommon richness, even if Johnson's weak lip allowed others to assume the lead when he was forced to drop out, and thus offer textures unintended by those attempting to recreate New Orleans music of the pre-recording era. On the other hand, their constantly evolving melodic variations retain the sought-after link with the past, and the music as a whole possesses a satisfying emotional depth. CS

BUNK JOHNSON & HIS SUPERIOR BAND
(Good Time Jazz GTJCD 12048 2)

KING OF THE BLUES
(American Music AMCD 1)

BRASS BAND & DANCE BAND
(American Music AMCD 6)

JAMES P. JOHNSON
CAROLINA SHOUT
(Biograph BCD 105)

James Price Johnson was nicknamed the 'Father of Stride Piano' because he was the fountainhead for the style played by mostly Harlem-based men in the 1920s, of whom perhaps the greatest and most inspired was Thomas 'Fats' Waller. The style, comprising complex melodic variations played over 'oompah' left hand figures, grew up and prospered on the rent party. That was a device whereby people raised the landlord's dues by hiring itinerant pianists, buying in booze, throwing open their doors to neighbours and charging entry fees. It therefore had a mission to entertain, but the very best of its practitioners (see: Willie 'The Lion' Smith) also created music of great depth, and influenced such important musicians as Count Basie and Duke Ellington, who both made dramatic changes to the style. And the lineage continues to Thelonious Monk and Cecil Taylor. So, on the one hand, Johnson originated the Charleston, and allowed a virile dance feeling to pervade much of his music. On the other, a desire grew alongside these to dabble in more serious composition, based on the clear architectural quality of his solo work. CS

SNOWY MOUNTAIN BLUES
(MCA/GRP 16042/GRP-604)

JAY JAY JOHNSON
THE EMINENT JAY JAY JOHNSON VOLS. 1 & 2
(Blue Note CDP 81505/6 2)

LETS HANG OUT
(EmArCy 514 454)

Jay Jay Johnson was a genuine pioneer of bebop trombone. Blessed with great technical facility, he successfully ran Charlie Parker's alto lines through the trombone slide and produced a style that remains inimitable. His bebop alacrity is superbly captured on the Blue Note double (actually separate issues), the svelte tone, the superbly lubricated phrasing and a creative talent to rival even his mentor. In the fifties he successfully co-led Jay & Kai, a quintet with a two bone front line, in which he showed to the obvious advantage of his colleague. In the sixties and seventies he was absent from the jazz parade ground, as he worked as educator, composer and conductor with MBA in New York.
His return to active jazz service came in the late eighties and, somewhat amazingly, his instrumental powers were undiminished. As before, he surrounded himself with worthy talents and, although the solo 'Beautiful Love' could be the stand-out performance on *Let's Hang Out*, the entire album shows him at ease, be it with stalwart Jimmy Heath (ts) or with young tigers Terence Blanchard (tpt) and Ralph Moore (ts). With Johnson, the style is as ageless as the man. BMcR

LIVE AT THE CAFE BOHEMIA 1957
Fresh Sound FSRCD 143) [L]

STAN GETZ & J.J. JOHNSON – AT THE OPERA HOUSE
Verve 847 340 2) [L]

ELVIN JONES

ELVIN!
(Riverside 9409/OJC CD 259)

LIVE AT THE VILLAGE VANGUARD
(MCA MCAD 39136) [L]

YOUNGBLOOD
(Enja ENJ 7051-2)

JAZZ MACHINE LIVE IN JAPAN
(Konnex KCD 5044) [L]

Brother of Hank and Thad, Elvin Jones holds a vital position in jazz drum history. Like them, a product of the Detroit school, he steered a course between the emphatic punctuation and swing of Art Blakey and the rhythmic association colouring of the free percussionists. His style was never arrhythmic but he produced superb cross rhythms that gave the superficial impression of a more abstract concept. He joined John Coltrane in 1960 and *Live At The Village Vanguard* is magnificent, as much for his drumming as it is for the horn work of the leader. Away from Coltrane, his leadership dates were slightly more conservative but *Elvin!*, with sextet and trio tracks, takes the more orthodox, hard bop route with marked success. In the 70s, he led his Jazz Machine from a drum power base and albums like *'Live In Japan* demonstrate the effectiveness of his polyrhythmic barrage in a post-Coltrane climate. *Youngblood* offers a more faithful picture of his current work. Cut in 1992 it has its leader as the most unconventional performer but, significantly, demonstrates that the new guard of Joshua Redman and Javon Jackson (ts) and Nicholas Payton (tpt) benefit from having their conservative feathers ruffled. BMcR

HANK JONES

UPON REFLECTION
(EmArCy 514 898)

THE ORACLE
(EmArCy 846 376)

LAZY AFTERNOON
(Concord CCD 4391)

BLUEBIRD
(Vogue Savoy VG 655 650140)

Brother of Thad and Elvin, Hank Jones has worked with almost everybody. Five years Ella Fizgerald's accompanist, seventeen years a CBS staff pianist, he has recorded with an endless list of jazz masters. His style has grown from seeds sown by Teddy Wilson and Billy Kyle and fertilised by, firstly, Art Tatum and then Bud Powell. His light touch and immaculate articulation make all he does sound effortless and his improvised solos have a composer's sense of form. At ease in any company, fifties recordings such as *Bluebird* demonstrate his ability to support horns with melodic hints, harmonic direction and no little rhythmic thrust. In more recent times, his talent for trio work is showcased in *Oracle* where he takes on the virtuosity of Dave Holland (b) and the verve of Billy Higgins (d) and surfaces on equal terms by way of 'Trane Connections' and 'Blood Count'. Perhaps the presence of one horn still remains an added stimulent and Ken Peplowski's clarinet and

Jones' celeste excursion on the title track of *Lazy Afternoon* is an unexpected bonus. Recorded in 1993, *Upon Reflection* is a heartfelt tribute by Hank and Elvin to the writing talents of their late brother Thad. The most private of occasions, a moving performance of 'A Child Is Born' is but one of many gems. Bradley's Piano Bar in New York, with its magnificent instrument, could have been built for him. BMcR

QUINCY JONES

THE BIRTH OF A BAND
EmArCy 822 469 2

By the late '50s, the trumpet-playing Mr Jones had worked his way from being a sideman with the orchestras of both Lionel Hampton and Dizzy Gillespie to emerging as one of jazzdom's most respected arrangers. It was at this point that Mercury offered to finance the sesssions that resulted in *Birth Of A Band*. The dates resembled a poll-winners shindig, with Ernie Royal, Joe Newman, Harry Edison, Clark Terry and Joe Wilder forming the trumpet team, Phil Woods, Frank Wess, Benny Golson, Zoot Sims, and Sahib Shihab turning up for sax section duties, similar headliners (guitarist Kenny Burrell, trombonist Urbie Green, etc.) filling space in other departments. The material chosen mostly had pedigree in spades – 'I Remember Clifford', 'Whisper Not', 'Moanin'', 'After Hours', while Nat Pierce and Al Cohn helped Quincy out with the chart chores. The result was a much hailed big band operation that's remained in-catalogue ever since. Not that Q has ever made an album that's less than near-essential and you can dig and dive into any dumper box that contains any portion of his work,from soundtracks like *In The Heat Of The Night*, *The Pawnbroker* and *The Hot Rock*, through to his support jobs for Frank Sinatra, Michael Jackson and Miles Davis, *Miles & Quincy Live At Montreux* (Warner Bros 45221 2) plus such contemporary deals as Quincy's own rap-wrapped 'Back On The Block' (Qwest 926 020 2) FD

THE GREAT WIDE WORLD OF QUINCY JONES
EmArCy 822 470 2

WALKING IN SPACE
A&M CDA 0801

THE QUINTESSENCE
MCA MCAD 5728

THIS IS HOW I FEEL ABOUT JAZZ
Impulse GRP 11152

THAD JONES

THE FABULOUS THAD JONES
Debut 127/OJC CD 625

THAD JONES/MEL LEWIS
LRC CDC 9004

Brother of Hank and Elvin, Thad Jones was a musician appropriately acknowledged for his composing, arranging and band leading kills but not always as consistently for his excellent trumpet work. A product of Detroit's hard bop scene in the fifties, Jones later earned important but very different lessons in the bands of Charles Mingus and Count Basie. As a trumpeter, he was a very distinctive player, comfortable with bop but often with an intensity that gave his solos an extra dimension. As the 1954/5 *The Fabulous* shows, he put improvisation high on his list of priorities and his confrontational battle in duo with Mingus on 'I Can't Get Started' could be compared with any of the music's great duet moments. In 1965, Jones formed a big band with drummer Mel Lewis. It was to become a legend for its Monday night sessions at New York's Village Vanguard. *Thad Jones/Mel Lewis* shows its quality, its imaginative approach to arranging and the resultant distinctive sound. Jones left in 1979 and spent most of his last years in Europe. It was perhaps fitting that he returned to lead the late Count Basie Orchestra for one year before his death in 1986. BMcR

LOUIS JORDAN

LET THE GOOD TIMES ROLL
(Bear Family BCD 15557) 8-CD Box

A giant of jive, Jordan was *the* man to reckon with on jukeboxes during the '40s. In Britain, jazz pundits of ye olde school sussed that he was almost inventing rock 'n' roll and frequently slammed his records as "non-jazz". Not that the kids (anyone under 25) cared. Louis touted an alto sax that virtually jumped out of his hands and sang in a way that was both hip and happy. He notched 52 hits during his time with Decca (all of which are included here), 18 of which were R&B number ones. His Tympany Five swung with more power than most big bands and Jordan's only mistake during that period was when he formed a larger outfit and, for a short spell, found that he sounded like all the rest. But those small group sides never dated (they still sound more contemporary than those of Bill Haley's Comets, who attempted to update the Jordan style, using the same producer) and when Louis' greatest hits were assembled to form the basis for the stage show *Five Guys Name Moe*, audiences showed their appreciation by buying tickets forever more. A cheaper, alternative purchase is MCA's *Golden Greats* (DMCL 5005) but the box should be where the smart money heads. FD

THE COMPLETE ALADDIN SESSIONS
(EMI CDP 796567 2)

STANLEY JORDAN

CORNUCOPIA
(Blue Note CDP 7 92356 2)

Guitarist Jordan's energetically marketed advent in the late eighties was accompanied by claims that he was the vanguard of the (new) guitar revolution. His claim to fame was the fact that he sounded the guitar by tapping its fretboard with both hands. This enabled him to expand somewhat on Joe Pass's concept of orchestral guitar playing and effectively play bass lines, chords and top lines simultaneously. Few claims were made for his expansion of the jazz language, and rightly so. Apart from the rather thin tone occasioned by the need to use thin strings, he produces on the quartet tracks here ('Impressions', 'Autumn Leaves' etc.) some exemplary jazz in the Pat Martino-Wes Montgomery mould but in terms of the notes played there's little to distinguish him from his excellent pianist Kenny Kirkland. The later George Benson styled soul-funk tracks are a good indicator of his short-term positioning in the marketplace, and Blue Note were right. MG

WYNTON KELLY

KELLY BLUE
(Riverside 1142/OJC CD 033)

PIANO
(Riverside 254/OJC CD 401)

By playing on one title on Miles Davis' classic 'modal break-through', *Kind Of Blue* (CBS 32109), Wynton Kelly claimed his immortality. He made no attempt to match Bill Evans' understated relevance on the remainder; 'Freddie Freeloader' was a blues and that is what this fine bop pianist did best. A Jamaican raised in New York, Kelly was happy in R&B bands and, as his technique developed, he became more ambitious. He worked in support of Dinah Washington and was present on her fine *Bessie Smith Songbook* (EmArCy 826663 CD). His graduation to bop had Dizzy Gillespie as an aid and from 1959 to 1963 he worked productively with Davis. Kelly was never more at home than in the hard bop combo and *Kelly Blue*, with the Davis rhythm team, finds him soloing inventively and backing the horns of Nat Adderley (c), Bobby Jasper (f) and Benny Golson with urgent conviction. He was similarly at ease in a piano trio, although perhaps his best smaller group work was in a quartet as on *Piano*, with the added voice of Kenny Burrell's guitar. This is a musician's album, themes good ('Whisper Not', 'Dark Eyes', 'Ill Wind' etc,), players interacting sympathetically and not an ugly phrase in sight. BMcR

STAN KENTON

RETROSPECTIVE
(Capitol CDP 7 97350 2) 4-CD

THE COMPLETE CAPITAL RECORDINGS
OF THE BILL HOLMAN AND BILL RUSSO CHARTS
(Mosaic MD4 136) 4-CD

The Kenton big band was simply that – BIG! Often it sounded even bigger than it actually was because Stan chose to enhance all early recordings by means of an echo chamber. Which meant even a standard 16 piece sounded HUGE. And, thanks to a steller brass section that frequently aimed to dismantle the walls of Jericho, the band could also surface as a live monster as the following albums recorded between 1953 and 59 loudly corroborate – *Stan Kenton Orchestra Vol. 1 & Vol. 2* (Vogue 655905/6), *Festival Of Modern American Jazz* (Status CD 101), *Kenton '56* (Artistry CD 002), *At The Rendezvous Vol. 1 & 2* (Status CD 106 &108), *Roadshow* (Capitol CDP 7 96328 2). By 1960, Kenton's brass obsession resulted in the introduction of four 'mellophoniums' which boosted the brass backline to a threatening 14 strong *Mellophonium Moods* (Status STCD 106). But back in the late '40s/early '50s, it was just simple riffs that came highly powered, tuneful mindworms such as 'Artistry In Rhythm', 'Eager Beaver', 'Intermission Riff', 'Southern Scandal' and 'Peanut Vendor' – *Kenton In Hi-Fi* (Capitol CDP 7 98451) and *New Concepts Of Artistry In Rhythm* (Capitol CDP 7 92865) . But the plan was to shift away from the ballroom towards the concert hall, via tone-poems, neo-classical suites (Bob Graettinger's advant garde *City Of Glass*) and even an album dedicated to the music of Wagner! As with any phenomenon, loyalties were noisily divided. Criticis, for the most part, damned Kenton's innovations as pretenious and unswinging, leaving his fanatical devotees to applaud the adrenalin rush of his numerous wide-screen, echo-enhanced impressionistic 'skyscraper' creations. In turn, Kenton's orchestral voicings exerted a marked influence on such as Elmer Bernstein's *The Man With The Golden Arm* and *Staccato* while Leonard Bernstein's *West Side Story* (later interpreted by Kenton) owes much to Stan The Man. Though a fine arranger himself, Kenton brought in the likes of Shorty Rogers, Bill Russo, Bill Holman, Lennie Niehaus and Johnny Richards to continually refurbish the 'book'. Depending on the mood, the premise was to use heavy splashes of densely orchestrated sound, anchored by precision drumming (Shelly Manne, Stan Levey, Mel Lewis), dramatically punctured by a seering burst of alto sax (Art Pepper, Lee Konitz), a stratospheric trumpet (Maynard Ferguson, Conte Candoli, Buddy Childers, Chico Alvarez), the rattle of latin percussion *Cuban Fire* (Capitol CDP 7 96260), or, if the moment was pastoral, a reflective tenor solo (Zoot Sims, Bill Holman, Bill Perkins), alternativly the burnished burr of a trombone (Frank Rosolino, Milt Bernhart, Carl Fontana). But whatever he did was never less than intriguing. And much of what he achieved is encapsulated on the all-embracing boxed history lessons from Capitol and Mosaic. FD

BARNEY KESSEL

THE POLLWINNERS
(Contemporary 7535/OJC CD1562)

SOARING
(Concord CCD 6033)

A self-taught guitarist, Barney Kessel might have been a comedian instead, his first professional work having been with the Chico Marx band in 1943, during which he developed a routine with Groucho's musical brother. Instead, while retaining a flair for satire, he became one of the first to carry the message of Charlie Christian, and, in a career spanning more than 50 years, he has been one of the most consistent and consistently recorded. Even in his late teens, he had recognised the thrust of Christian's work, though his use of the latter's compellingly long lines has perhaps been most expressive in ballads. His reputation was sharply enhanced by a stint with the original Oscar Peterson trio from 1952-3, after which he made a string of excellent records for the West Coast Contemporary label while working Hollywood's television and radio bands. It was during his tenure with Contemporary, that Kessel linked up with ever-popular Ray Brown (b) and Shelly Manne (d) to record a series of best selling albums under the collective title, The Poll Winners. And, as *The Poll Winners* illustrates they brought a fresh slant to (over)familiar material like 'Satin Doll' or 'On Green Dolphin Street'. Throughout his career, Kessel's playing has evolved, the long, linear phrasing of old slowly surrendering to more fragmented lines marked by a highly percussive chordal technique. CS

EASY LIKE
(Contemporary 3511/OJC CD153)

VOL. 3: TO SWING OR NOT TO SWING
(Contemporary 3513/OJC CD 317)

POLL WINNERS THREE!
(Contemporary 7576/OJC CD 692)

RED HOT & BLUES
(Contemporary CCD 14044)

PETER KING

CHARLIE WATTS QUINTET: FROM ONE CHARLIE
(UFO CD 2)

BROTHER BERNARD
(Miles Music MMCD 076)

Since the untimely passing of Joe Harriott and Derek Humble, by far the most powerful alto saxist on the British scene has been Peter King. For all his efforts, King isn't the first to suffer from inverted snobbery. Were he American, rather than local hero, his obvious world-class status would be undisputed. While King's alliegence to Bird doesn't pass unnoticed, the true test of his ability emerged when cast as the key player in a quintet assembled by Rolling Stones' drummer Charlie Watts for *From One Charlie* – the soundtrack to Watts' simplistic cartoon book biography of Charlie Parker, *Ode To A High Flying Bird* (with which it is boxed) and subsequent successful showcase engagements in Japan and the USA. Though it contains but seven tracks, 'Bluebird' and 'Relaxin' At Camarillo' are the only Bird originals. But you wouldn't know that, for King fashioned a beret-full of fresh sounding themes in the bop tradition ('Practising, Practising, Just Great', 'Blackbird – White Chicks', etc) rather than cranking out faded facsmilies. But then, the intention wasn't slavish imitation, rather a heartfelt celebration without a cobweb in sight. Previous to this, the 1988 *Brother Bernard* date was King's best available representation, but the Bird project plus his work on Stan Tracey's albums *Portraits Plus* (Blue Note CDP 7 80696) and *Live At The QEH* (Blue Note CDBLT 1010) have brought him back into prominence and, in doing so, refocused his undeniable talent and given him a zestful sense of purpose. TH

CHARLIE WATTS QUINTET:
A TRIBUTE TO CHARLIE PARKER WITH STRINGS
(Continuum CD 19201)

WARM & TENDER
(Continuum CD 19310)

JOHN KIRBY

THE JOHN KIRBY SEXTET 1939-1941
(Columbia COL 472184 2)

'The Biggest Little Band In The World' ran the tag. And the John Kirby Sextet certainly thought in terms of major league. Everyone in the band was a star, from bassist-leader Kirby and singer Maxine Sullivan through to drummer O'Neil Spencer. Russell Procope (as), Buster Bailey (clt), Billy Kyle (p) and Charlie Shavers (tpt) – there wasn't a weak link in the line-up. They were a team. They played together and stayed together. And, come payday, Kirby wasn't mean. The arrangements were slick, the playing tight and if everything was a mite polite then that went down well at the Onyx Club on New York's 52nd Street, where the band held sway. The music they played sounds a bit Mickey Mouse these days. Shavers was usually confined to mute, while the material was frequently of a novelty nature, spotlighting tunes stolen from Grieg, Chopin and Shubert, a typical example being a touch of Tchaïkovsky dubbed 'Bounce Of The Sugar Plum Fairy'. But, in terms of '40s combo swing, the Kirby Sextet is fondly remembered. FD

ANDY KIRK

ANDY KIRK & MARY LOU WILLIAMS – MARY'S IDEA
(MCA GRP 16222)

Andy Kirk captained The Clouds Of Joy, one of the great Kansas City bands of the '30s and '40s. Initially there was just one true instrumental star in the band – Mary Lou Williams, who wrote, arranged and played piano in a style that owed much to the rent party scene. Vocally, Pha Terrell (known to his detractors as Pha Terrible) was a ballroom idol who raised a zillion ooohs and aaahs every time he paraded 'Until The Real Thing Comes Along' (missing from this compilation), but everything was really down to Mary Lou, whose work is ably demonstrated on such tracks as the delightful 'Twinklin'', 'Bear Down' and, to lesser effect, on the Harry Mills-sung tribute that is 'The Lady Who Swings The Band'. After Mary Lou's departure, the band began employing more major names from the local MU's books, such as saxmen Jimmy Forrest (who later wrote the slinky 'Night Train') and future R&B honker (Big) Al Sears plus trumpet giants Shorty Baker, Fats Navarro and Howard McGhee. But it was the early band that grabbed the headlines and swung the Savoy Ballroom silly. FD

KANSAS CITY BOUNCE
(Black & Blue 59 240)

ROLAND KIRK

RIP RIG AND PANIC/NOW PLEASE DON'T YOU CRY, BEAUTIFUL EDITH
(EmArcy 832164)

THE INFLATED TEAR
(Atlantic 81396)

DOES YOUR HOUSE HAVE LIONS
(Rhino/Atlantic R2 71406) 2-CD

CHARLES MINGUS: OH YEAH!
(Atlantic 790 667)

A great one-off, there has never been another artist quite like Roland Kirk. A tenor player and a man possessed, he added two obscure reed instruments to his arsenal, the manzello and stritch; an odd-looking pair of battered turn-of-the-century Spanish military band instruments and close relatives of the soprano and alto respectively. When the spirit moved him, Kirk frequently stuffed all three saxes into his mouth at one time and through a combination of 'circular-breathing' and fancy-fingering simultaneously wailed on all three in harmony for anything up to half-an-hour without pausing, as on 'Sack O' Woe' (*We Free Kings*) and 'Hog Calling Blues' (*Oh Yeah!*). Unfortunately, those reactionaries unable to see further than their own prejudices, dismissed Kirk as a 'novelty' act rather than a visionary talent. In his quest to "catch the sound of the sun", Kirk honked, hooted and hollered while feverishly incorporating everything from whistles and sirens to breaking glass, a nose flute and a cassette recorder that emitted Fats Waller's 'Ain't Misbehavin'' to heighten the mood and intensify the texture. About the only piece of music-making hardware he didn't have strapped to his body was a flute from which he produced the much-imitated style of simultaneously humming or growling while improvising ('You Did It, You Did It' *We Free Kings*).

Rahsaan (Mercury 846630) an 11-CD box covers his years with Mercury and includes familiar albums such as *We Free Kings*, his personal *tour de force Rip Rig And Panic*, *Domino*, *I Talk With The Spirits*, encounters with Tubby Hayes, Benny Golson, Quincy Jones plus a knockabout 'live' set in Copenhagen with pianist Tete Montoliu and legendary bluesman Sonny Boy Williamson. It was on Atlantic that he reached an even wider international audience heading The Vibration Society and producing albums like the deeply moving *The Inflated Tear* – a reference to his childhood blindness, plus the socially-aware *Prepare Thyself To Deal With A Miracle* and *Volunteered Slavery* (Rhino R2 71407). Such was Kirk's driving life-force that, in 1976, he refused to allow a stroke that paralysed one side of his body to sideline him. For the last year of his life, he played one-handed. Hardly anyone noticed! Very few musicians have ever established such a close rapport as the one Kirk shared with his fans. When, in December 1977, Kirk died, age of 40, to many it was like a death in the family. RC

JIMMY KNEPPER

I DREAM TOO MUCH
(Soul Note 121092)

Trombonist Jimmy Knepper's technical facility earned him jobs in the fifties with nearly all the top band leaders of the day. The most significant, however, was Charles Mingus and to the Chazz man's music Knepper added an arranger's hand as well as his considerable solo skills. *The Complete 1959 CBS Charles Mingus Sessions* (Mosaic MQ4-143) present the best of their association, with the trombone preaching through a plunger on 'Song With Orange', smoothly inquisitive on 'Mood Indigo' and truculent on 'New Now, Know How'. The sixties and seventies had him in the arranger's playgrounds led by Gil Evans, Thad Jones/Mel Lewis and also employed to good effect with Lee Konitz. His arranging talent and natural solo skills are well showcased on Konitz's *Yes, Yes, Nonet* (SteepleChase SCS 1119) or *Live At Laren* (Soul Note 121069). The former especially notable for the charts and their immaculate execution and the latter for stunning solos on 'Who You', 'Without A Song' and 'Times Lie'. Knepper's contribution to Mingus Dynasty in the eighties was crucial. His (mixed) experience with Mingus had given him considerable insight into Chazzland and the 1982 *Reincarnation* (South Note 121042) offers a living, vital continuation of the Mingus legacy and not a tired retrospective. Even better as a complete package is the 1984 *I Dream* by his own band, if only because it has textural qualities that are pure Knepper. The sound of the brass is trombone inspired, yet is brilliantly executed by trumpet, trombone and french horn. BMcR

LEE KONITZ

SUBCONSCIOUS-LEE
(Prestige 7004/OJC CD 186)

THE LEE KONITZ DUETS
(Milestone 9013/OJC CD 466)

LIVE AT THE HALF NOTE 1959
(Verve 521 659 2)[L]

ZOUNDS
(Soul Note 121219)

The Adam's rib of Lennie Tristano's music, Lee Konitz was almost unique in ignoring the all pervading influence of Charlie Parker in the process of becoming one of the music's outstanding alto saxophonists. *Subconscious-Lee* has him, with Tristano, in the comfort of his stylistic home. Various groups from 1949 to 1950 show how well he fitted into this home, his tone sounding strangely vulnerable but the flow of his ideas at times breathtaking. The newly-discovered two-disc *Live At The Half Note* is the 1959 Tristano quintet with Bill Evans depping on the pianist's night off. Here, with Warne Marsh (ts) plus Jimmy Garrison (b) and Paul Motian (d) rounding out the fivesome, Konitz takes command of the situation for a *tour de force* performance. Konitz always seemed to embrace the risk factor when improvising and, perhaps because of this, excelled in the duet situation. He responded superbly to the sympathetic support of pianist Hal Galper on the 1974 *Windows* (SteepleChase SCS 1057) but the chance to hear him with various stylistic challenges on Duets from 1967 makes it irresistible. Konitz worked well with his Nonet in the late seventies and *Yes, Yes, Nonet* (SteepleChase SCS 1119) shows how effectively he promoted loose limbed solos within his exactly performed but never pedantic ensemble. He had always sought out freer elements in his music and saw nothing incongruous in juxtaposing harmonically harnessed tunes with free improvisational excursions. This is successfully accomplished on the 1990 *Zounds* where 'Sythesthetics' and the title track, in particular, allow him totally free rein. Konitz's infractions of jazz world normality make him a much admired nonconformist. He is the paroled figure, torn between traditional incarceration and running for deliciously illicit freedom. BMcR

KONITZ MEETS MULLIGAN
(Pacific Jazz CDP 7 46847 2)

GENE KRUPA

UPTOWN: ROY ELDRIDGE & GENE KRUPA
(Columbia 466310 2)

KRUPA & RICH
(Verve 521 643 2)

COMPACT JAZZ: GENE KRUPA
(Verve 833 286)

COMPACT JAZZ: GENE KRUPA & BUDDY RICH
(Verve 835 314)

One of the most emulated of all jazz musicians, Krupa's influence stretched from the mid-30s as far as Keith Moon, late drummer with The Who, who with great affection, freely adapted Krupa's extrovert stance and mannerisms. Krupa may have gained attention with the McKenzie-Condon Chicagoans (1927), but from the moment he joined Benny Goodman as featured attraction (1935) Krupa's destiny was set. An abundance of natural charm and charisma coupled with a streak of good-natured exhibitionism instantly won over audiences and, aside from his role in Goodman's legendary trio and quartet, subsequent showcase hits such as the frenzied 'Sing, Sing, Sing', resulted in the Drummer Man upstaging the Swing King himself. In terms of matinee idol good-looks, he had more going for him than most of Hollywood's leading men which resulted in Krupa guesting in a number of movies.
Uptown stands witness to the fact that between 1938 and 1943 (and again in 1945-51), Krupa's fan base was large enough for him to

front his own wildly percussive Big Band; a visually exciting outfit featuring singer Anita O'Day and trumpet star Roy Eldridge which livened up the charts with 'Let Me Off Uptown' and 'Disc Jockey Jump'. He even tried his hand at Big Band bop. However, by the '50s, Krupa's drums/sax/piano trio had become a regular Jazz At The Philharmonic fixture while his drum battles with Buddy Rich noisy showstoppers. As the Verve material illustrates, from 1952 until the mid-60s, producer Norman Granz took every opportunity to use him on a diversity of sessions – some, more appropriate to Krupa's swing-era style than others. And, when the phone rang, Krupa was also on call for media-intensive reunions with Goodman, Teddy Wilson (p) and Lionel Hampton (vbs). Somehow it seemed only right that this Showman supreme and all-round likeable guy should be the subject of a Hollywood bio-pic *Drum Crazy/The Gene Krupa Story* (1958) with Sal Mineo in the role of the master-drummer. In later years Krupa's swing based two-in-the-bar may have sounded of its time, but his pioneering technique along with his considerable achievements were always beyond question. RC

STEVE LACY

MORNING JOY
(hat Hut 6014)

SCHOOL DAYS
(hat Hut 6140)

THE CONDOR
(Soul Note 121135)

Steve Lacy and Sidney Bechet are the only two major jazzmen to realise their true, musical ethos through the soprano saxophone. Once a Dixielander, Lacy jousted with Cecil Taylor before finding true comfort in the didactic environment of Thelonious Monk and his music. His Monk-cred is perfectly displayed on *School Days* and it motivated one of the most prodigious recording careers in jazz. It was a career that supported a style based on lengthy lines in melodic free fall. Nothing was in deliberate, sequential order and momentary inspiration was its fuel. Monk lore remained an important factor and, as recently as 1989, his solo *More Monk* showed that it could still be the bare bones of his playing method. The most outstanding of Lacy's day-to-day work through the seventies and eighties was with his quintet/sextet, including wife Irene Aebi (vocals/violin) and his saxophone alter ego Steve Potts. While awaiting the appearance of certain LP classics on CD (*Stamps* hat Hut) the best examples available are either the 1986 *Morning Joy* by a quartet (without Aebi) or the full sextet on the 1985 *The Condor* with poetry reading added. Both have the Lacy-Potts contest in high profile and show that it was a pleasure for Lacy. The superb 1985 *Chirps* (FMP CD 29) is a similar competition with the challenge provided by Evan Parker (ss) and the two men somehow making musical polemics sound like a friendly discussion. BMcR

LAMBERT, HENDRICKS AND ROSS

SING A SONG OF BASIE
(Impulse! GRP 11122)

In 1945 Buddy Stewart and Dave Lambert, vocalists with the Gene Krupa Band, recorded 'What's This?' the first bop vocal recording. Seven years later jazz singer Annie Ross added surreal lyrics to

'Twisted' – vocalizing not just the top line but the entire improvised tenor sax solo made famous earlier by Wardell Gray. Surprisingly, the Ross version entered the US Pop charts . The third piece of the jigsaw was added in 1957 when Jon Hendricks and Lambert, both former drummers, collaborated on a 'vocalese' version of Woody Herman's flagwaver, 'The Four Brothers'. Later that year, Ross joined them to emerge as the most successful jazz vocal group since The Four Freshman, winning a new jazz audience and, in due course, influencing the likes of Eddie Jefferson, Al Jarreau, Bobby McFerrin and Manhattan Transfer. By virtue of Hendricks and Lambert's knack of custom-writing lyrics to the section parts and solos from instrumental jazz classics and Ross' incredible five octave vocal range, fame was of the instant variety and they toured extensively, peaking in 1959 with 'The Jazz For Moderns' tour. All their recordings maintain the same degree of excellence but *Sing A Song Of Basie* remains the pick of a still-fresh crop. Here they are joined by the Count's rhythm section, Freddie Greene (gtr), Eddie Jones (b), Sonny Payne (d) and pianist, Nat Pierce, with 'Little Pony', 'Avenue C' and 'Everyday' just having the edge. In 1962, sadly due to illness, Ross was replaced by Yolande Bavan, but without the same success. An era ended when, in 1964, Dave Lambert was the victim of a fatal road accident. JF

HAROLD LAND

HAROLD IN THE LAND OF JAZZ
(Contemporary 7550/OJC CD162)

THE FOX
(Contemporary 7619/OJC CD 343)

Tenorman Harold Land is present on five of the 10-CDs that comprise *Brownie/The Complete EmArCy Recordings Of Clifford Brown* (EmArCy 838 306). The quintet Brownie co-lead with drummer Max Roach is regarded as the last of the great bop bands – Hard Bop was waiting in the wings to pick up the banner dropped with Brownie's death and run with it. One in a long line of Texas tenors, Harold Land kicked in hard as the quintet nailed one classic performance after another: 'Parisian Thoroughfare', 'Joy Spring', 'Daahoud' before handing over to Sonny Rollins in time for Xmas 1955. Six months later, Brownie was dead in the wreck of an automobile. Despite such a pedigree, Harold Land's decision to remain on the West Coast frequently left him out of the running when the subject of heavyweight tenor players was debated. No slacker, Land's contributions to the Curtis Counce Quintet were often the highspots but a brace of albums he made under his own name further carved his reputation in stone. *Harold In The Land Of Jazz* (aka *Grooveyard*) is basically the Counce group, but *The Fox*, taped in August 1959, is indispensable. Fronting a group that help define West Coast Hard Swing, Land's front-line partner was enigmatic Brownie-inspired trumpeter Dupree Bolton whose only other recording date before disappearing into prison was with another local tenorman, Curtis Amy. Pianist Elmo Hope, who also supplied most of the charts proves the lynchpin, enabling Herbie Lewis (b) and Frank Butler (d) to drive the group relentlessly. But, as the title track drives home, it's still Land and Bolton who remain the centre of attention. In later years, Land reflected Coltrane concepts during his association with vibesman Bobby Hutcherson (*Total Eclipse* Blue Note B21Y 84291, *Damisi* Mainstream MDCD 714 and *San Francisco* Blue Note CDP 28268), but *The Fox* will forever remain his moment in a somewhat hazy LA sun. RC

EDDIE LANG

JOE VENUTI & EDDIE LANG VOL. 1 & 2
(JSP CD 309 & 310)

The guitar is the clearest link between jazz and its folk-blues roots, so it is ironic that its establishment as a jazz solo instrument should have been the achievement of an Italian-American in the mid-1920s, when jazz development had already picked up considerable momentum. Salvatore Massaro – he changed his name to Eddie Lang after a childhood baseball hero – was originally a violinist, with Joe Venuti as a classmate. They frequented Atlantic City as a violin-playing duo after leaving school and it was not until he was about 21 that Lang picked up the guitar.

Despite his origins, he had a natural feeling for the blues and, although his determination to maintain a singing sound occasionally disrupted his rhythmic momentum, its voicings were distinctly 'modern'. Sometimes, he played rhythm in a walking, single-string fashion that augured the way the double bass would be used. His work with Venuti is always charming, coherent and swinging, but it was a handful of Bix Beiderbecke sides that saw some of his most ingenious playing. Venuti, though fluent and articulate, remains a minor league violinist, behind Eddie South, Stuff Smith and Claude Williams of the pre-War era. Lang died in 1933 from post-operative complications after a tonsillectomy (see Bennie Moten) but, by then, he had given the guitar a jazz voice, developing a hornlike solo style that enabled it to challenge more established frontline instruments for a hearing. CS

EDDIE LANG: JAZZ GUITAR VIRTUOSO
(Yazoo YAZCD 1059)

BIX BEIDERBECKE VOL. 1: SINGIN' THE BLUES
(CBS 466309 2)

JOE VENUTI: JAZZ VIOLIN
(Yazoo YAZCD 1062)

JOE & ZOOT
(Chiaroscuro CRD 142)

PEGGY LEE

BLACK COFFEE
(Decca 25P2 2829)

MINK JAZZ
(Capitol TOCJ 5342)

The greatest-ever white jazz singer? Possibly. Though La Lee now suffers from ill-health, from the '40s through to the late '60s she was the one that mattered most. A former Benny Goodman band singer, she could tease a ballad into something approaching pure heartbreak, yet, without striving, she could sound like the blackest of R&B singers. Additionally, Peg swung with a nonchalance that left others for dead. *Black Coffee*, made with a tasty yet unobtrusive jazz combo, is simply one of the greatest vocal albums ever made and demonstrates every aspect of the Lee oeuvre. She turns 'I've Got You Under My Skin' into the epitome of swing, does her sultry blues thing on 'Gee Baby Ain't I Good For You', defiantly insists 'My Heart Belongs To Daddy' and honey-hushes 'Easy Living' in such a way that you almost forget that Billie got there first. *Mink Jazz*, which stems from 1963, is lighter but almost as compelling, the tracks pitting Peg's voice against the perky, unique trumpet sound of Jack Sheldon being of the kind that would bring smiles to Mount Rushmore. Though neither record is currently available in the UK except on import, *The Best Of Peggy Lee 1952-1956* (Music Club MCCD 157) contains several tracks from *Black Coffee* and is therefore near-essential. FD

PERFECT-LEE
(MCA DMCL 1794)

PEGGY LEE – COLLECTORS SERIES
(Capitol CDP 7 93195 2)

WITH GEORGE SHEARING: BEAUTY AND THE BEAST
(Capitol CDP 7 98454 2)

GEORGE LEWIS

GEORGE LEWIS WITH KID SHOTS
(American Music AMCD 2)

TRIOS & BANDS
(American Music AMCD 4)

The teetotal, non-smoking, religious George Lewis was perhaps more responsible than any other New Orleans revivalist bandleader for sparking off the excesses, musical and social, of the 1950s 'trad' boom. By then, his own music had become bogged down in the familiar, narrow repertoire of a whole generation of New Orleans bands, but, at its best, it was a deeply expressive dance music. Rooted deeply in the blues, it is geared directly to particular dance steps so that, whereas Bunk Johnson's martial approach may contain only an occasional reference to an old-time dance form, such rhythms as the polka found greater currency in George Lewis's performances (e.g. the archaic waltz-time introduction to 'Over The Waves', and the two-stepping quadrille feeling of 'High Society'). Being a folk music, of course, its emotional flavour lurches wildly between tense, moving passages ('San Jacinto Blues No 1') and moments of toe-curling sentimentality ('This Love Of Mine'). Nonetheless, this basic approach masked more complex musical characteristics, when his improvising pulls beyond mere New Orleanian melodic embellishment to hint at certain practices of the Swing Era. Thus, 'Ice Cream' is a polyphonic masterpiece, revealing how its use by many 'trad' bands as a flagwaver misses the rhythmic point of Lewis's original. CS

THE COMPLETE BLUE NOTE RECORDINGS
(Mosaic MD3-132)

JAM SESSIONS
(Storyville STCD 6019)

DAVE LIEBMAN

DOUBLE EDGE
(Storyville SCD 4091)

THE TREE
(Soul Note 121195)

ONE OF A KIND
(Core/Line COCD 9.00887)

Dave Liebman's affair with jazz has sometimes been a tad fickle. He studied theory with Lennie Tristano and, in the seventies, worked with Elvin Jones and Miles Davis as well as with the rock group Ten Wheel Drive. The group Lookout Farm with Richie Beirach looked at a special brand of John Coltrane/Indian fusion and suggested a desertion from the jazz cause. This movement away increased during the decade and it was not until the eighties that he fully returned to the jazz world. He was in his element, again with Beirach on the 1985 *Double Edge*; an album that, in using well known themes 'Naima', ''Round Midnight', 'Green Dolphin Street' etc,), allows the listener easy access to the variations provided. The mood is one of understated drama, yet there is a sense of latent menace that suits both players. Liebman also scored as a solo saxophonist and *One Of A Kind* showed his comfort with the form. More challenging was *The Tree*, another solo work but one offering two takes of each theme, appearing in reverse order. The parts of the tree are conceptualised rather than depicted but it shows how Liebman prefers to work with musical impressions and not with descriptive, sound painting. BMcR

ABBEY LINCOLN

WE INSIST! FREEDOM NOW SUITE
(Candid CCD 9002)

STRAIGHT AHEAD
(Candid CCD 79015)

YOU GOTTA PAY THE BAND
(Verve 511 110-2)

Vocalist/composer/bandleader/actress Abbey Lincoln is one of jazz's most politically outspoken female artists, as well as one of its most talented and original. She participated in the 1960 *We Insist!* project with her husband, legendary drummer Max Roach, she has performed and recorded with many of post-bop's most notable instrumentalists, and has always preferred to sing from within a true jazz setting. *Straight Ahead*, from 1961, represents her first date as leader, and features an astonishing line-up of stars, including avant-garde reeds virtuoso Eric Dolphy, trumpeter Booker Little, tenor legend Coleman Hawkins and her husband behind the kit. *You Gotta Pay The Band* is a good example of her more recent work. This 1991 session (highlight track 'A Time For Love') features the late Stan Getz in one of his last recordings, as well as immaculate piano veteran Hank Jones and bassist Charlie Haden. LC

CHARLES LLOYD

DREAM WEAVER
(Atlantic AMCY 1010)

NOTE FROM BIG SUR
(ECM 1465 511 99 2)

Unfortunately, Charles Lloyd became jazz's standard bearer in the 'Flower Power' movement. He came to prominence in the groups of Chico Hamilton and Cannonball Adderley but, leading a fine group with Keith Jarrett (p), Cecil McBee (b) and Jack DeJohnette (d) in the late-60s, found himself as popular at rock venues as he was in jazz rooms and a headline attraction at the Newport and Monterey festivals when not hanging out with The Beach Boys! In retrospect, this is not easy to understand. Sartorially, he did acknowledge the 'world of peace' but his John Coltane inspired style on *Dream Weaver* was about straight ahead jazz, albiet with a touch of the exotic. A period away from music for much of the seventies led many to assume his absence as permanent but, during the eighties, he re-appeared in good, musical shape. *Note From Big Sur* finds him happy in the company of pianist Bobo Stenson, his musical travelling company. The Coltrane inspiration remains undeminished, his light tenor tone exudes genuine, emotional commitment and whether at the medium clip of 'Sam Song' or on the appropriately named 'Monk In Paris', he shows that he can still match that commitment with a comparable, creative flair. BMcR

JOE LOVANO

LANDMARKS
(Blue Note CDP 7 96108 2)

WORLDS
(Label Bleu LBLC CS24) [L]

Stints with the Paul Motian Trio and John Scofield's post-fusion quartet brought Lovano to international prominence, although his background – in Woody Herman's seventies band – was by comparison curiously conservative. It's interesting to note, in his playing on the ballad 'Emperor Jones' on *Landmarks*, occasional echoes of an earlier incumbent of a Herman sax chair, Stan Getz, and that says something about Joe Lovano as the renaissance man of contemporary saxophone, a musician able to play old and new with equal authenticity and conviction. *Landmarks* is generally of the more contemporary persuasion, a blend of fierce hard bop and angular riff music ('Here And Now') in which Lovano and his fellow soloists, including the ever-melodic Kenny Werner (p) and an unusually aggressive John Abercrombie (gtr), hold the form while pummelling it towards disintegration.
Worlds is a recording from the 1989 Amiens jazz festival which presents Lovano's writing for a larger ensemble including his singer wife Judi Silverman, and old trio partners Bill Frisell (gtr) and Paul Motian (d). Trumpeter Tim Hagans and trombonist Gary Valente flesh out a band which represents another, yet more abstract aspect of Lovano's art. MG

SOUNDS OF JOY
(Enja CD 7013 2)

UNIVERSAL LANGUAGE
(Blue Note CDP 7 99830 2)

FROM THE SOUL
(Blue Note CDP 7 98363 2)

JIMMIE LUNCEFORD

BLUES IN THE NIGHT
(Jazz Roots CD 56013)

In November 1940, no less than 28 of America's greatest big bands were assembled at New York's Manhattan Center and scheduled to play short sets. All got off-stage on time – except for one. For the fans simply screamed until Lunceford's exhuberant crew was allowed to blow into extra time. Prompted by trumpeter Sy Oliver's outstanding two-beat (but decidedly not two bit) arrangements, the band had an instantly recognisable sound of its own.

Solo-wise, Willie Smith blew a kind of distinctive acid-blues alto, Jimmy Crawford was simply a great drummer who did all the simple things and made them swing, while Paul Webster kept the trumpet section exciting. And if the band singers contributed less than most – lead singer Dan Grissom was known as Dan Gruesome – then it didn't really matter. For such rifferoles as 'For Dancers Only' kept the kids sweet and the more azure 'Uptown Blues' and 'Outskirts Of Town' steadied the buffs. FD

STOMP IT OFF
(MCA GRP 16082)

JIMMY LYONS

BURNT OFFERING
(Black Saint (120130 2)

CECIL TAYLOR – UNIT STRUCTURES
(Blue Note BCT 84237 2)

CECIL TAYLOR – FONDATION MAEGHT NIGHTS
(Jazzview COD 001/3)

GIVE IT UP
(Black Saint 120087)

Buster Bailey gave Jimmy Lyons his first alto saxophone, Charlie Parker contributed a stylistic direction and Cecil Taylor provided a less than well paid career but, more significantly, an educating hand. Lyons recorded with Taylor, on and off, from 1961 to 1984. He came to the partnership with his bop inspired method; one that was not only harmonically and rhythmically incompatible but perhaps also pitched at the wrong level of intensity. He rapidly adjusted, his studied application perhaps reasonably acceptable on the aptly titled *Unit Structures* but, by 1969 and *Fondation Maeght Nights* the stylistic transition was complete. Ironically, it was out of his Taylor-made situation that Lyons' recognisable style came about. The 1982 *Burnt Offering* duo with Andrew Cyrille finds him reacting superbly to the drummer's oblique, rhythmic references and soaring freely through three minor themes to launch into an examplary free flow. The sextet on his *Give It Up* uses no piano and perhaps hints at the fact that, much as he owed to Taylor, relief from that 'authority' was a welcomed. BMcR

HUMPHREY LYTTELTON

BACK TO THE SIXTIES
Philips 834458 2)

HUMPHREY LYTTELTON & HIS BAND 1960-63
Philips 838764 2)

BEANO BOOGIE
Calligraph CLG 026)

The most important name in British jazz? Certainly there's a case to be made for Humph's part in the scheme of things. A trumpet-playing old Etonian, he proved great newspaper fodder right from the start and even grabbed a chart hit in 1956 with 'Bad Penny Blues', a trumpet and boogie piano item that owed much to the

Harry James Boogie Woogie Trio. Having set his personalised version of New Orleans jazz on its feet, Lyttelton then led the charge into mainstream, the two Philips albums spotlighting a band that included Basie's Buck Clayton and leading Brit tenor modernist Jimmy Skidmore in its line up. Ellingtonia, soul-jazz ('Sack O'Woe'), bebop ('The Champ'), Humph tossed them all together with impunity and lost the allegiance of a zillion banjo-lovers. Since that time, he's continued on his own individualistic way, forming his own record label (Calligraph) and heading wherever he feels like heading in the company of whoever he chooses to befriend musically, *Beano Boogie* linking him with sax-playing one-time young lion Alan Barnes. Another day, he'll record with the likes of Helen Shapiro or Acker Bilk, maybe hurtle back in time to link with former colleagues Wally Fawkes (clt) and Kathy Stobart (ts), but that's Humph. Skip the 'file under' classification, in this case catergories don't count. FD

MACHITO & HIS AFRO CUBAN ORCHESTRA

THE ORIGINAL MAMBO KINGS/
AN INTRODUCTION TO AFRO-CUBOP
(Verve 314 513 876)

The incessant clatter of Latin percussion has long become as much an everyday urban American pulse as a fatback rock beat. Like all innovations, it's absorbtion into the mainstream soundtrack was of a casual nature. As with all types of popular immigrant dance music, its stars – in this instance, Cuban-born bandleader Machito (Frank Grillo) and his trumpet playing brother-in-law, Mario Bauza – already enjoyed a strong local following around Manhattan and the success, in 1947, of 'Tanga' and 'Killer Joe' promptly caught the Big Apple's more adventurous jazz ears: the most notably being Dizzy. The opening shot was the ultra-rare 'Cubop City Parts 1 & 2' (included here): an historic date which had the great tenorman Brew Moore and the fiesty trumpets of Bauza and protobopper Howard McGhee framed by the soon-to-become-familiar bitter-sweet blast exclusive to blood vessel-busting Cuban trumpet sections. It even earned a UK release on Vogue as a brittle 10-inch single. Almost immediately, J.A.T.P.'s tenor honkin' Flip Phillips ('Tanga'), Charlie Parker ('Okiedoke'), drummer Buddy Rich and arranger Chico O'Farrill got on the Cubop case , but more so, Dizzy Gillespie who, with the custom-composed 'Manteca' (here, transformed into a full-blown suite) and 'Cubano Be-Cubano Bop' quickly shaped the genre into the most exciting sound in town. Long overdue, this well-focused compilation amounts to an important addition to the recorded history of indiginous contemporary American music. Elsewhere, numerous contemporary Machito mambo dance dates and Salsa sessions are to be found (mostly on Charly) replete with smoking trumpets, raucous saxes and vocals that vary between sultry and swaggering according to taste. RC

JUNIOR MANCE

SMOKEY BLUES
(JSP CD 219)

If anyone could be said to personify the fifties Chicago school of hard bop pianists, it would be Junior Mance. Richard Abrams moved on, Jodie Christian went many years without recording, but Mance remains a living monument to the style. He fuses left with right hand in a way that is fundamentally simple but he spices it with something of the baptist rock, the basis of blues steeped piano since the earliest days. His experience in the late forties had been with tenor stars Gene Ammons and Lester Young but his residency at Chicago's Bee Hive lounge moulded his effortless blend of legato blues and the more urgent bop elements. He was at home in any company and had productive periods with Dizzy Gillespie (1958-60), and a twin-tenor combo fronted by Eddie 'Lockjaw' Davis and Johnny Griffin. He was also at home with the piano trio and *Smokey Blues* typifies his work up to the present day. Blues like 'In The Evenin'' and 'Deep' are bespoke material for him but the novel way in which he takes 'Small Fry' back to Chicago's South Side is the work of a man who has paid his dues. BMcR

ALBERT MANGELSDÖRFF

ROOM 1220
(Konnex KCD 5037)

THREE ORIGINALS
(MPS 519 213 2) [L]

Albert Mangelsdörff has seen a great deal of trombone history slide by since his days as a J. J. Johnson disciple in early fifties Hamburg. He has been credited as the god father of trombone multiphonics when the facts of the matter suggest that, following pioneer work by Paul Rutherford, Mangelsdörff played a vital role in bringing coherence to the style. There were no 'voice over' effects on the 1970 *Room 1220* but the title track does accommodate sensible, chromatic licence as well as a slice of ''Round Midnight'' containment. Mangelsdörff was a prominent member of the Globe Unity Orchestra and the United Jazz And Rock Ensemble but his very finest work has always been in the small, free combo. There are high spots on all three concerts that make up *Three Originals*. By 1975 he was well into multiphonics, his technique was awesome and he used the colossal range of musical colours available to enhance the creative aspects of his solo building. BMcR

HERBIE MANN

EVOLUTION OF MANN
(Rhino-Atlantic 71634) 2-CD

MEMPHIS UNDERGROUND
(Atlantic 7567 81364)

Whether originating trends or capitalizing on existing ones, flautist Herbie Mann once sold albums in pop-like quantities. A perennial poll winner (*Down Beat* Magazine 1957-70) his peak years were during the '60s, when the kind of jazz performed by Herbie Mann, Ramsey Lewis, Cal Tjader, Ahmad Jamal, Stan Getz, Charles Lloyd, Les McCann and Jimmy Smith frequently crossed-over into the mainstream and onto Swingin' Sixties Hollywood soundtracks. Though a commonplace instrument, few jazz flautists have ever managed to hold the listener's attention for more than a couple of selections. That's where Mann scored. Aside from the half-dozen albums recorded 'live' at the Newport Jazz Festival and the Village Gate that regularly kept his name on the charts, the man here dabbled in all kinds of exotica, covering bases as diverse as authentic Brazilian, African and Middle Eastern rhythms to jazz-rock, reggae and deep soul grooves. Furthermore, Mann was just as likely to throw in a chart cover ('Comin' Home Baby') for guaranteed radio play. It wasn't only his flair for double-guessing public taste, but his bands acted as incubators for the likes of Roy Ayers (vbs), and Sonny Sharrock (gtr). 'Hold On, I'm Comin' on *Memphis Underground* as with *Muscle Shoals Nitty Gritty*, demonstrates that Mann had devised an equally acceptable alternative soul-jazz sensibility to that common to Blue Note. RC

SHELLY MANNE

AT THE BLACKHAWK VOL. 1-4
(Contemporary 7577-78-79-80/OJC CD 656-57-58-59)

AT THE BLACKHAWK VOL. 1-4
(OJC CD 660)

As everyone from Chick Webb and Gene Krupa to Art Blakey and Chico Hamilton affirmed, give the drummer the date and he'll turn in a highly 'musical' record. Former Kentonite Shelly Manne was no exception. Upon leaving Shorty Rogers' Giants (1955), he immediately hit paydirt when linking up with Andre Previn (p) and Leroy Vinnegar (b). Billed as Shelly Manne & His Friends, this threesome's good humoured jazz interpretations of the score of *My Fair Lady* (Contemporary/OJC CD 336) became one the biggest selling jazz albums ever. Further 'interpretations' followed: *Pal Joey*, *West Side Story*, *The Bells Are Ringing*, *Gigi* etc, with either Manne or Previn taking top billing. Arguably the most accomplished all-round drummer of his generation (and also the most recorded), Manne was to fulfil his destiny when both forming his California Hard-style combo Shelly Manne And His Men and operating his own Hollywood club, The Manne Hole (1960-74). A West Coast equivalent of the Jazz Messengers, Shelley Manne always attracted the right sidemen to essay the equally distinctive closely-knit 'Men' sound. For the monumental *At The Blackhawk*, Joe Gordon (tpt) and Richie Kamuca (ts) with Victor Feldman on piano (depping for Russ Freeman) plus Monty Budwig (b), all perform with great valour. The first four discs are straight vinyl-to-CD transfers (plus bonus tracks), while Volume 5 is all new, representing almost five hours of the finest prime cut straight-ahead jazz. This is jazz of Olympian stature for, whereas so many live blowin' dates degenerate into absent-minded cliches, the music performed at this San Francisco club in September 1959 had a genuine sense of purpose. No drifting off at a tangent, no falling back on licks, just inventive playing of an inspired nature on a book that includes 'Our Delight', 'Whisper Not', Horace Silver's 'How Deep Are The Roots' plus a brace of Feldman top-lines 'Eclipse Of Spain' and 'Pullin' Strings'. Always mindful of the needs of his fellow players, Shelly Manne was as much an architect of modern drumming as Art Blakey, Max Roach, Elvin Jones or Ed Blackwell, and the reissue of the *Blackhawk* legacy should guarantee him his rightful place in the drum pantheon. RC

THE THREE & THE TWO
(Contemporary 3584/OJC CD 172)

THE WEST COAST SOUND
(Contemporary 3507/OJC CD 152)

AT THE MANNE HOLE VOL. 1 & 2
(Contemporary 7593/OJC CD 714 & 7594/OJC CD 715)

BRANFORD MARSALIS

TRIO JEEPY
(CBS 465134 2)

CRAZY PEOPLE MUSIC
(CBS 466870 2)

Although he has said that he owes his major label status to the hyperventilation occasioned by his younger brother Wynton, Branford (ts/ss) has probably followed a more creative and open career path than his puritan sibling, happy to live with both Sting's pop-jazz band and the authentic if somewhat self-conscious iazz of these two sessions. *Trio Jeepy* is the cosier of the pair, featuring Branford with drummer Jeff Watts and venerated bassist Milt Hinton in a fond, somewhat wry postmodernist reconciliation of the swing era virtues of Coleman Hawkins, Don Byas and Paul Gonsalves with the modernism of the leader's generation. *Crazy People Music* is no more original, but no less fun either, offering a convincing, often exhilarating demonstration of Branford's credentials in the era which first interested the Marsalis brothers. It's a muscular mix of *Impressions*-styled Coltrane ('Mr. Steepee' and 'The Ballad of Chet Kincaid'), Blue Note-era Wayne Shorter ('The Dark Knight') and freeish jazz ('Rose Petals') much enhanced by the presence of the compelling Kenny Kirkland on piano. MG

THE BEAUTYFUL ONES ARE NOT YET BORN
(Columbia 468896 2)

WYNTON MARSALIS

WYNTON MARSALIS
(Columbia 468708 2)

MARSALIS STANDARD TIME: VOL. 1
(Columbia CK 47346)

Wynton Marsalis has enjoyed the extraordinary achievement of being hailed as one of the world's top trumpeters in both classical music and jazz. Early in his career he was splitting his time between Blakey and Haydn, but he now concentrates on jazz, electing himself as the music's spokesman and establishing a powerful American movement of young, black tradition-conscious 'neo-classicists'. His eponymous début, from '81, has his brother Branford on saxophones and features Herbie Hancock (p), Ron Carter (b) and Tony Williams (d). It comes after a period spent on the road with the Jazz Messengers and captures the Marsalis pair on blistering form. The first of three *Standard Time* albums came five years later, and is a quartet recording with pianist Marcus Roberts, bassist Robert Leslie Hurst III and drummer Jeff Watts. The trumpeter's virtuosity and ideas are breathtaking as he puts the band through its paces on a series of standards, complicated by some exciting and unexpected changes of time signature. A two disc set, *In This House, On This Morning* (Columbia 474552 2) sounds like the culmination of a period spent concentrating on an Ellingtonian swing and blues mixture. A musical representation of the traditional African-American church service, it is a superbly arranged septet performance, lacing stirring compositions with exciting improvisation. LC

BLACK CODES (FROM THE UNDERGROUND)
(Columbia 468711 2)

WARNE MARSH

NE PLUS ULTRA
(hat Art 6063)

It was the confluence of Lester Young's tone, Charlie Parker's harmonic instruction and Lennie Tristano's seemingly capricious
sense of timing that produced a Warne Marsh. There were some
occasions when that sense of timing suggested Pee Wee Russell;
the product of a technique that suddenly failed to accommodate
the mind's conception. At best, it was a factor that lent a distinct
magic to a style that was based on instantaneous inspiration. His
natural association with Lee Konitz on the latter's *Subconscious-Lee*
(Prestige 7004/ OJC CD 186) set the highest standards and used a
rhythm section fully couched in Lennie Tristano language. Marsh
often demonstrated that he could build his personal 'new tunes'
onto established, chordal frames without such suitable support.
Fortunately, the 1969 *Ne Plus Ultra* was blessed with second generation Tristano disciples (altoist Gary Foster), who produced the
totally apposite background. Marsh responded with a magnificent
series of subtly re-fragmented solos of which 'Lennies Pennies'
was especially ambitious. He worked with Supersax through most
of the seventies and, despite failing health, continued to play well
in the last decade of his life. He still remained something of an
enigma, however, and his endlessly investigative mind was not
matched by a similar sense of professional commitment. His highly
personal style was bolstered by diligent practice sessions but
restrained by his deliberate avoidance of what he regarded as being
over-exposure. Marsh's life came to abrupt halt in December 1987,
on stage at Donte when, during a rendition of 'Out Of Nowhere',
he breathed his last. BMcR

PAT MARTINO

CONSCIOUSNESS
(Muse MCD S039)

While George Benson was making octave-playing, in many ways
the most obvious and superficial element of Wes Montgomery's
style, into a bankable asset, the job of furthering Montgomery's
innovations fell to the brilliant Pat Martino. The 1974 *Consciousness*
is a thing of legend, a modern guitar session uncompromised either
by commercialism or a dull reliance on tradition. Though there has
been talk since the early seventies of John McLaughlin's assimila-
tion of the Coltrane vocabulary, it is evident from Martino's extraordinary roastings of 'Impressions' and the skulking title track just
where the accolade 'Coltrane of the guitar' properly sits. At fast
tempos he can be repetitive and takes little breath between
phrases, but neither reservation is at all significant when the ideas
and momentum are so strong. The session is made all the more
valuable by the fact that Martino's powers were all but erased by a
cerebral aneurysm in 1980. He has since been relearning from his
own records and his latest for Muse, *Interchange*, is encouraging evidence of a return to form, but *Consciousness* remains his finest statement, an essential modern guitar record. Light blue touchpaper
and retire. MG

INTERCHANGE
(Muse MCD 5529)

LES McCANN

RELATIONSHIPS – AN ANTHOLOGY
(Rhino-Atlantic 71279) 2-CD

Relationships tells the full story. At the start of the '60s, Les McCann's star rose faster than the blood pressure of those detractors who regarded his run of deep fried West Coast soul-jazz 'hit' tunes as nothing more than cliched opportunism. An adequate enough pianist (and later, vocalist), he might never have posed a threat to Horace Silver but, he knew how to work effectively within the limits of his style and regularly strayed back across the tracks for jazz dates with tenormen Roland Kirk, Teddy Edwards and Stanley Turrentine *Les McCann In New York* (Pacific Jazz CDP 7 792929 2), The Jazz Crusaders, Lou Rawls and organ grinder Richard 'Groove' Holmes etc.One of the more successful soul-jazz populists, McCann's bag was groove cutting. Steeped in gospel grease hallelujahs and driven by a pulpit polite baptist backbeat, tunes such as 'Vasushna', 'The Truth', 'The Shampoo', 'A Little 3/4 For God And Co' etc, turned a fast buck in jukebox territory until the formula dried up and he moved to Atlantic Records.
But, like so many who munched on the received wisdom of the cosmic cookie, the sound produced had a hollow echo. Hippy platitudes apart, the out-of-leftfield, 'Compared To What?' – a track taken from *Swiss Movement* (Atlantic 781 365) recorded with tenorman Eddie Harris at the Montreux Jazz Festival pushed the album into the charts and well beyond one million sales. God looks after his own. RC

BROTHER JACK McDUFF

HOT BARBEQUE/LIVE
(Ace CDBGPD 053) [L]

Screamin' Brother Jack McDuff was an apt moniker for this particularly agile organist. Piloting a customised B-3 Hammond, McDuff came hurtlin' out of the sun at full throttle like an attacking jet fighter. Nobody slept when he was in the house, for in keeping with heavyweight hornmen Lou Donaldson, Illinois Jacquet and their ilk, every night was Saturday when McDuff hit the stand. Club crowds adored him and especially more so when he added young, gifted guitarist George Benson to share the front line with the jagged-edged tenor of Red Holloway. By the mid-'60s, McDuff's quartet was one of America's top dollar jazz acts and selling albums in quantities that reflected their status. The formula seldom diviated. Soul jazz riffs ('Hot Barbeque' and'Rock Candy'), gospel grooves and fatback drums occasionally giving way to a then current torch song 'Cry Me A River.' It worked then, and, as recent releases on Muse and Concord confirm, it's still working now. RC

HOWARD McGHEE

THE BOP MASTER
(Affinity AFF 765)

SHARP EDGE
(Black Lion BL 760110)

TEDDY EDWARDS & HOWARD MCGHEE –
TOGETHER AGAIN!
(Contemporary 7588/OJC CD 424)

The arrival of bebop in the middle forties presented established players with a major problem. Howard McGhee was a trumpeter who faced the challenge better than most and Coleman Hawkins' *Hollywood Stampede* (Capitol CDP 793201 2) shows that he could handle the new music with confidence as early as 1945. In fact, McGhee retained the appropriate parts of his swing era legacy, rounding his phrases in a natural manner, and employing a tone that breathed an added 'hot' quality.

McGhee's hands-on involvement with Bird on the infamous 'Loverman' date and, under much happier circumstances 'Relaxin' At Camarillo' *The Complete Dial Sessions* (Spotlite SPJ 4101), to be followed by the two-way trumpet tear-up with Fats Navarro on 'Double Talk' *The Fabulous Fats Navarro* (Blue Note CDP 7 81532/3 2) was sufficient to earn him top trumpet status in *Down Beat* magazine's 1949 poll. As with so many of his contemporaries, drug addiction did not help his career in the fifties but titles like 'Loverman' from *The Bop Master* are typical of his creative work and fully justify the album title.

Increasing Health problems meant enforced periods of inactivity and come-backs became something of a way of life. As a result, the record catalogue does not fully do him justice. When the company was right, as with the 1961 *Sharp Edge*, he was a coherent and swinging bopper, happy with the medium blues of the title track, always wise in his choice of tempos and as 'Arbee' and 'Ill Wind' show, capable of changing improvisational patterns from one take to another. Unfortunately, self-abuse had taken its toll and, touring in London in 1982, he conceded that, following stomach surgery, he was playing against medical advice. The crunch was, he was playing well. BMcR

CHRIS McGREGOR/BROTHERHOOD OF BREATH

LIVE AT WILLISAU
(Ogun OGCD 001) [L]

TO BE FREE
(District Six – Editions EGECD 53)

To see the unsung heroes of Brotherhood Of Breath standing in single line and playing collective 'all in' was a completely daunting experience. Life for that remarkable band actually began when pianist Chris McGregor brought his combo the Blue Notes from their native South Africa via Switzerland to Britain. This group included the explosive talents of Mongezi Feza on trumpet, Dudu Pukwana's eternally pursuasive alto and a rhythm driven by the drums of Louis Moholo and incapable of quitting. These men were at the heart of the Brotherhood and they helped make it one of the most exciting big bands, world wide. Too few recordings were made but *Live At Willisau* is a fine example of their work. It declares the band's tremendous riff based swing, its collective power and the commitment of soloists like Evan Parker (ts) and Radu Malfatti (tb), as well as the above. McGregor was as much at home with 'changes' as he was free flow but, like the Brotherhood, received less than his due. A fine, driving pianist, his jabbing, harmonic instructions and flowing clusters sat comfortably alongside his calm bop piano both with combo and with Brotherhood alike. The 1987 *To Be Free* shows his more conservative side and the calm resolve of his playing on 'Into The Light', in particular, marks him out as a small group guv'ner. BMcR

JOHN McLAUGHLIN

EXTRAPOLATION
(Polydor 841 598 2)

INNER MOUNTING FLAME
(Columbia 31067)

FREE SPIRIT – TOKYO LIVE
(Verve 521 870 2) [L]

The 1968 *Extrapolation*, McLaughlin's debut as leader, resonates with the burgeoning experimentalism of the period. The playing is more enthusiastic than polished, and McLaughlin plays more rock than jazz, but the adventurous amalgam of jazz. rock, folk and odd time-signatures provided a summation of the decade's styles and pointed towards fusion to come and his involvement with Tony Williams' Lifetime. Except for Jan Hammer's piano solo on 'The Noonward Race', there isn't much evidence of jazz in the 1971 Mahavishnu Orchestra's *Inner Mounting Flame*. Well served by the era's infatuation with highly amplified guitar, McLaughlin relates to Coltrane in as much as he plays pentatonic scales, but here, at any rate, he lacks Trane's harmonic ingenuity and accuracy. The awkward time signatures, rude juxtapositions of style ('The Dance of Maya') and bludgeoning rock power amounted to the most transparent kind of fusion, but Mahavishnu delivered previously unimagined sound combinations with great force, virtuosity ('Awakening') and spirituality. There followed more reflective periods for McLaughlin, and in the 80s a time of retrenchment for jazz in general. It was perhaps the latter which prompted McLaughlin to produce the best evidence yet of his early love of such beboppers as Tal Farlow. Recorded in 1993, *Tokyo Live* has him swinging mightily in a classic organ trio format with Joey De Francesco, playing authoritative chromatic jazz lines ('JuJu At The Crossroads') with echoes of Scofield but perhaps just a little too much vibrato bar. MG

JACKIE McLEAN

FREDDIE REDD: MUSIC FROM 'THE CONNECTION'
(Blue Note B2 89292)

BLUESNIK
(Blue Note B21Y 84067)

LET FREEDOM RING
(Blue Note CDP 7 46527 2)

ONE STEP BEYOND
(Blue Note 7 46821 2)

When, between 1959 and 1961, McLean joined pianist Freddie Redd for a playing/acting role in both the New York and London stage productions (and later the movie version) of Jack Gelber's controversial drugs drama *The Connection* it truly was a case of art imitating life. As there seemed little difference between McLean's on stage problems and those he confronted away from the footlights, it came as no real surprise that the music performed nightly proved as tormented and unpredictably knife-edged as the characters themselves. Regrettably, as with Bird, an all-consuming drug dependency meant that young McLean's alto seemed to spend more time in the pawn shop than in his possession. Prior to *The Connection* and, when not perfecting his smarts with George

Wallington (1955), Charles Mingus (1956) and The Jazz Messengers (1956-57), McLean spent the second half of the '50s as an integral part of the no-rehearsals-conveyor-belt blowing sessions that were the penny-pinching hallmark of Prestige Records. If Bird personified bebop, then McLean's anguished, unsweetened wail was synonymous with hard bop. Later, Ornette Coleman would fulfill much the same role of guru in McLean's artistic development. McLean's transfer to Blue Note coincided with the label embracing the avant garde while simultaneously still cornering Hard Bop.

The fearless McLean explored both these routes: the tense coiled spring modern blues bop of *Swing Swang Swingin'*, *Bluesnik* (propelled by the unrelenting drumming of Pete La Roca), and *A Fickle Sonance* placed him beyond the reach of would-be contenders while his grasp of New Thing tendencies – first evident, in 1959, on *New Soil*, further gained confidence with *Let Freedom Ring* (1962), *One Step Beyond* (1963) and *Destination Out* (1963). The basic horn and three rhythm line up of 1962's *Let Freedom Ring* is deceptive, for here McLean cuts back noticeably on hard bop devices to flag up his future statement-of-intent on three originals ('Melody for Melonae', 'Rene', 'Omega') plus Bud Powell's 'I'll Keep Loving You'. Recorded in 1963, (almost a year prior to Eric Dolphy's *Out To Lunch*), McLean's *One Step Beyond* pre-dates that session in many aspects. With the exception of trombonist Grachan Moncur III partnering McLean (Freddie Hubbard consorts with Dolphy), not only are the two albums identical instrumentally, but Bobby Hutcherson (vib) and Tony Williams (d) fulfill similar duties on both dates with (two takes of) 'Saturday And Sunday' proving a fine example of McLean still retaining a hard bop footing while pressing a shoulder firmly against the barricades. As chronicled on *The Complete Jackie McLean Blue Note Sessions 1964-66* (Mosaic MD4 150) McLean's approach became infinitely more hyper-active as he embraced the avant garde. In the process, his tone took on an even more hard-edge which, coupled to the searing intensity of his attack was capable of melting the vinyl on which his (new) music was (then) pressed. Mosaic's four-pack incorporates *It's Time* (1964), *Right Now* (1965), *Action!* etc, with a supporting cast including Lee Morgan (tpt), Bobby Hutcherson (vib), Herbie Hancock (p) Billy Higgins (d). McLean's intonation may have irritated some, yet, for all his efforts there appeared to be little return. Self-exile in Europe during the early '70s, followed by the role of University jazz educator led back to regular jazz work in the late '80s , with *Dynasty* (Triloka 181), heralding his return to greatness. *The Jackie Mac Attack: Live* (Birdology 519 270) proved it wasn't just a one-off, while reports concluded that McLean is currently positioned as one of the most exciting of all in-person performers. RC

MARIAN McPARTLAND

PLAYS THE BENNY CARTER SONGBOOK
(Concord CCD 4412)

Marian McPartland successfully overcame two major obstacles in building a reputation as a jazz piano soloist – being a woman and being non-American (i.e. British). She also remained unanchored by former husband Jimmy McPartland's Dixieland work, developing instead an individual mainstream-modernism that allowed her to play alongside stylists as disparate as Eubie Blake, Oscar Peterson and Bill Evans in her long-running NPR radio series, *Piano Jazz Hour*. Influenced initially by Johnny Guarnieri, Duke Ellington, Teddy Wilson and Art Tatum, McPartland has remained an eclectic, with a sufficiently broad sense of jazz history to give her playing a wide range of mood and emotional content. She also retains a sense of careful structure, of spontaneous composition, which is why her interpretations of major jazz composers' works are so rewarding. The former Marian Turner remains a thinking player, who, despite turning out many excellent solo and trio recordings, is spurred to even greater heights by the presence of a major leaguer in the group. CS

WITH DIZZY GILLESPIE
(Jazz Alliance TJA 12005)

CARMEN McRAE

SINGS GREAT AMERICAN SONGWRITERS
(MCA GRP 16312)

CHRIS CONNOR/CARMEN McRAE
(Charly CDCD 1081) [L]

CARMEN SINGS MONK
(Novus PD 83086)

YOU'RE LOOKIN' AT ME
(Concord CCD 4342)

More reasonably represented in the CD catalogue than some of her contemporaries, McRae has maintained a high standard of jazz vocalism for many years without grabbing much in the way of kudos. Indeed, though Joe Public is familiar with the names of Fitzgerald, Holiday and Vaughan, few would even have heard of McRae, despite her recording career spanning some forty years. On her earliest sides, represented by the MCA compilation which places her in settings devised by Ray Bryant, Ralph Burns, Tadd Dameron, Mat Mathews and others, she laid instant claim to star status, phrasing daringly on such standards as 'You Took Advantage Of Me' and 'Blue Moon', other examples of her singing and equally accomplished piano playing of this period appearing on such releases as *Here To Stay* (MCA GRP 16102 CD) and the more commercially disposed (but still invaluable) *Invitation* (Official 83 027). The split Charly release (oddly on the label's Classic Soul off-shoot) is less essential but remains, nevertheless, a worthy example of Carmen live (at London's Flamingo Club in 1961) rendering a thoughtful reading of 'Round Midnight', a song reprised at length on the difficult project which comprised the singer's 1990 *Sings Monk* tribute. The collection of Sarah Vaughan songs, recorded during the same year, comes easier and benefits from the accompaniment of a trio headed by Shirley Horn, another underrated singer-pianist. And if the record is as much about McRae as it is about Sassy, then that's to be expected from a singer who's always had much that is her own to offer, even if only her peers realised the singer's true greatness and individuality. FD

JAY McSHANN

BLUES FROM KANSAS CITY
(MCA/GRP 16142 (GRD-614))

James 'Jay' McShann brought the last great big band out of Kansas City, completing the musical equation that led to Bebop. For, in that band was another KayCee resident, alto saxist Charlie Parker.

McShann, also known as 'Hootie', had arrived in that wide open midwest city from Oklahoma in December, 1936, just after the departure of the Basie band, which took the seeds of modernism north in the playing of tenorman Lester Young and drummer Jo Jones. A pianist with a percussive, strongly blues-based style, McShann formed his own big band in 1939, after working in trios and sextets. His instrumental style translated to the ensemble, and the orchestra retained the lightness of foot combined with power that characterised KayCee bands. Its success with both its blues format ('Confessin' The Blues') and the presence of Parker has overshadowed McShann's subsequent career as a pianist (he was drafted in 1942 and was unable to re-form on demob), which has lasted 50 years and revealed a strong individuality, sparked by the blues, with standard material. CS

EARLY BIRD
(Stash STCD 542)

SWINGMATISM
(Sackville SKCD 2 3046)

MULGREW MILLER

FROM DAY TO DAY
(Landmark LCD 1525)

The band of Mercer Ellington, Betty Carter's notorious workshop and Art Blakey's Jazz Messengers were Mulgrew Miller's route to jazz-cred. A first call pianist in New York in the eighties, led to his being an ever present figure on the world festival tour. The Messengers' *New York Scene* (Concord CCD 4256) showed his hard bop chops in most testing circumstances; his swing was powerful, his touch remorselessly aggressive and his solos agreeably cliché free. If there is a criticism, it is that his trio LPs employ a formula for presentation that results in overall blandness. It is not a lack of light and shade on individual titles but, despite excitement and instrumental facility, a certain emotional predictability. The 1990 *From Day To Day* is certainly an exception. Miller is in an inventive frame of mind and the rhythm team are firing on all cylinders. Live performances in the nineties have been consistent with this and suggest that the prodigious Miller still has doors to open. BMcR

MILLS BLUE RHYTHM BAND

BLUE RHYTHM
(Hep 1008 CD)

The Mills of the band's name was actually Irving Mills, their manager. And though they made records that, during the early '30s, were often as hot as sides made by Duke Ellington or Cab Calloway, for whom they sometimes substituted, many of the musicians were faceless while such over-employed session vocalists as Chick Bullock hasn't provided the band's more commercial sides with any patina of longevity. Even so, MBRB moved on to become swing kings during the mid-30s, delivering over a dozen major hits, many of them cover-versions. Several years later, trumpeter Charlie Shavers, who was a member of the mid-30s alumini, returned to play with an extraordinary revival of the Mills Blue Rhythm Band that recorded eight Van Alexander arrangements using musicians such as Lucky Thompson, Stan Getz, Herbie Haymer (ts), Willie Smith (as), Juan Tizol (tmb), Barney Kessel (g),

Jimmy Rowles (p) and Don Lamond (d). Unfortunately, none of these sides are currently available on a UK CD release, which leaves just those early sides, which, though sometimes flawed, explain why Louis Armstrong employed MBRB as his Coconut Grove Orchestra. FD

CHARLES MINGUS

JAZZ WORKSHOP
(Vogue VG 655 650132)

PITHECANTHROPUS ERECTUS
(Atlantic 81456)

NEW TIJUANA MOODS
(RCA PL 85635 2CD)

CHARLES MINGUS PRESENTS CHARLES MINGUS
(Candid CS 9005)

BLACK SAINT AND THE SINNER LADY
(MCA MCA D 5649)

A larger than life figure, Charles Mingus was a magnificent bass player, functional pianist, imaginative composer/arranger but, above all else, a true leader. He took that position seriously and led spiritually, instrumentally and, ultimately, vocally. His first major leadership task came in the days of the 'cool' jazz movement and, as the 1954/5 *Jazz Workshop* clearly illustrates, was devoted to the ideal of meticulous organisation, calm delivery and carefully pre-designed solos. The following year, in fact, saw a complete about face. With *Pithecanthropus Erectus*, a stormy description of the first man to stand upright, written parts were largely abandoned and sidemen were encouraged to regard their solos not as personal statements but as intrinsic parts of the whole. The jazz world was in shock and it set Mingus off on an inspired bout of composing, with superb themes such as 'Ysabel's Table Dance' (*New Tijuana Moods*), and fashioning 'East Coasting' (*New York Sketchbook* Charly CD 19) to demonstrate the organic importance of his soloists. 'Haitian Fight Song' (*The Clown*) showed how to make a musical mountain from a simple, thematic molehill while 'Wednesday Night Prayer Meeting' (*Blues & Roots*) deposited the listener in the front pew of a Southern Baptist Church. Mingus' live performances were no less potent and his concert at Antibes (1960) presented excellent new material (with Bud Powell guesting) with a line-up that included saxists Eric Dolphy and Booker Erwin and Ted Curson on trumpet. *Presents* had no pianist (just Curson, Dolphy and drummer Dannie Richmond) but was recorded in a studio with the mood of a club prevailing. Including 'All The Things You Could Be By Now If Sigmund Freud's Wife Was Your Mother' and 'Original Faubus Fables', it became one of the man's finest works. Multi-instrumentalist Rahsaan Roland Kirk added his unique dialect to the Mingus language on *Oh Yeah*, but it was 1963 that saw Mingus' finest hour. *Black Saint* is a major work, Ellingtonian in basic concept but totally Mingusian in spirit. Saxophonist Charlie Mariano comes near to the mood of Johnny Hodges but the strength of the composition, its adroit tempo changes and the spirit of involvement that the sidemen produce takes it near to being a perfect example of the Mingus ethic. *Mingus, Mingus Minus, etc*, is an outstanding brother album, less focussed in overall approach but full of the bassist's minor miracles. The majority of Mingus sides from 1964 to the time of his death in 1979 were on location. He toured copiously but *Town Hall Concert 1964* recorded prior to a barnstorming Euro-junket, can be recommended unconditionally because of its superior personnel and because Johnny Coles (t), Eric Dolphy (as/f) and Jaki Byard (p) play superbly. Penned in 1971, Mingus' provocative autobiography *Beneath The Underdog* is as much wishful thinking as it is fact. BMcR

THE CLOWN
(Atlantic 790142 2)

BLUES & ROOTS
(Atlantic 7567 81336 2)

OH YEAH
(Atlantic 7567 90667)

MINGUS AT ANTIBES
(Atlantic 90532 2) [L]

MINGUS MINGUS MINGUS MINGUS MINGUS
(MCA MCAD 39119)

TOWN HALL CONCERT (1964)
(Jazz Workshop 005-S/OJC CD 042) [L]

HANK MOBLEY

SOUL STATION
(Blue Note CDP 7 46528 2)

ROLL CALL
(Blue Note B21Y 46823)

To even the casual observer, Hank Mobley appeared to be in the right place at the right time: a founder Jazz Messenger (1954-56), he then took his tenor sax on active service with Horace Silver (1956-57) Max Roach (1957-58), the Messengers again (1959), Miles Davis (1961-62) and more Blue Note sessions than most any one else could handle, and yet, because Mobley ran directly counter to the Coltrane-Rollins dictum, his efforts were often underrated. To what extent is difficult to gauge because, judging by the number of praiseworthy albums he made under his own name for Blue Note, sales must have warranted such a steady flow of his product. Lyrical to a fault, smooth where others might prove abrasive and, when least expected, rhythmically idiosyncratic, Mobley's solos were thoughtful constructed, occasionally intro-spective looking, but hard-hitting if needed. *Soul Station* (1960) stands as his finest moment with an intuative interplay between drummer Art Blakey and Mobley on 'This I Dig Of You' plus an emotive interpretation of 'If I Should Lose You' combining as the centrepiece. Unquestionably, in the same rarefied league as *Saxophone Colossus* (Rollins) and *Giant Steps* (Coltrane), its success in entirely due to the empathy that existed between all four players whose careers frequently crossed. But, on this occasion, Wynton Kelly (p), Paul Chambers (b) and Art Blakey (d) each brought something extra to the *Soul Station* session with staggering results. *Soul Station* wasn't a one-off encounter. Nine months later, the same line-up, with the addition of Freddie Hubbard (tpt), came close to scaling similar creative heights on *Roll Call* featuring the self-explanatory 'A Baptist Beat'. The all-too familiar curse of drugs and alcohol prematurely ended Mobley's career. He was out of action between 1975 and 1986, then, as he attempted a comeback a bout of double pneumonia proved fatal. RC

MODERN JAZZ QUARTET

MODERN JAZZ QUARTET
(Giants of Jazz CDJT 56)

MJQ 40
(Atlantic 782330-2) 4CD

MJQ & FRIENDS
(Atlantic CD 7567-2538 2)

It seems an odd circumstance that the first revisitation of a really
European form of jazz – the original being the Hot Club of France
– was made by four black Americans. Pianist John Lewis, an active
cerebral participant in Third Stream music and an arranger for the
Miles Davis / Gerry Mulligan *Birth Of The Cool* sessions, realised his
ambition to create small group improvisations based on themes
drawn from the Italian Renaissance's *Comedia del Arte*. These
Baroque styled vignettes emphasised classical form and structure,
leaned heavily on counterpoint and were above all, intensely
melodic. The early Quartet which included Milt Jackson (vibes)
Ray Brown (bs) and Kenny Clarke (drms) was altered with Percy
Heath replacing Brown and Connie Kay, a less intrusive player,
later taking over from Clarke. The sound suffered not one whit. In
fact it sounded better. The Giants of Jazz reissue has all the classic
(in the full sense) pieces from the early 50s. 'Django', 'Concorde', 'Milano', 'Fontessa', 'Delaunay's Dilemma',
all epitomise the MJQ at their creative and fashionable peak, even
the titles themselves having an almost umbilical connection with
the group's style. Milt Jackson provides most of the improvisation
within these decorous structures and he achieves this brilliantly.
John Lewis, a more judicious player, is, nevertheless, the catalyst
for the direction of the music and has a remarkably sensitive ear for
the blues. If you have to choose only one collection of the Modern
Jazz Quartet, this is it.
The 40th Anniversary 4-CD set of 54 tracks covering the group's
career is a definitive package with a mouth-watering list of guests
including Clark Terry, Paul Desmond, Kai Winding, Jimmy
Guiffre, Phil Woods, Richie Kamuca, Laurendo Almeida and the
Swingle Singers. The most obvious changeover in recent years has
been Jackson's ascendancy to the leadership. As one of the most
fecund of jazz performers his domination of the group has been
inevitable and has led to a less buttoned-up presentation. The
Friends collection from 1992/3 features guests as disparate as the
Marsalis brothers, Phil Woods and Harry 'Sweets' Edison in a more
relaxed mood than usually associated with the Quartet. Sadly, in
1994 Connie Kay passed away, the drumstool being taken over by
Micky Roberts. JM

THELONIOUS MONK

THE GENIUS OF MODERN MUSIC VOL. 1 & 2
Blue Note CDP 7 81510/11)

THELONIOUS MONK TRIO
Prestige 7027/OJC CD 010)

THELONIOUS MONK QUINTET
Prestige 7053/OJC CD 016)

The most enigmatic figure in jazz, sometimes it seems as though
we know more about Buddy Bolden than Thelonious Sphere

Monk. Like The Duke, he is as much a composer as a pianist. Indeed, it's difficult to separate the two. Those who heard him before he made it onto record speak of a technically adept keyboard-covering musician, with a good line in stride and an affection towards Teddy Wilson. By the time he turned up in a starring role on Blue Note, his playing was full of discordant jagged shapes, obtuse angles, awkward pauses and misplaced notes that didn't have a logical resting place. Monk's approach was that of the minimalist. He'd stripped away all the residue to leave a skeletal structure upon which to hang improvisations. All but a few could make them fit as envisaged by the composer.

As many musicians attest, the aura of simplicity was misleading.

Few musicians could comfortably manoeuvre around such material as 'Ruby My Dear', 'Well You Needn't','Off Minor', 'In Walked Bud', 'Round Midnight', 'Monk's Mood', 'Evidence', 'Misterioso', 'Epistrophy', 'I Mean You', 'Criss Cross', 'Eronel', 'Straight No Chaser' and come to terms with Monk's fuzzy logic. From Monk's Blue (Note) period (1947-52), two dates with vibesman Milt Jackson that produced prototypes of 'Epistrophy', 'Evidence', 'Criss Cross' and 'Straight No Chaser' demonstrated that Jackson had a much better handle on Monk's material than most.Though, he helped shape modern music, Monk didn't garner the accolades or create a dynasty in the same manner as Bird or fellow pianist Bud Powell. Many couldn't see beyond the funny hats, the quirky dance steps and the weird eyes of this amiable but eccentric bear of a man. At Prestige (1952-54) he added 'Blue Monk', 'Bemsha Swing', 'Reflections', 'Little Rootie Tootie', 'Monk's Dream', 'Locomotive', 'Hackensack' to his repertoire. This, together with his Blue Note portfolio comprised most of the music he would constantly rework for the remainder of his career.

By the time he reached Riverside, Monk set about further exploring much of the material he recorded for his previous labels. Musicians seldom had an easy ride with Monk who never signalled his left-turns. For instance, even with a line-up of Clark Terry (tpt), Ernie Henry (as), Sonny Rollins (ts), Oscar Pettiford (b) and Max Roach (d), *Brilliant Corners* (Riverside 226/OJC CD 026) almost ended in a shambles. Even after two dozen takes, the title track had to be edited together from a number of attempts. Nevertheless, such tension yielded one of Monk's best-ever sessions. Despite also involving himself in a few Big Band dabblings with varying results, Monk really wasn't a team player, preferring his own company on *Solo Monk* (Vogue 111502) *Thelonious Himself* (Riverside 235/OJC CD 254) and *Thelonious Alone In San Francisco* (Riverside 1156/OJC CD 231) where the programme was split almost evenly between his own material and him 'picking out' familiar standards at the keyboard.

The year 1957 presented a busy schedule. Whether the pressure proved too intense, but the likes of tenor titans Sonny Rollins, John Coltrane and Johnny Griffin didn't stay around too long. In Coltrane's case *Thelonious Monk With John Coltrane* (Jazzland 46/OJC CD 039) and *Monk's Music* (Riverside 242/OJC CD 084) reveal that it was very much a highly personal trial-by-ordeal scenario and once he'd covered the assault course, as vividly enshrined on the privately-taped *Discovery! Live At The Five Spot 1957* (Blue Note CDP 799786), he swiftly moved on and a year later Johnny Griffin was onstage in 'Trane's place at the Five Spot (*Thelonious In Action* Riverside 1190/OJC CD 103) and *Misterioso* (Riverside 1133/OJC CD206)). It wasn't the first occasion Griffin had worked with Monk, being on hand in July 1957, for one of the pianist's greatest achievements *Art Blakey's Jazz Messengers with Thelonious Monk* (Atlantic 781332) where items from his familiar repertoire were treated to a once-in-a-lifetime make-over. In 1959, Charlie Rouse took over permanent tenor duties and stayed around until 1970 without attracting too much attention. In 1962, Monk signed to Columbia and once he'd made the cover of *Time* Magazine to coincide with the aptly titled *It's Monk's Time* (Columbia 4712405) the (jazz) world became his oyster. But, as his star glowed brighter, Monk became entrenched in mainly reprising his greatest hits. Not note-for-note, but constantly approaching them from new and oblique angles (*Live At The It Club* 1964 (Columbia 4691862) and *L'Olympia 23 May 1965* (Trema 710377/8)). The results were often hit or miss. But then, how many versions of 'Round Midnight', 'Epistrophy' or 'Blue Monk' did anyone other than trainspotters want? During a Giants Of Jazz tour, Monk undertook what proved to be his last recording session in November 1971 (*The London Collection Vol. 1-3* (Black Lion BLCD 760101/16/42). Performing either solo or with Al McKibbon (b) and Art Blakey (d), he offered one last insight into to his own private world before finally closing the door. He would die eleven years later. A decade after Monk's passing, few have genuinely cracked his cypher. Infact, his repertoire has become something of a musical obstacle course with entire albums and repertory bands given over to attempting passable interpretations of Monk's musical maze. The frustration continues. . . RC

THE COMPLETE RIVERSIDE RECORDINGS
(Riverside 15RCD 022) 15-CDs

J.R. MONTEROSE

THE MESSAGE
(Fresh Sounds FSR CD 201)

J.R. MONTEROSE
(Blue Note B2 29102)

Never the easiest of albums to find, *The Message* stands shoulder-to-shoulder with *Giant Steps* (Coltrane), *Saxophone Colossus* (Rollins), *Introducing* (Griffin) and *Soul Station* (Mobley) as a classic grand-standing tenor-with-rhythm workout. Trane's *Giant Steps* pianist, Tommy Flanagan and his future bassist Jimmy Garrison may have been on hand, together with the elusive Pete La Roca on drums, but, in common with Mobley, JR's determination not to come off as a second rate copy of 'Trane and Rollins forced this Detroiter to create a strong personal identity. Even so, it's very much a set of close-to-the-chest tactics right down to such equally personal writing on 'Straight Ahead' (replete with stark trades between sax and drums) and 'Green Street Scene' As with his equally energetic eponymous Blue Note one-shot that had him engaged with Horace Silver and Art Blakey (*J.R. Monterose*), the world foolishly yawned and looked the other way. RC

WES MONTGOMERY

THE INCREDIBLE JAZZ GUITAR
(Riverside 1169/OJC CD 036)

FULL HOUSE
(Riverside 9434/OJC CD 106) [L]

JAZZ MASTERS 14
(Verve 519 826 2)

Despite touring his best Charlie Christian licks with Lionel Hampton in 1948-50, Montgomery had to wait until Cannonball Adderley recommended him to Riverside in the late fifties to attract national attention. By then, as the 1960 *The Incredible Jazz Guitar* shows, the elements of his genius had coalesced – the warm, thumb-driven tone, the unerring melodic sense, the Trane inflected bop vocabulary, the funky drive, the unfailing stamina, the three-tier solo formula (single lines, octaves, then chords) all displayed to perfection on 'Airegin', 'D-Natural Blues' and the like. However, Wes felt uneasy in studios and relished the opportunity in 1962 to record live with the rhythm section of one of his favourite musicians, Miles Davis. Although Joe Henderson might have been stylistically more appropriate, Wes and the Wynton Kelly Trio were joined by tenorist Johnny Griffin at Tsubo's in Berkeley for the *Full House* date, one of Wes's most spontaneous sessions. The same rhythm section and another live setting help to make the sublime 1965 'No Blues' more than sufficient reason for acquiring the *Jazz Masters* compilation. This is unsurpassed Wes, a tour de force of sustained invention and masterly pacing. Much of the rest is Wes's octave style sugared in strings for mass consumption, but in the absence of the complete *Smokin' At The Half Note* (from which 'No Blues' is drawn) it remains essential. MG

A DYNAMIC NEW SOUND
(Riverside 1156/OJC CD 034)

TETE MONTOLIU

TETE!
(Steeplechase SCS CD 1029)

SWEET 'N' LOVELY VOL. 1 & VOL. 2
(Fresh Sound FSR CD 161 & 162)

It has become apparent that some of the most dynamic piano stylists no longer come from the usual urban-American traditional schools, but have perfected their approach outside of the United States. Cuban nationals Gonzalo Rubalcaba and Chucho Valdes plus Frenchman Michel Petrucciani being the highest profiled. But, in many ways, it was Barcelona born Tete Montoliu who first demonstrated that it was possible for non-American players to attain international headline status. Having begun his career on long-forgotten Spanish labels in the late '50s, it was a gloriously ramshackled affair, taped live at Copenhagen's Club Montmartre in 1963, matching Montoliu with a highly boisterous Roland Kirk that attracted attention. The only thing not up to scratch that night was the piano which had long since enjoyed better days, but, Montoliu appeared unfazed by it all and dug straight in. With 45 minutes of newly-discovered music, this session currently occupies two entire CDs on *Rahsaan-The Complete Mercury Recordings Of Roland Kirk* (Mercury 846 630). A year later, he was performing similar duties for Dexter Gordon but on a better instrument (*I Want More*, Steeplechase SCCD 36015). Of the extensive recordings Montoliu made for Enja, Steeplechase, Timeless and Soul Note, the mid '70s sessions with Niels-Henning Orsted-Pedersen (b) and Albert 'Tootie' Heath (d) are the most attractive in that they benefit from the blind pianist's Catalonian background and his ability to control the passionate side of his nature so that it never veers into cabaret. The more recent Fresh Sound tracks with veteran guitarist Mundell Lowe are more reflective, as if Montoliu is reviewing his role, anticipating a new direction. Or maybe he isn't! JF

JAMES MOODY

NEW SOUNDS-ART BLAKEY/JAMES MOODY
(Blue Note CDP 7 84436 2)

HI FI PARTY
(Prestige 7011/OJC CD 1780)

HONEY
(Novus PD 83111)

James Moody is a bebop saxophonist, flautist and quirky singer. He was in on the bop ground floor and *New Sounds* introduces a player with still a little swing era baggage left in his musical ruck sack. His big, comfortable tone is the item he has never surrendered from that era and there are moments on *Hi Fi Party* from 1954 when the lyrical legacy sits just a tad uncomfortably with his bebop urgency. Not many of his quite impressive list of recordings have survived into the CD era but this was not helped by a period of disillusionment during what he saw as barren rock and fusion years. He was, for many years, associated with Dizzy Gillespie and his name crops up with him in various eras. He flirted with the music of John Coltrane briefly but in the main remained true to his bop colours. The 1990 *Honey* shows a player of undimished skills with fine soprano on 'Someone To Watch Over Me', gambolling alto on 'I Can't Get Started', and tenor items that just won't quit. BMcR

LEE MORGAN

CANDY
(Blue Note CDP 7 46508)

THE SIDEWINDER
(Blue Note CDP 7 84157)

SEARCH FOR THE NEW LAND
(Blue Note CDP 7 84169)

LIVE AT THE LIGHTHOUSE
(Fresh Sound FSR CD 140/2) [L]

Seen by many as Clifford Brown's heir apparent, Lee Morgan's was a precocious (almost brattish) trumpet talent. As with Brownie, Morgan possessed the same air of confidence that comes with youth and a full-fat tone part Dizzy, part Navarro. There seemed little to stop him. As an 18-year old, his dues paying was done in Dizzy Gillespie's Big Band and on John Coltrane's *Blue Train* (Blue Note CDP 7 46095) until he joined Art Blakey's Jazz Messengers in 1958 where, over the next four years, he rapidly realised his potential on such material as 'Blues March', 'Moanin'' while on the numerous recordings of 'Whisper Not' and the atmospheric vignettes that comprised the Messengers soundtrack to *Des Femmes Disparaissent* he proffered an alternative Harmon mute sound to that of Miles Davis. But when tenor player Wayne Shorter joined The Messengers in 1960, Morgan was at his peak. Brimming with ideas he was never to again quite capture the moment. *Candy*, may stand as a feisty, self-assured quartet date with pianist Sonny Clark but his finite blend of hard bop and soul jazz struck paydirt in the guise of the sizeable 1964 juke-box hit 'The Sidewinder' and its formularised follow-ups 'The Rumproller' and 'Cornbread'. Nevertheless, eight weeks after *The Sidewinder* session Morgan found time to record the more challenging *Search For The New Land* with Shorter and Grant Green before (briefly) re-joining the

Messengers. While coasting along on his success in the singles stakes, Morgan was aware of the winds of change and *Live At The Lighthouse* shows him being well prepared for all eventualities. However, his personal life was still in a mess. While drugs hadn't actually robbed Morgan of his talent, his few remaining friends seemed to be of the undesirable element. And, it was one such female acquaintance who fatally gunned-down the 33-year old Morgan, outside of Slug's club, on New York's Lower East Side, on February 19, 1972. RC

THE BEST OF LEE MORGAN
(Blue Note CDP 7 91138)

JELLY ROLL MORTON

THE COMPLETE JELLY ROLL MORTON 1926-1930
(RCA Bluebird ND 82361) 5-CD box

RED HOT PEPPERS, NEW ORLEANS JAZZMEN & TRIOS
(Giants Of Jazz CD 53018)

He claimed to have invented jazz in 1902 and, even if he didn't, Jelly was a master of the New Orleans idiom, a superb pianist, arranger, songwriter and singer whose sometimes bluesy soft-ped-alled vocal approach is still influential today. When you hear Jelly deliver 'Winin' Boy Blues' then it's a short walk stylistically to Mose Allison or maybe Dr John. As a bandleader he vied with Ellington in the manner in which he could personalise each and every session and there's little on the Bluebird box set that can be considered less than essential, even though some may rail at the number of extra takes included on the five discs. Ever-boastful but well able to prove his ability as an entertainer and then some, Jelly and his Red Hot Peppers, two-beat their way to glory on the glorious Charleston that is 'The Chant', set up the world's greatest hot-line on 'Dr Jazz' ("Hello Central, give me Dr Jazz"), delivered ballsy renditions of such classics as 'Beale Street Blues', 'Wolverine Blues' and 'Shreveport Stomp' and generally fashioned a strain of New Orleans jazz that was never to be surpassed. The Giants Of Jazz issue grabs some of the best sounds from the same period, adds them to half a dozen sides made in 1939 with Morton's New Orleans Jazzmen and, for practically the price of a burger and large fries provides something Creole that really cooks. FD

JELLY ROLL MORTON 1923-1924
(Classics 584)

JELLY ROLL MORTON 1930-1939
(Classics 654)

THE PEARLS
(Bluebird/BMG ND 86588)

BENNIE MOTEN

BASIE BEGINNINGS
(RCA/Bluebird 9768 2 RB)

Bennie Moten started out by playing a peculiarly ferocious dance music, veined with novelty effects, and ended up encapsulating the innovations of jazz in Kansas City and the South West. The cat-alysts that propelled him from *derriere garde* to *avant garde* were twofold: Count Basie and Eddie Durham. They joined what was the area's leading band attraction in late 1929 after it had been drubbed in a band battle by their own, Walter Page's Blue Devils. What Moten could not beat he bought and, from 1930, Basie and Durham produced progressive charts that revolutionised rhythm and set a pattern for Swing. From the 1929 'Jones Law Blues' to the remarkable 1932 'Lafayette', 'Moten's Swing' etc, they wrote sophisticated ensembles that swung in 4/4 like a KayCee tenorman's solo [see Lester Young] instead of the hopping 2/4 of earlier jazz. Along the way, Durham also invented amplified guitar by adding a resonator board to his instrument ('Oh Eddie' etc). It all ended on the operating table in 1935 when Moten, under local anaesthetic, moved during a routine tonsillectomy and died of blood loss from a wound to his jugular vein. CS

SOUTH
(RCA/Bluebird ND 83139)

PAUL MOTIAN

MISTERIOSO
(Soul Note SN 121174)

PAUL MOTIAN & THE ELECTRIC BEBOP BAND
(JMT 514004 2)

Despite being party to the intimate worlds of pianists Bill Evans, Paul Bley and Keith Jarrett, Paul Motian is a long way from being a mere trio drummer. The masterful *Sunday At The Village Vanguard* (Riverside 9376/OJC CD 140) by the trio of Evans, Motian and bassist Scott La Faro is a model of the way that three men can interrelate. More pointedly, it demonstrates Motian's ability to ignore the role of pace maker and, instead, relate his accentation and phrase shapes to reciprocal counterpoint. This structural rather than loosely swinging approach enhanced his composing and arranging work and his groups with horns are particularly impressive. The excellent 1986 *Misterioso* has the strong presence of saxophonists Jim Pepper and Joe Lovano plus guitarist Bill Frisell on the aptly titled 'Gang Of Five' and confirms the Motian magic on 'Folk Song For Rosie'. For well over a decade Motian, Lovano and Frisell have been the core of most of Motian's recordings. Sometimes they perform strictly as a threesome (*It Should've Happened A Long Time Ago* (ECM 1283)) or have invited either Charlie Haden (*Paul Motian On Broadway Vol. 1 & 2* (JMT 834430/40)) or Marc Johnson (*Bill Evans* (JMT 834445)) to bring along their bass. To prove that the Motian method is ageless, the 1992 *Electric Bebop Band* includes tenor saxophonist Joshua Redman and takes a more harmolodic route to its exciting conclusions. The whole thing is based on Motian's adaptability. BMcR

JIM MULLEN

SOUNDBITES
(EFZ 1003)

Though best known for his long partnership with tenorist Dick Morrissey, Jim Mullen, probably the most distinctive guitarist in British jazz, has his roots in the hard bop he studied and played before leaving Glasgow in 1969. When Morrissey-Mullen finally split in 1990 after some 15 years, both principals began to develop their small group work. Mullen's first post-Morrissey solo project,

Into The 90's, actually pursued a highly produced jazz-funk ideal, but the 1992 *Soundbites*, while retaining electric bass and backbeats, often suggested a cross between the light funk approach of John Scofield's 1979 *Who's Who* and the American's more abstract latter-day style. Mullen has confessed his admiration for Scofield, but in fact at this point the signature Mullen mix of Cornell Dupree inspired blues and public domain bebop is to the fore once again. His own voice is certainly strong enough to stand alone. Dave O' Higgins (ts), Laurence Cottle (b) and Ian Thomas (d) show total sympathy with the leader's vision. MG

GERRY MULLIGAN

THE BEST OF GERRY MULLIGAN WITH CHET BAKER
(Pacific Jazz CDP 7 95481 2)

CALIFORNIA CONCERTS VOL. 1
(Pacific Jazz 7 46860 2)

CALIFORNIA CONCERTS VOL. 2
(Pacific Jazz CDP 7 46864 2) [L]

THE COMPLETE PACIFIC JAZZ AND CAPITOL
RECORDINGS OF THE ORIGINAL GERRY MULLIGAN
QUARTET AND TENTETTE WITH CHET BAKER
(Mosaic MD3 102) 3-CD

COMPACT JAZZ:
GERRY MULLIGAN CONCERT JAZZ BAND
(Verve 838 933)

NEW YORK-DECEMBER 1960
(Jazz Anthology 550072) [L]

RE-BIRTH OF THE COOL 1992
(GRP GRD 9679)

As architects of the 'West Coast Sound', the common denominator shared by East-Coast composer/arrangers Shorty Rogers and Gerry Mulligan was the influence of the 1949/1950 recordings of the Miles Davis Nonet – later to become known as 'The Birth Of The Cool'. Shorty Rogers & The Giants more or less replicated the instrumental texture for their Capitol debut, but Mulligan was closer to the source, having scored just under half of the original 'Cool' repertoire ('Jeru', 'Venus de Milo', 'Rocker', 'Godchild', and 'Darn That Dream') and played baritone sax on all three sessions. Nonetheless, it is for both his innovative 'piano-less' quartet which, in 1952, also introduced the talents of Chet Baker, plus his equally distinctive baritone work that Gerry Mulligan is continually honored. Against a firmly anchored bass, Chico Hamilton's highly-detailed, tuneful brushwork set up a rhythmic flow against which Mulligan's agile baritone sax and Baker's crisp, dry trumpet interweaved playfully on a succession of jukebox 78s – 'Bernie's Tune', 'Walkin' Shoes', 'Nights At The Turntable', 'Freeway' while Baker's haunting showcase, 'My Funny Valentine' sidelined almost any other available treatment. In marked contrast to the commonplace tightly-knit sound of tenor/trumpet and three rhythm just running changes, the attractive deployment of baritone sax and trumpet and the lack of a chording piano produced an entirely fresh attention-grabbing sound that immediately found favour with audiences due to its great depth of presence and a genuine sense of purpose. A unique partnership, Mulligan and Baker persistently second-guessed one another during the many contrapuntal 'chases' that characterised the music they made together. It most certainly wasn't bop. And, though it was as contemporary as tomorrow, in essence it contained elements of (modern) dixieland and swing -'Makin' Whoopee', for one, conjures up haunting empty ballroom nostalgia of a previous era. And, because their partnership was so shortlived it never had sufficient time to run out of ideas and stagnate. Even as those initial quartet sides were making headlines worldwide, Mulligan hankered after expanding his line-up. He incorporated Stan Kenton's then alto star Lee Konitz into the quartet with emaculate results *Konitz Meets Mulligan* (Pacific Jazz CDP 7 46847 2) and while 'Walkin' Shoes' was burning up the airwaves cut a 10-inch LP for Capitol with his Tentette -a rehearsal band which was basically the quartet combined with the ensemble instrumentation of the Miles Davis nonet. Volume one of the *California Concerts* reveals Jon Eardley to be a inspired (but all-too-brief) replacement for Chet, while the second volume adds Bob Brookmeyer (v-tmb) and Zoot Sims (ts) to the line-up to flag-up Mulligan's route for the remainder of the '50s as he switched between quartet and sextet line-ups. *At Storyville* (Pacific Jazz CDP 7 94472 2) a 1956 club set featuring Brookmeyer is this line-up's best representation and further explores the *nouveau-retro* tactics. By 1960, Mulligan's energies were channelled into his Concert Jazz Band and the Compact Jazz anthology is certainly the best available representation with Bob Brookmeyer, Zoot Sims, Clark Terry (tpt) among the many soloists working on a book that includes a large chunk of the score to the movie *I Want To Live*. And, though he regularly returned to a small group format (co-leading a quartet with Dave Brubeck) it's when arranging for much large instrumenation that Mulligan is truly in his element. RC

MARK MURPHY

RAH!
Riverside 9395/OJC CCD 141)

BOP FOR KEROUAC
Muse MCD 5253)

WHAT A WAY TO GO
Muse MCD 5419)

Damn record companies! Many of Mark's finest moments still remain unavailable on CD. Thankfully there's enough around to prove that Murphy is just another word for vocal genius. Ever inventive - sometimes too inventive - he's an ace musician kitted out with a voice, instead of a instrument. He phrases like Coltrane, Rollins, Miles, anyone he wants to be. And given a ballad he can weave a tremendous depth of feel into its lyric. Not that he ever settles, ever waits to be catergorised. On *Rah!*, his most potent offering to date, he links with the arrangements of Ernie Wilkins and a dream band that includes Clark Terry, Blue Mitchell, Ernie Royal (tpt), Urbie Green (tmb), Bill Evans (p) etc, to fly on a lyrically and melodically inventive 'My Favourite Things' and scatdoodles dextrously through 'Milestones'. *Bop For Kerouac* finds him donating a version of Mingus' 'Goodbye Pork Pie Hat' that shows Joni Mitchell just how her words should have been handled and hitches 'Parker's Mood' to a reading from Jack Kerouac's *The Subterraneans*. Finally, *What A Way To Go* has two tilts at the Sinatra songbook ('I Fall In Love Too Easily', 'All My Tomorrows') then closes on a rap ('Ding Walls') that describes Mark's acceptance by London's acid-jazz community of the late 80s and early '90s. These days, the Singing M (as he was dubbed) is into Brazillian sounds. But, he'll move on again, assimilating everything. As always. FD

THAT'S HOW I LOVE THE BLUES
(Riverside 9441/OJC CCD 367)

DAVID MURRAY

SWEET LOVELY
(Black Saint BSR 120039)

MING
(Black Saint BSR 120045)

LIVE AT SWEET BASIL VOL. 1 & 2
(Black Saint BSR 120085/95) [L]

David Murray is one of the most prolific recording artists. As well as sessions under his own name, he has worked with Special Edition, Clarinet Summit, the World Saxophone Quartet and the Music Revelation Ensemble. His admiration of Albert Ayler did show in his earliest work and his 1977 album for India Navigation was entitled *Flowers For Albert* (West Wind 2039) and featured that oft recorded piece. In reality, Murray's similarity to Ayler was largely superficial. Murray's timing was more regular and his attention to melodic projection far more concerned with note placement that would make him swing. His tone on the 1979 *Sweet Lovely* still had a hint of the grainy Ayler sadness but, as his career developed, he achieved a sound that was very much his own. Murray is also a superb arranger and, although *Ming* is outstanding, all of his octet sessions were successful. Brass outnumbered reeds three to two and Murray fully exploited the tonal textures available. He showed similar imagination with his big band and made full use of its impressive personnel. The book was challenging with specially tailored material from Jelly Roll Morton and Duke Ellington and with originals such as 'Bechet's Bounce' that were realistically modern tributes to the dedicatee concerned. *Live At Sweet Basil* shows how well Black Saint captured live dates. An important feature when one considers how exciting this band sounds live. BMcR

THE HILL
(Black Saint BSR 0110)

SPECIAL QUARTET
(DIW CD 843)

FATS NAVARRO

THE FABULOUS FATS NAVARRO VOL. 1 & 2
(Blue Note CDP 7 81531 2/32 2)

FATS NAVARRO FEATURED
WITH THE TADD DAMERON BAND
(Milestone M 47041) [L]

BIRD & FATS – LIVE AT BIRDLAND
(Cool & Blue C&B CD 103) [L]

Being saddled with a monstrous drug habit and the nickname 'Fat Girl' didn't do anything for Theodore Navarro's self esteem. Navarro, six years junior to Dizzy, was but 22, when he took over Gillespie's gig with Billy Eckstine's historic blues 'n' bop big band

(1945-46), demonstrating that he possessed the chops for such a demanding role. As with Dizzy, he organised his solos meticulously, while his big band experience not only built up his physical power, but instilled in Navarro the knowledge how best to improve his sound, project himself and the value of shading. However, in less than five years he would be dead. Second only to Dizzy as the complete bop trumpet player, Navarro's recording career was often as a sideman for Eddie 'Lockjaw' Davis, Tadd Dameron, Bud Powell etc. His Blue Note legacy may fill two CDs, but in truth, Navarro only ever taped one sessions for the label under his own name and even that he co-led with trumpeter Howard McGhee supported by the Tadd Dameron band minus its pianist leader. The remainder stem from two Dameron dates (1947) and (1948) and finally, Bud Powell's famous quintet session from 1949 that included Sonny Rollins (ts) working out on 'Bouncing With Bud', 'Wail', 'Dance Of The Infidels' and '52nd Street Theme'. The 1947 date had Ernie Henry (as) and Charlie Rouse (ts) sharing the frontline on 'The Chase', 'The Squirrel', 'Our Delight', 'Dameronia', while the 1948 features two laconic bop tenors Allen Eager and Wardell Gray on multi-takes of 'Jahbero', 'Ladybird' and 'Symphonette'. But, on every occasion, it's always Navarro that streaks straight to the fore. The Milestone set comes from a plethora of airshots again featuring Tadd Dameron's seven piece band which revisits some of the Blue Note repertoire and together with tapes of his collaboration with Bird give a true measure of Navarro's worth. Perhaps, he knew time was fast running out, for the 1950 Roost sessions (Savoy/Vogue 650126) often depict a somewhat melancholic Navarro as having the edge over Bird and it all happened again at Birdland in May just a week before Navarro's death. The Hard Bop trumpet linage may well be traced back to Brownie, but everything from tone and articulation, speed and balance, derived first from Fats Navarro. No argument. RC

LENNIE NIEHAUS

THE QUINTETS VOL. 1
(Contemporary 3518/OJC CD 319)

Today, Lennie Niehaus may be best known as soundtrack supplier to Clint Eastwood (*City Heat, Bird, Unforgiven* etc), but in the mid-'50s, he was amongst the coolest on the Coast. A studious looking altoist, with an aloof yet cutting tone and a nice line in casual shirts, he deservedly bagged *Down Beat* Magazine's 1955 New Star Award within a year of making his presence known with a 10-inch album of genuinely inventive performances. Taking the Mulligan Quartet's encounter with Lee Konitz a stage further, Niehaus used a three sax /two rhythm voicing to execute his meticulously constructed yet fluent arrangements on both originals and standards such as 'I Remember You'. In Jack Montrose (ts) and Bob Gordon (bs), Niehaus had found like-minded frontline partners. Octet and (with) Strings sessions soon followed. All this high-profile activity ran concurrent to his role as featured soloist and arranger with Stan Kenton. It was but a short step to Hollywood and a profitable reunion with his former army, piano-playing buddy, Clint Eastwood. For a low-key comeback taped for Fresh Sound, in 1989 (*Patterns*), Niehaus teamed-up with former Kentonite Bill Perkins on a set including some of the themes from *Bird* and, despite its Parkeresque structure, still proved instantly recognisable. RC

THE OCTET *2: VOL. 3
(Contemporary 3503/OJC 1767)

JIMMIE NOONE

COMPLETE RECORDINGS VOL. 1
(Affinity AFS CD 1027 3)

Praised by no less a figure than Maurice Ravel, Jimmie Noone was
a prime force in the 'liberation' of jazz clarinet from its traditional,
somewhat decorative role. A New Orleanian of quite original out-
look, and eminently capable of matching the classic standards of
New Orleans clarinet as personified by Sidney Bechet and Johnny
Dodds, Noone learned from Louis Armstrong's example. The
result was the band he formed towards the end of the decade in
which the customary trumpet was replaced by Joe Poston's underrated alto saxophone, which contrived to combine a decorative role
with the cornet ensemble lead as developed by Armstrong. Greater
rhythmic freedom demonstrated a much more forward-looking
approach to music-making, showing up especially clearly on the
virtuosic, uptempo 'Monday Date' and the tremendous duets on 'I
Know That You Know' (which were to be echoed by Soprano
Summit in the 1970s). Noone was also praised for the beauty of his
tone, and its poised luminosity lends these creations a superb
sheen, from which it becomes easier to trace Noone's place as a
stepping-stone between New Orleans and Dixieland and the later
clarinet styles of the Swing Era as personified by Benny Goodman
and Artie Shaw. CS

RED NORVO

KNOCK ON WOOD
(Affinity CD AFS 1017)

MOVE
(Savoy SV 0168)

Kenneth Norville – 'Red Norvo' – sort of sneaked up on the vibraharp after Lionel Hampton had established it as a jazz instrument
during the latter 1930s. Throughout that period, Norvo had stuck
to the unamplified xylophone, creating the pianistic solo style that
he transferred to the vibraharp after 1943. It was an alternative to
Hampton's approach as strong and distinctive as that offered by
Lester Young to the prevailing tenor style created by Coleman
Hawkins. Just as Hampton and Hawkins favoured a hot, vertical
style of phrasing, so Norvo and Young leaned towards a cooler,
legato, more melodic approach. In the 1930s, he created a body of
'chamber jazz' of lasting value, its swirling impressionism auguring
the 'hot v cool' debate to come. When he switched to vibes, his
work retained this adventurousness (in 1945 he recorded with Bird
and Diz), and the trio recordings (made in the early '50s with guitarist Tal Farlow and bassist Charles Mingus), with their densely-
woven melodic fabrics of supple counterpoint and subtle rhythmic
contrasts touched the work of trios in coming decades. CS

RED NORVO TRIO VOL. 2
(VJC 1008)

LIVE FROM BLUE GARDENS
(MM 65090) [L]

BENNY GOODMAN SEXTET: SLIPPED DISC
(CBS 463337 2)

WOODY HERMAN: THUNDERING HERDS
(CBS 460825 2)

ANITA O'DAY

ANITA O'DAY 1956-1962
(Giants Of Jazz CD 53145)

ANITA SINGS THE MOST
(Verve 829 577 2)

'It's not true about me and the whole Stan Kenton Orchestra!' claimed Anita in one her many revealing moments. What is true is that she's never been anything other than a jazz vocalist, even when working basically as band singer with Gene Krupa and parading the pops back in the early '40s. Maybe her pitch is a bit suspect, but it's the imperfections in her ever-husky voice that make her far more interesting than many who are endowed with faultless but more unfeeling delivery. The Giants Of Jazz release is a marvellous compilation that links tracks from her scintillating Cole Porter album (with Billy May) with cuts culled mainly from big band sessions with Buddy Bregman, Russ Garcia, Marty Paich and others. Included are show-stopping work-outs on 'Take The A Train', 'Early Autumn' and a scat-happy interpretations of 'Four Brothers' and 'Hershey Bar'. Conversely, the Verve set, with the Oscar Peterson Quartet, will satisfy those who insist Anita, who's been known to bend a tune or two in the name of personalisation, works better with a combo that provides freedom to move. Those who admire such singers as June Christy and Chris Conner need seek no further than here to locate the source of inspiration for those singers. For additional pleasure O'Day is featured in the movies *Drum Crazy: The Gene Krupa Story* and *Jazz On A Summer's Day* while her warts-and-all autobiography *High Times Hard Times* is compulsive reading. FD

KING OLIVER

KING OLIVER VOL. 1 1923-1929
(BBC CD 787)

THE KING OF NEW ORLEANS 1923-1930
(Jazz Portraits CD 14547)

The first influential cornet player/trumpeter to stem from New Orleans (Buddy Bolden is merely a legend while Freddie Keppard has few recordings to his name), Joe Oliver also led the first jazz supergroup – King Oliver's Creole Jazz Band.
While the recording techniques of the day provide but a constricted version of what was taking place in the studio, the interplay of Oliver and Louis Armstrong, woven into place by the thread of Johnny Dodd's clarinet remains breathtaking on such tracks as 'Dippermouth Blues'. The budget-label Jazz Portraits release covers some of the same ground but expands to cover sessions by Oliver's Dixie Syncopators (a favourite with Al Capone) and includes a several of the tracks recorded for Victor during 1929-30. Though his playing was in decline by this time and he was no match for the ever-soaring Armstrong (check Oliver's 'West End Blues' against Louis' Hot Five version), he nevertheless retained much of his original (and much-copied) style, his mute work being particularly accomplished. FD

THE NEW YORK SESSIONS 1930-1931
(RCA Bluebird ND 90410)

ORIGINAL DIXIELAND JAZZ BAND

THE FIRST JAZZ RECORDINGS
(Timeless CBC 1 009)

Nick LaRocca boasted that he invented jazz when his band cut the first 'jass' records for Columbia in 1916. Indeed, the advertising proclaimed 'Original Dixieland Jazz Band – the creators of Jazz'. In fact, their music merely reflected their black neighbours' developments without being directly influenced by them. Black musicians in New Orleans were creating an improvised dance music by instrumentalising the blues over martial and ragtime syncopations, and their white neighbours had begun to hear the possibilities. But the blues were not an integral part of the white man's culture, so they relied on the ragtime and marching band ingredients. As a result, their music lacked emotional depth. Moreover, ragtime was a written idiom, with no space for improvised solos, so white 'jazz' ensembles were equally rigidly worked out, leaving very little room for solos.

Melodically, their music was crammed with activity to the point of being febrile. And a misunderstanding of blues 'vocalese' led to novelty effects like the crowing clarinet, whinnying cornet and neighing trombone of 'Livery Stable Blues'. There are elements here, in the playing of clarinettist Larry Shields and cornetist LaRocca, that would be echoed in the Chicago School playing of such as Frank Teschemacher and Bix Beiderbecke. But the ultimate ODJB legacy was more cabaret than anything.

The release on Timeless is recommended over the RCA/Bluebird reissue, *75th Anniversary* (ND 90650), with identical contents, for having the better sound. CS

ODJB IN LONDON
(KJ 118FS)

KID ORY

KID ORY'S CREOLE JAZZ BAND, 1944-45
(Good Time Jazz GTJCD 120 22)

Edward 'Kid' Ory was the founding father of the 'tailgate' style of New Orleans trombone playing and remained unsurpassed as an exponent throughout a long life. Strictly an ensemble style using smears and glissandi to generate rhythmic momentum, it is technically simple. It is the timing that is critical and, in this, Ory was a virtuoso. He was also a master of mutes, adding another layer to a style that made up for adequate technique with emotional expressiveness. One of the earlier musicians to depart New Orleans, he was spreading the jazz message in California from 1919-1925.

It was his move to Chicago that year which brought him into contact with important New Orleanians like Armstrong (JSP CD 312) and Dodds (JSP CD 319) and provided the first recordings on which his reputation was built. Like many NO masters, he left the music in 1933, in his case to farm chickens, but returned with the Revival of the early 1940s to work with Mutt Carey (tpt), Darnell Howard (clt) etc , when the *op cit* proved he had lost none of the powers he retained until retiring in 1966. CS

THE GREEN ROOM
(American Music AMCD 42)

THE LEGENDARY KID
(Good Time Jazz GTJCD 12016)

ORAN HOT LIPS PAGE

HOT LIPS PAGE 1938-1940
(Official CD 83047)

Oran 'Hot Lips' Page was the trumpet voice largely lost to history, ironically by being plucked from obscurity to work as Louis Armstrong's 'double'. Half brother to the great bassist, Walter Page, he should have joined him in the Count Basie band that made its fame in New York after 1936; instead, he went ahead as a single hired by Satchmo's manager, Joe Glaser, who wanted to repeat Louis' commercial triumph fronting big bands with grandstanding trumpet. But Page's forte was blues playing, sharpened in work with his half brother's Blue Devils and Bennie Moten (*Basie Beginnings* RCA/Bluebird 9768 2RB), where he earned himself the billing 'Trumpet King Of The West'. This was something less appreciated by a more appreciated northern audience bent on distancing itself from its poorer roots. The venture failed, even hits records with Artie Shaw ('St. James Infirmary Blues') and Pearl Bailey ('Baby, It's Cold Outside') proved fleeting and Page's career remained in a vacuum until drink claimed him via a heart attack at the early age of 46. Such recorded glimpses as remain reveal an expansively expressive style, brimming with tonal effects and subtle rhythmic infections. At times, he crams so much emotion into his blowing that the instrument seems barely able to contain it. In fact he came as close as anyone to becoming the soul of jazz. CS

CHARLIE PARKER

THE CHARLIE PARKER STORY
(Savoy SV 0105)

CHARLIE PARKER MEMORIAL: VOL. 1
(Savoy SV 0101)

CHARLIE PARKER MEMORIAL: VOL. 2
(Savoy SV 0103)

THE GENIUS OF CHARLIE PARKER
(Savoy SV 0104)

CHARLIE PARKER ON DIAL/
THE COMPLETE SESSIONS 1946-47
(Spotlite SPJ CD 4-101) 4-CD

THE COMPLETE DEAN BENEDETTI RECORDINGS
OF CHARLIE PARKER
(Mosaic MD7 129) 7-CD [L]

BIRD AT THE ROOST VOL. 1-4
(Savoy Vogue 650124/5/6/7) [L]

JAZZ AT MASSEY HALL
(Debut 124/OJC CD 044) [L]

BIRD: THE COMPLETE CHARLIE PARKER
ON VERVE JAN 46-DEC 54
(Verve 837141) 10-CD

Alto-saxophonist Charlie 'Yardbird' Parker stands as one of the very few musicians (Armstrong, Miles, Coltrane, Ornette and Hendrix) who've wiped clean and then redrawn the roadmap. At the heart of all these innovators way of things could be located a deep rooted blues sensibility. In Parker's instance it was matched by a complete overhaul of rhythm and harmony. Nobody has ever swung so hard, so fluently and with as much purpose as Bird. And though the tempos could be torrid and his assault on tunes-the-way-they-were almost vicious, his approach was deceptively effort-less – as though the instrument was playing itself. Parker emerged from the hedonistic Kansas City fleshpots of 24-hour jam sessions and unlimited sex and substances. In the pre-Pearl Harbour days (1939-42), the already errant Parker jumped and jived with the band of Jay 'Hootie' McShann (*Early Bird* Stash STCD 542), moved on to Earl Hines (1942-43) where he linked up with like-minded Dizzy Gillespie. At which point the pair joined 'Sepia Sinatra' Billy Eckstine's blues 'n' bop big band (1944) before deciding to form their own ill-fated combo (1944-45).

Though there's a seemingly confusing proliferation of Bird product (much of which overlaps), it's possible to neatly assemble his prime-cuts into into three distinct periods; the sessions he cut for Savoy (1945-48), Dial (1946-47) and Clef/Verve (1946-54).The material on the earlier labels demonstrating just how Bird achieved maximum lift-off. Surprisingly, Bird's official studio recordings with Dizzy are minimal (though there's a plethora of airshots), the bulk of the Savoys and Dials being cut with a fledgling and often faultering Miles Davis. Those at the keyboard included Bud Powell, John Lewis, Errol Garner and Duke Jordan. Tommy Potter and Curley Russell were the regular bassists while drummer Max Roach remained constant. It's been suggested that Bird intention-ally avoided working with stars of the calibre of Dizzy and Fats Navarro for apart from the expense, there was the possibility of them stealing the limelight. Basically, Bird hired trumpet players such as Davis, Kenny Dorham and Red Rodney for the purpose of beefing up the themes and affording him a rest between solos.

Whereas Thelonious Monk was to create new music from the ground up, Bird built an impressive book by frequently plundering Broadway show tunes or dancehall standards, and annexing exist-ing chord changes to such as - 'I Got Rhythm' ('Anthropology'), 'Honeysuckle Rose' ('Marmaduke'), 'How High The Moon' ('Ornithology') 'Indiana' ('Donna Lee'), 'Embraceable You' ('Meandering') 'Cherokee' ('Koko'), Lover Come Back To Me' ('Bird Gets The Worm'), 'S' Wonderful' ('Stupendous'), 'All the Things You Are' ('Bird Of Paradise') 'Out Of Nowhere' ('She Rote') etc, then overlaying them with entirely original riffs and melody lines often performed at sonic speeds in an effort to weed out bop wannabes or unwanted intruders. Amid it all there was the inevitable bluesware; acid azure beauties like 'Parker's Mood', 'Cool Blues' or maybe 'Now's The Time', a riff so R&B based that it eventually graced jukeboxes in the guise of 'The Hucklebuck'.

The Savoy sessions produced many classics including 'Billie's Bounce', 'Now's The Time', 'Koko', and 'Parker's Mood'.

The Dial dates accounted for 'Moose The Mooche', 'Yardbird Suite', 'Ornithology', 'A Night In Tunia' (including the legendary 46-seconds alto break), 'Cool Blues', 'Relaxin' At Camarillo', 'Cheers', 'Klact-oveeseds-tene', 'Scrapple From The Apple', 'Out Of Nowhere' and much more. Though chronically dependent of drugs (and later alcohol), Bird seldom let his illness interfere with recording, on the rare occasion that it did – the infamous 'Loverman' session on Dial -the results possessed deep passion.

The first modernist to be extensively recorded (unauthorised) by the likes of obsessive fans such as Dean Benedetti these recordings give one a detailed insight into Bird's creative process. The seven CD Mosaic collection covers the period March 1947 to July 1948, and while crudely recorded, it assembles 278 tracks culled from 461 live recordings Benedetti made on either a portable 78 rpm acetate disc cutter or a primitive paper-base tape recorder. These, to the faithful, represent the Holy Grail. They also represent a hefty financial involvement. The Royal Roost broadcasts profile free flying Bird in a nightly working environment. Often good humoured and frighteningly creative. *Inglewood Jam* is the only unedited document of Chet Baker's brief stint with Bird and also involves Sonny Criss (as) and Al Haig (p) on a typical club date. *Jazz At Massey Hall* (aka The Quintet Of The Year) has taken on legendary status for the fact, that in 1953, it gathered together Bird, with Dizzy and a rhythm section of Bud Powell, Charles Mingus (who taped the performance) and Max Roach. A freewheelin' event, it benefits from extended performances ('Perdido', 'All The Things You Are', 'Hot House' etc) and a genuine rapport between all concerned.

With Norman Granz in his (familiar) role of jazz Svengali. Bird's move to Clef (later renamed Verve) was to provide him with mass market appeal. Aside from Bird's constant need for ready-cash, the other incentive was the opportunity to fulfill a lifelong ambition to record with (cloying) Strings which he did quite often and with mixed results. Overall, the Verve sessions were often erratic, a reunion with Diz and Monk was sabotaged by Buddy Rich's unsympathetic drumming, but on the plus side there was a superb one-off with Coleman Hawkins ('Ballade'), a collaboration with Machito's latin big band for a performance of Chico O'Farrill's 'Afro Cuban Suite', several small group dates collated on *Swedish Schnapps* (Verve 849 393) plus historical Jazz At The Philharmonic encounters with Lester Young.

Both Blue Note and Fresh Sound sourced the same Hi-Hat sessions featuring Bird unhampered by a house band that includes unknown trumpeter Herbie Williams. The (slightly) better sounding Fresh Sounds also include material from a date six months earlier when Herb Pomeroy was trumpet man. It's standard bop fare ('Ornithology', 'My Little Suede Shoes' etc), while the late-hour casualness of the on-mike banter and the sax supremo's consideration towards his workmanlike accomplices produces better than expected results from all involved. The Parker legacy is peppered with intriguing oddities *The Complete Birth Of The Bebop: Bird On Tenor* (Stash STCD 535) is of particular interest to the Ornithologist in that it contains early '40s discoveries such as a crude hotel room recording of Bird on tenor ('Body And Soul' and 'Honeysuckle Rose'), a coin-in-the-slot recording booth souvenir of Sweet Georgia Brown' plus Bird cheerfully playing along with 78rpm recordings of Benny Goodman's 'Avalon' and 'China Boy'. This is but the tip, to collect everything is a full-time occupation and one that could benefit loan sharks! RC

BIRD AT THE HI-HAT 1953-54
Blue Note CDP 99787 2) [L]

BIRD IN BOSTON/LIVE AT THE HI-HAT 1953-54 VOL. 1&2
Fresh Sound FSR CD 1006/7) [L]

BIRD AT ST. NICK'S
Jazz Workshop JWS 500/OJC CD 041)[L]

BIRD ON 52ND STREET
Jazz Workshop 501/OJC CD 114)[L]

THE GREAT SESSIONS 1947-48
Jazz Anthology 550082) [L]

BIRD AT CARNEGIE HALL
Cool & Blue C&B CD 105) [L]

EVAN PARKER

CONIC SECTIONS
(ah um 015)

There is something about the rather odd European free music scene that makes it quite normal for a saxophonist like Evan Parker to take part in very contrasting, big band dates like the Brotherhood of Breath's *Live At Willisau* (Ogun OGCD 001) and the Globe Unity's *Rumblin'* (FMP CD40). The same man was on the Spontaneous Music Ensemble's *Karyobin* (Chronoscope CPE 2001), Tony Oxley's sadly deleted *Baptised Traveller* and with Greg Goodman on the similarly deleted *Abracadabra*. He also took part in a breathtaking string of intimate duos with the likes of Derek Bailey (gtr) and John Stevens (d) and, when present, was a tower of strength in the Company team. Parker's self motivating style fitted into each of these situations. The degree of coalescence was of a very special kind; there was mutual respect but there was also a need for a confrontational element. Parker avoided melodic continuity, used circular breathing to add a contrapuntal dimension and presented a tapestry of sound that was insistently creative. At times, his playing related closely to his colleagues; at others, not at all. In real terms, all free improvisation is ageless; there can be no progress in the crass sense. For that reason *Conic Sections*, a recording that grew out of a successful practice session, is an ideal introduction to Parker's work. It is a solo performance but, in a sense, so were many that found him in a big band. BMcR

JOE PASS

VIRTUOSO
(Pablo PACD 2310 708)

Virtuoso was not mistitled. The first in a series of solo guitar recitals which revitalised Pass's career in the mid-seventies, it was an exhaustive introduction to his fluent contrapuntal style. However, the title also inadvertently signalled a problem: such is the preoccupation with technique that the rococo flourish tends towards automatic gesture, the bebop vocabulary is systematised to the point of formula, and dynamic, rhythmic and timbral variation are overlooked in the pursuit of mere articulacy. But Pass plays with vigour on eleven standards ('Night And Day', 'Here's That Rainy Day' 'How High The Moon', 'Round Midnight' etc), and a blues, inspired perhaps by his new Pablo deal, and this, combined with a slight distortion on some chords, produces rugged moments in a sometimes rather mechanical display. Pass seemed more relaxed, and more likely to swing, away from the solo spotlight. The small group session *Tudo Bem* (Pablo 2310 824/OJC CD 685 2) was such an occasion, and the repertoire of sambas, bossas and light funk also provided relief from his usual diet of bop and Broadway standards. 'Corcovado' has Pass in buoyant form over a grooving rhythm section including Paulinho Da Costa and Don Grusin. His death, in 1994 left shoes only a brave person would attempt to fill. MG

JACO PASTORIUS

JACO PASTORIUS
(Epic 81453)

JACO
(Improvising Artists Inc. 123846 2)

Given the evidence of his eponymous 1976 debut, it's difficult to argue with Jaco's introduction of himself to Joe Zawinul as "the greatest bass-player in the world". *Jaco Pastorius* is not only a consistently brilliant piece of music, but a comprehensive survey of the past, present and future of jazz bass. There's bebop in the casual duet reading of 'Donna Lee', R&B in Sam & Dave's 'Come On Over', Caribbean music in the steel-pan feature 'Opus Pocus', world music before its time in the Afro-Cuban 'Okonkole Y Trompa', and stunning expositions of Jaco's bass-line revolution in the liquid harmonics, rich chord work and orchestral conception of 'Portrait of Tracy' and the funky drive, fretless slurring and guitar-like agility of '(Used To Be A) Cha-Cha'. Jaco's bass method and the notion of stylistic inclusiveness are commonplace now, but you probably heard it here first. Like his work with Joni Mitchell, the 1974 *Jaco* is another illustration of Pastorius's versatility, setting him in a loose, often abstract environment with Pat Metheny (gtr), Paul Bley (p) and Bruce Ditmas (d). The playing is impromptu and unfocused, but there are rewarding moments and novel perspectives on Bley (untypically playing funky electric piano) and Metheny (playing rock-inflected jazz with phase-shifter and barely a sign of country music). MG

HOLIDAY FOR PANS
Sound Hills SSCD 8001)

LIVE IN ITALY
(Jazzpoint JP 1036) [L]

BIG JOHN PATTON

THE ORGANIZATION! THE BEST OF
(Blue Note 8 30728)

BLUE PLANET MAN
(King KICJ 168)

Jimmy Smith and Horace Silver may have been scoring the juke-box hits, but during the 'soul jazz' years, the resourceful Big John Patton was the sound of Blue Note. A Kansas City-slicker, not only did his Hammond B-3 bomber record prolifically for the legendary New York label but with guitarist Grant Green and drummer Ben Dixon in tow made up the house rhythm section that funked. Far from being intimidated by Jimmy Smith's giant-killer reputation, Big John carved out an equally distinctive approach. For, whereas labelmate Larry Young looked towards Coltrane for divine inspiration, Patton followed the bebop gospel according to Bud Powell and Hampton Hawes. The antithesis of keyboard flash, Patton slowly cooked up a mess of blue bop on a back burner as he carefully evaluated each note and pause. *The Organization!* cherry-picks the Blue Note back-catalogue to bring you everything you need to know about Patton with 'The Silver Metre', 'Along Came John', 'The Turnaround', 'Latona' and 'Fat Judy' among the highlights. The advent of Acid Jazz in Europe and the sudden 'discovery' by Japan's jazz fraternity of the organ (an instrument they previously shunned) has turned the spotlight on seemingly forgotten Hammond B-3 bombers such as Patton. Lonnie Smith and Mel Rhyne, *Blue Planet Man* gives notices that, three decades on, Big John remains true to his original formula on 'Congo Chant' and Archie Shepp's 'U-Jama', where his signature licks are offset by John Zorn's alto squawks, Ed Cherry's plummy guitar runs, a pair of crunchy hot fudge tenors and some kicking rhythm business. RC

ART PEPPER

SURF RIDE
(Savoy SV 0115)

THURSDAY NIGHT AT THE VILLAGE VANGUARD
(Contemporary 7642/OJC CD 694) [L]

Art Pepper was a fine saxophonist who waged an on going war with
the romanticism that lurked in his musical psyche and could never
be totally suppressed. Schooled in the Stan Kenton Orchestra, he
emerged in the early fifties as the typical West Coast clinician, cool
of hand, organised of mind and playing with a light but buoyant
swing. *Surf Ride* finds him in ideal company and shows how his creative processes were used to refashion themes like 'Foolish
Things' and to turn 'Indiana' into a jaunty 'Suzy The Poodle'.
Drug addiction had entered into the equation before the 1957 *Meets
The Rhythm Section* (Contemporary 7532/OJC CD 338) was made
but, despite being ill prepared for that particular date, Pepper
responds superbly to the Miles Davis rhythm team of the day and
produces one of his most passionate performances. The impact of
incarceration and the music of John Coltrane attended the Pepper
method in about equal proportions in the seventies. He was, at
times, directed by a fervant intensity and the *Living Legend*
(Contemporary 7633/OJC CD 408) could be seen as a natural
prospectus for Pepper, the reluctant romantic and realistic achiever.
The 1977 *Vanguard* date, however, takes this process a stage further. Elvin Jones (d), George Cables (p) and George Mraz (b) light
fires that Pepper takes into outright conflagration. It is a live date
that sums up the man; a musician tragically dead at 57 and a player
who swam a highly personal midstream between the bop currents
of Bird and the swirling, musical eddies of Lee Konitz. BMcR

OSCAR PETERSON

PETERSON & FRIENDS
(Pablo 8385315)

O.P. AT ZARDIS'
(Pablo 2620118)

Oscar Peterson is one of the few pianists with the technique to be
genuinely Influenced by Art Tatum, rather than inspired by him.
He joined Jazz At The Philharmonic in 1949 and became the ultimate 'house pianist', supporting a wide range of the music's finest
musicians and showing himself, on albums like *Peterson & Friends*,
to be a model accompanist and the chassis around which the entire
JATP band wagon was built. He was as much at home with Louis
Armstrong – *Meets Oscar Peterson* (Verve 825713-2) as he was Dizzy
Gillespie – *Diz & Getz* (Verve 833559-2) and on the latter actually
upstages Stan Getz. His other natural métier, however, was as a trio
player. It was an environment that accommodated his expansive
improvisational skills and put emphasis on his ability to swing. *At
Zardis'* presents him with Ray Brown (b) and Herb Ellis (g) in the
most integrated unit he ever led. All three men get to express
themselves and there is no trace of virtuosic intimidation. On *Night
Train* (Verve 821724), drummer Ed Thigpen replaced Ellis in 1959
and his arrival changed the musical approach. Peterson assumed a
more central role, the piano became the focal point of the unit and
there was a discernible increase in intensity. Contrasting items like
'Moten Swing' and 'C-Jam Blues', in particular, show that there
remained a comparable, creative virility. In the late sixties,

Peterson fell in love with Hans-Georg Brunner Schwer's piano and made a superb series of records in the German's studio. The general standard was first rate but, with solo performances like *My Favourite Instrument* (MPS 821843) the Peterson mastery really blossomed and his Tatumesque 'disciple-ship' was confirmed once and for all. The early eighties found Englishman Martin Drew in the drum chair for what proved to be another productive period. *Time After Time* (Pablo 2310947) typifies the degree of rapport that grew in the trio and, in its finest moments, showed that the new line-up rivalled the Thigpen unit. Arthritis crept into the music via Peterson's knuckles in the nineties but *Live At The Blue Note* (Telarc CD 83304) with old stalwarts like Ellis and Brown and drummer Bobby Durham shows that genuine, emotional input, life time keyboard cunning and good old fashioned jazz know-how can be the salvation of a player of Peterson's quality. At his peak, he was master but the restricted 1990 edition tips his hat to no one. *The Will To Swing* (Verve 2 CD 847 203 2) takes Peterson from 1949 to 1971 and offers the opportunity to trace his development during that period. BMcR

FLIP PHILLIPS

FLIP WAILS: THE BEST OF FLIP PHILLIPS
(Verve 521 644)

Flip Phillips may have made his name as featured tenorman with Woody Herman's (Thundering) First Herd (1944-46) as a result of his no-sense solos on 'Caldonia', 'Apple Honey' and 'Northwest Passage', but upon enlisting as a Jazz At The Philharmonic combatant for a ten year stretch, this Brooklynite (and noisy neighbour Illinois Jacquet) honked his way into history during a midnight matinee at Carnegie Hall in 1947, with the rabble-rousing marathon 'Perdido' and it's 'Mordido' and 'Endido' encores which, at the time, was spread over *eight* 78s.

Henceforth, this performance, which he had to re-run almost nightly, marked Phillips as a tenor equivilant of one of Buddy Rich's shed-building drum solos of the time. An unfortunate piece of brutish typecasting, which for far too many years diverted attention away from his joyous Lestonian skills. Ironically, half of the 20 tracks on *Flip Wails* include Rich and provide some of the best moments on a collection that doesn't so much re-write history but puts events into their correct perspective. The many small group sessions Phillips undertook for Norman Granz reveal him to be a tempered player, who never once hides his admiration for his mentor ('Salute To Pres'), in fact he wallows in it. A wistful reading of 'If I Had You' and a mischievous 'Blues For The Midgets' feature pianist Oscar Peterson in attendance and demonstrating why he is one of the greatest of all accompanists. The finale, a 'live' treatment of 'Topsy' (taken Buddy Rich's 1957 *Live In Miami*) affords Phillips the space to confidently unravels a finely structured solo before a few emaculate trade-offs with the drums. RC

COURTNEY PINE

THE VISION'S TALE
(Antilles ANCD 8746)

Recorded in 1989, *A Vision's Tale* proves to be this valiant young player's most focussed effort to date. This is due in no small measure to the skill of an All-American rhythm section directed by

Ellis Marsalis – the piano playing father of Wynton, Branford and this session's producer Delfeyo. It's not that Marsalis leads Pine by the hand, but affords him the kind of disciplined (as opposed to stressful) support that allows the saxman to broaden a vision that has become blurred by too much genre hopping.

Aside from reworking material usually associated with 'Trane and Rollins (covering the latter's 'I'm An Old Cowhand' might seem foolhardy, until recalling that the *Way Out West* album first inspired the young Londoner to take up the sax), Pine grabs the opportunity to not just incorporate stylistic touches common to these players but evoke shades of Hawkins, Webster, Byas and other ballad sax kings into the preceedings as he attempts to move forward while frequently casting an eye of one shoulder. RC

JEAN-LUC PONTY

HUMAIR/LOUISS/PONTY VOL. 1
(Dreyfus Jazz Line 191018-2) [L]

Given Stephane Grappelli's legacy and the European orchestral tradition, it seems natural that the pioneer of the modern jazz violin should be French. Although Ponty is best known for his American jazz-rock recordings, from a jazz point of view he never improved on the work he did with drummer Daniel Humair and organist Eddy Louiss at the Cameleon club in Paris in 1968. Even at that early stage, the essence of his modernism – the successful amplification of the instrument and the co-option to it of bebop and a good part of Coltrane's vocabulary – was already firmly established. Of the five standards here, 'Summertime' and 'Nostalgia In Times Square' provide muscular straight ahead settings for Ponty's rueful violin, powered by the reassuring thrum of Louiss's organ, but the fragmentation and evident comedy of the 15-minute 'So What' shows the trio's awareness of freer dimensions. The mid-fi sound is quite acceptable, but the grudging 46 minutes of this volume is curious, considering that Yves Chamberlain recorded 'a great number' of reels during that memorable fortnight. MG

KING KONG
(Blue Note CDP 7 89539 2)

BUD POWELL

THE BUD POWELL TRIO PLAYS
(Roulette CDP7 93902 2)

THE AMAZING BUD POWELL VOL. 1 & 2
(Blue Note CDP 7 81503 2 & CDP 7 815042)

Tormented by the early death of his younger brother, Richie, in the same car crash that claimed Clifford Brown, Earl 'Bud' Powell was the genius of Bop piano whose brilliance was dissipated by repeated mental and physical breakdowns. Like Earl Hines, Powell transposed the innovations of the dominant horn of the day to the piano – for Armstrong, read Charlie Parker. He used this as the basis of a style of enormous inner momentum, creating headlong necklaces of notes, punctuated by rhythmic whirlpools, and carried over moody, intensely personal harmonies. His earliest period, covered here, was one of great creative richness. The blistering 'Indiana' and 'Bud's Bubble' (Roulette) are breathtaking examples of cohesion at speed. Other masterpieces include 'Un Poco Loco' and 'Ornithology' (Blue Note), the former driven by volcanic Max Roach drumming. After 1953, his playing grew ever more inconsistent as his inner torments took hold and he became more withdrawn. Occasionally he muddled harmonic sequences, and phrasing that would once have been rifled off was often fumbled. Even then there was often a most moving emotional depth to his later playing which persisted until his death in 1966. Much of this time, especially after brother Richie's death in 1956, was spent in Paris, where his life (more so than Lester Young's) became the model for Oscar-nominee Dexter Gordon's (Dale Turner) acting debut in the film *Round Midnight*. However, his early triumphs remain the measure of his unquestioned brilliance, which peered into an uncertain future through such titles as 'The Glass Enclosure', 'Oblivion' and 'Hallucinations'. CS

THE COMPLETE BLUE NOTE & ROOST RECORDINGS
(Blue Note CDP 7243 8 30083 2 2) 4-CD

THE COMPLETE BUD POWELL ON VERVE
(Verve 521669 2) 5-CD

TITO PUENTE

FIESTA CON PUENTE
(Charly CD HOT 506)

LIVE AT THE VILLAGE GATE
(Tropijazz CDZ 80879) [L]

Brilliant Latin percussion virtuoso Tito Puente grew up in New York's unique musical melting pot environment, where mambo, salsa, modern jazz and soul where being fused into a funky, rhythmically incessant, improvisatory hybrid. A master *timbalero*, he is Latin music's most prolific leader, and has released countless albums of a consistently high standard. *Fiesta Con Puente* covers a vast, brassy selection of the Fania mambo and boogaloo hits that made him famous. Catchy, soulful dance music at its very best, there is plenty of excitement and more than a little charm here. *Live At The Village Gate* is a recent all-star project bringing together some of the music's great leaders, including *conguero* Mongo Santamaria, flute virtuoso Dave Valentin, pianist Hilton Ruiz and saxophonist Paquito D'Rivera. It is a well-recorded disc, with stunning solo work, imaginative arrangements and exhilarating, propulsive percussion. The emphasis is firmly on Latin jazz (rather than salsa), with performances of Miles Davis's 'Milestones' and a superb version of Freddie Hubbard's 'Little Sunflower', featuring memorable solos by Valentin and Ruiz. MG

IKE QUEBEC

BLUE AND SENTIMENTAL
(Blue Note CDP 7 84098 2)

Quebec comes from the school of heavy-breathing tenormen as exemplified by Ben Webster and Coleman Hawkins with whom he'd worked and after a long stay with Cab Calloway (1944-51) spent the remainder of the '50s driving a cab. That is until Alfred Lion (for whom he had recorded in the mid-'40s) invited Quebec to rejoin the label as a dual capacity. From 1959 until falling victim to lung cancer four years later, Quebec was as close to an A&R man as Blue Note ever got; doubling as everything from the label's arranger and session fixer to Good Samaritan by bringing Dexter

Gordon and Leo Parker (bs) back into the fold. Though Quebec cut a handful of romantically-inclined albums including one of the more palatable forays into Bossa Nova (*Soul Samba*), Alfred Lion viewed Quebec as being somewhere between King Curtis and Gene Ammons – a perfect jukebox jumper for the 1960s and proceeded to cut over two dozen sides such as 'If I Could Be With You' and 'For All We Know' all of which are gathered together on two CDs *The Complete Blue Note 45 Sessions Of Ike Quebec* (Mosaic M 118). And while Quebec's 1961 *Heavy Soul* should be rushed onto CD, *Blue And Sentimental* (also from the same year) lives up to its title as with a stylish flourish he wantonly cuts across current fashion for a spot of unshamed heart-string tugging. RC

THE COMPLETE BLUE NOTE FORTIES RECORDINGS
OF IKE QUEBEC AND JOHN HARDEE
(Mosaic MD3 107) 3-CD

DEWEY REDMAN

RED & BLACK IN WILLISAU
(Black Saint BSR 120093)

As a saxophonist who worked with Ornette Coleman for seven years and who, effectively, filled the Coleman shoes in Old & New Dreams, Dewey Redman has received scant, critical acclaim. Coleman had been a major influence but Redman was no stylistic mugger. His phrase organisation and tonal idiosyncrasies on titles like *Willisau* confirm his background as a member of the Texas free school but he was a man who had travelled his own path. Old & New Dreams was formed in 1976 and Redman's reflective investigation of a fine programme on *Old And New Dreams* (ECM 1154) showed him sharpened both by the Coleman experience and by his often underrated work with pianist Keith Jarrett. His growth in maturity since his recording debut as a leader in 1966 was very evident. Gone was the oriental tinged conservative of the second generation avante garde and, on the 1988 *Living On The Edge* (Black Saint 120093), the fine, open ended improvisation of 'Mirrow Window' and the basic blues of 'J.A.M.' are by a man using tools forged in a less than easy career. If the listener detects a trace of the pre-blues field holler in his style; it is intentional. BMcR

DON REDMAN

MCKINNEY'S COTTONPICKERS:
THE BAND DON REDMAN BUILT
(RCA/Bluebird ND 90517)

With Fletcher Henderson, Donald Matthew Redman set the style for all future big band development (whether jazz or not) and, in so doing, revolutionized the music. A conservatory-trained music prodigy and multi-instrumentalist, he joined Henderson in 1922, immediately building the band on four interdependent units still used today – trumpets, trombones, reeds and rhythm. He then evolved a jazz style for big band, using Louis Armstrong's trumpet style as a starting-point for ensemble writing.

More businesslike than Henderson, who enjoyed carousing, Redman left in 1927 to front McKinney's Cottonpickers, a band based in Detroit, but with an RCA-Victor contract. Immediately, Redman began experimenting with his newly-created arranging rules, combining elements of brass and reeds for added contrast.

Among his other trademarks was a habit of contrasting smooth, sweet saxophone unisons with choppier phrases; using chanting off-beat figures to generate rhythmic propulsion; or mood pieces like his own 'Gee, Baby, Ain't I Good To You?'. The result was one of the most important big bands in jazz, though its existence was fleeting, extinguished like so many by the Great Depression, and unmatched by any of Redman's subsequent bands. CS

JOSHUA REDMAN

WISH
(Warner Bros. 45365)

JOSHUA REDMAN
(Warner Bros. 45242)

Winner of the prestigious Thelonious Monk International Saxophone competition in 1991, Joshua Redman has not looked back. Son of Dewey, he is, nevertheless, virtually self taught. He cites Dexter Gordon as an influence but avoids practice routines to ensure his own individuality. Harvard educated and a recipient of a Warner Brothers recording contract, his early records showed genuine promise. *Joshua Redman* teams him with other contemporary, young tigers on a set that embraces Thelonious Monk and James Brown and, for all its authority and hard bop know-how, takes off in a rather guarded manner. In contrast, *Wish* teams him with old 'pros' and the interaction works. Perhaps not yet the stellar figure his fans would have, Redman plays himself out of his father's shadow by upping the emotional ante. Part studio, part club, it has Pat Metheny at full bore and a rhythm, super team of Charlie Haden (b) and Billy Higgins (d). 'Whittlin'' and 'Blues For Pat', in particular, find Redman in red-blooded, musical health but the whole album speaks of virility. BMcR

DJANGO REINHARDT

DJANGOLOGY
(Blue Note CDP 7 80659 2) 10 CDs

Django Reinhardt started out as a violinist and overcame a hand injury to become one of the most virtuosic guitarists in history. A Belgian gypsy, Reinhardt was maimed in a caravan fire which twisted the little and adjoining finger on his left hand. The accident happened in 1928 and it was six years later that Django's star began rapidly to ascend with the formation of the Quintet du Hot Club De France with which he began a long series of jousts with Stephane Grappelly's flamboyant, often nectarine violin. Reinhardt electrified the world of jazz guitar with solos that usually opened with a simple melodic or rhythmic fragment, rapidly developed to climax in percussive chordal passages. Few contemporaries had such a catlike sense of where the pulse lay and his gifted melodies ('Love's Melody', 'Nuages', 'Djangology' etc,) were expressed with the most beautiful acoustic tone. His position in jazz is unique: he was not only the idiom's first guitar virtuoso, he was also the only European to have had such an impact, even to this day. CS

THE LONDON DECCAS
(JSP CD 342)

THE DEFINITIVE SERIES VOL. 3
(JSP CD 343)

BUDDY RICH

BUDDY RICH: ILLUSION
(Sequel NXT CD 181) 3CD set

Legend has it that, while Rich was drumming with the Tommy Dorsey band, he broke his arm but continued playing at gigs, even delivering the usual array of pyrotechnics on his nightly 'Not So Quiet Please' show-stopping feature. But that was Rich, tumble-tough and pugnacious (he once fought Frank Sinatra, while both men were with Dorsey, and later he acquired a black belt in karate) a musician who had little time for minor talents and ever endeavoured to remain the premier percussionist on the block. He did the rounds of the all the big bands, Artie Shaw, Bunny Berigan, Harry James etc., but, when called upon to do so, could equally drive a small group without overpowering his chosen cohorts. The Sequel set presents a near perfect view of Rich's career from the mid-'40s through to the early '70s, encompassing his work with the Metronome All-Stars, JATP and small combos led by Count Basie, Teddy Wilson, Lionel Hampton and Bud Powell, the *Bird With Strings* sessions, the drum battles with Gene Krupa (*Compact Jazz* Verve 835 314) a late date with Woody Herman and a guest shot with Britain's Bobby Lamb-Ray Premru line-up, plus various live and studio cuts by Rich's own hard-driven big band of the '60s and '70s. Full of tour-de-force percussion sorties, the set pans out as not only a brilliant aural guide to one man's contribution to the world of jazz but also a manual of the highest order presented by a drummer considered by many to be the finest ever to grace Jazzdom. FD

SWINGIN' NEW BAND/
KEEP THE CUSTOMER SATISFIED
(BGO BGOCD 169)

LEE RITENOUR

WES BOUND
(GRP GRD 97052)

Fusion guitarist Lee Ritenour's long-running contract with GRP has tended to be more a case of surface polish than artistic content – shiny, snappy jazz-pop in which the real artist is the studio technician. *Wes Bound* is untypical in several ways. A big band session dedicated to the great Wes Montgomery and casting an affectionate eye over Montgomery's own series of big band recordings, it draws the best out of Ritenour and a number of collected fusion heavyweights, including keyboardist Bob James, bassist John Patitucci and drummer Steve Gadd. For a sampler of Ritenour's more typical style, GRP have released a compilation of material recorded during the '80s entitled *Collection* (GRP GRD-9645). LC

SAM RIVERS

SAM RIVERS/DAVE HOLLAND
(Improvising Artists Inc. 123843 2)

In 1964, saxophonist Sam Rivers chose to work with Cecil Taylor rather than the 'restricting' music of Miles Davis. It was not the action of a conservative but, for all that, Rivers has never abandoned himself totally to the free form cause. At Boston Conservatory he had played viola in a string quartet, studied composition and had always maintained that the truly free music could be notated – if required. His own performances, however, erred toward the free end of the spectrum. He worked on the Taylor treadmill for almost four years and then further supported the music by opening the Studio Rivbea, a performance area that typified the loft movement in New York during the seventies. Recorded in 1976, the Holland duos are a superb example of Rivers' work on tenor and soprano (123843) and on flute and piano (123848) at the time. They show his instrumental facility when operating in the false, upper register and highlight his awareness of the harmonics available to each horn. He fronted his Harlem Ensemble and Winds Of Manhattan groups in the eighties but his more recent work has not been well covered on CD. *Lazuli* (Timeless SJP 291) finds him as the only horn; although pleasing, it gives the impression that Rivers is a conservative. In fact, Rivers has always been looking around the next musical corner. BMcR

MAX ROACH

DEEDS NOT WORDS
(Riverside 1122/OJC CD 304)

WE INSIST! FREEDOM NOW SUITE
(Candid CS 9002)

Max Roach was Charlie Parker's first drum choice on the legendary Dial and Savoy recordings of 1947/8. He was in Miles Davis' Birth Of The Cool band in 1948 but also worked successfully with swing era's Red Allen, Coleman Hawkins and Benny Carter. Roach had picked up the historical baton from Kenny Clarke. He retained the legato cymbal beat as a basic but became more extravagant as he shifted the pattern of accentation through the entire kit. On the West Coast, he teamed with trumpet genius Clifford Brown and that seminal group is dealt with elsewhere. Back in New York, he formed his new hard bop group with trumpeter Booker Little and *Deeds Not Words* endorses the stylistic statement made in California. Roach also gave a musical compass reading to the sixties human rights navigators with *We Insist!* Though it involved Booker Little, tenor legend Coleman Hawkins and Roach's wife, singer Abbey Lincoln, in retrospect, its message is somewhat affected but it remains an important work and confirms the drummer's awareness of the disadvantaged position of black Americans. In the seventies, Roach led his percussion ensemble M'Boom and made brilliant duo recordings with the likes of Anthony Braxton *Birth And Rebirth* (Black Saint BSR 0024), Archie Shepp *The Long March, Part 1* (hat Art CD 6041) and Cecil Taylor *Historic Concerts* (Soul Note 121100/1). He toured world-wide in the seventies and eighties with his quartet, well documented by *In The Light* (Soul Note 121053) but also with groups of other sizes including a String Quartet. The scope of his music seems boundless and *To The Max* (Enja 702 1222) provides a perfect re-cap of his career. BMcR

MARCUS ROBERTS

THE TRUTH IS SPOKEN HERE
(Novus 3051)

Marcus Roberts replaced Kenny Kirkland in Wynton Marsalis' band of the late '80s, and remains most associated with the famous trumpeter. One of the most talented followers of Marsalis' outspokenly traditionalist beliefs, he is a sombre, technically flawless pianist playing conservative but attractive and engrossing music. *The Truth Is Spoken Here* was recorded in 1989, and includes drummer Elvin Jones and guest appearances by tenor saxophonist Charlie Rouse and Wynton Marsalis. The best moments include a lively rendition of 'Blue Monk' and a touching solo performance of Duke Ellington's beautiful 'Single Petal Of A Rose'. LC

SPIKE ROBINSON

AT CHESTERS VOL. 1 & 2
(Hep CD 2028 & 2031) [L]

With Stan Getz, Zoot Sims, Al Cohn, Brew Moore and Bob Cooper no longer with us, the ranks of first generation Lestonian 'Grey Boys' has been greatly depleated to the point where unruffled tenorman Spike Robinson stands almost alone as one of the few remaining torch bearers. Having been professionally inactive for year's, 1982's unexpected *The Music Of Harry Warren* (Discovery DSCD 937) served notice of his re-emergence. With the contents of the Chester sets, recorded live, in the UK, two years later, Spike threw his hat in the ring as serious contendor. Though he often comes close, on record, Robinson has never quite bettered this quartet date with pianist (the late) Eddie Thompson. RC

RED RODNEY

FIERY
(Savoy SV 0138)

THEN AND NOW
(Chesky JD 79)

Red Rodney graduated with honours from the been-there-seen-it-done-it-got-the-t-shirt school of hard knocks. Quickly travelling from swing to bop first, in the trumpet section of the big road bands of Elliot Lawrence, Jimmy Dorsey, Georgie Auld, Benny Goodman, he then refined his skills with the more demanding Gene Krupa, Claude Thornhill and Woody Herman's Second Herd, prior to his appointment, in 1949, as Charlie Parker's front-line partner (*Swedish Schnapps* Verve 849 39). An association (including the infamous 'Albino Red' episode) prominently featured in Clint Eastwood's *Bird* movie. Less hesitant in his role than Miles Davis and Kenny Dorham before him, he wasn't there just to play harmony lines or give Bird a breather. Bird may have worked him extremely hard, but this fluid, clear toned young, freckle-faced, redhead possessed sufficient skill and self-confidence to avoid becoming intimidated by the man he held in awe. At one point, Eastwood seriously considered producing a TV movie of Rodney's incredulous post-Bird lifestyle which had him masquerading as a top brass in the military for a crime spree prior to socially rehabilitating himself. *Fiery* (better known on vinyl as *Red Arrow*) – a 1957 pit-stop featured Rodney's long-time musical associate, Ira Sullivan – a remarkable player equally adept on trumpet and tenor sax. And, in the face of Hard Bop, this is one of Bop's last flings. For Rodney, there was life after Bird. Until his death in 1994, Rodney may have been regarded as bop's last great survivor, but he wasn't timelocked in the past. *Then And Now* on which Rodney and arranger Bob Belden refreshingly de-construct and then re-assemble a selection of 40's bop hits 'Woody 'n' You', 'Un Poco Loco', 'Confirmation', 'Marmaduke' proves that there was nothing vampiric about Rodney regularly re-stocking his working band with impressive youngsters such as emergent tenor star Chris Potter. Rodney rightful argued that they gave him the kind of challenge that musicians of his own age could no longer summon up. With Rodney's death following on so soon after Miles and Diz, it was most certainly the end of a trumpet dynasty. RC

SHORTY ROGERS

THE BIRTH OF THE COOL: VOL. 2
(Capitol CDP 7 98935 2)

Until the arrival of Issac Hayes' wah-wah drenched *Shaft* score, trumpeter Shorty Rogers was amongst the most influential men on Hollywood's sound stages. In the course of three highly controversial movies *The Wild One*, *Private Hell 36* and *The Man With The Golden Arm*, Shorty Rogers redefined the soundtrack to high drama screen action with a combination of frenetic jazz shapes, encompassing sky-scraper brass, yearning saxes and the hiss of flying hi-hat cymbals. Leith Stevens and Elmer Bernstein may have taken composer credits, but all they did was pen top lines in the familiar Rogers' milieu for him to remodel in the same manner he'd previously done for Woody Herman (1945-49), ('Keen And Peachy', 'Lemon Drop') and Stan Kenton (1950-51), ('Jolly Roger', 'Round Robin', 'Viva Prado') – it's said, that Rogers alone taught Kenton to swing! The acknowledged architect of the West Coast Sound, comparison's between Miles Davis' *Birth Of The Cool* sessions and the half-a-dozen tracks Rogers taped in 1951 for Capitol (*The Birth Of The Cool: Vol. 2*) are clearly evident. Two other 10-inch LPs from 1953 – the eponymous *Shorty Rogers & The Giants* and the wildly successful *Cool & Crazy* added more depth and texture to the Davis formula, though Rogers (and his sidekick drummer, Shelly Manne) insisted that Pres-period Basie to be their inspiration. *Short Stop* (Bluebird ND 90209) reassembles the aforementioned 10-inch albums plus four atmospheric items from the *Wild One* score. Highlights are many: the blues bop title track, Art Pepper, Bud Shank, Jimmy Giuffre and Bob Cooper all hunking down on baritone sax for 'The Sweetheart Of Sigmund Freud', the latin excursions of 'Diablo's Dance', 'Mambo Del Crow' and 'Tale Of An African Lobster' plus the ever-present sound of Rogers' crisp, citric tone trumpet . Much later Rogers proved there was more to life than soundtracking *Starsky & Hutch* and *The Love Boat*, forsaking studio security to resume a full time jazz career, recording *America The Beautiful* (Candid CCD 79510) and *Eight Brothers* (Candid CCD 79521) and with Bud Shank leading a new Lighthouse All-Stars until his death in '94. RC

THE COMPLETE ATLANTIC & EMI JAZZ RECORDINGS OF SHORTY ROGERS
Mosaic MD4 126) 4-CD

SONNY ROLLINS

TENOR MADNESS
Prestige 7047/OJC CD 124)

SAXOPHONE COLOSSUS
Prestige 7079/OJC CD 291)

WAY OUT WEST
Contemporary 7530/OJC CD 337)

On at least three separate occasions, Sonny Rollins has withdrawn
from public scrutiny to reassess his role in the scheme of things.
The first was prior to joining Max Roach-Clifford Brown
Incorporated in 1956, the second occured around 1960, when (for
two years) the only time you could catch Rollins was during mam-
mouth practice sessions on the windy Williamburg Bridge. The
third occasion commenced in the late '60s and lasted five years.
When in 1956, Prestige released *Saxophone Colossus*, it was about as
accurate a title as anyone could conceive. The sun-kissed
calypso'St. Thomas' might be the best remembered of the five
cuts, but it's the opening 'Blue Seven' that's indicative of the
album's title. An acknowledged improvisational masterpiece, 'Blue
Seven' became the yardstick by which not just other tenormen, but
Rollins himself would be judged. From that moment right until
mid-1959 Sonny Rollins produced a run of albums both as leader
and also with the Max Roach & Clifford Brown Quintet and
Thelonious Monk, that few have ever matched for sustained excellence. In contrast to following Coltrane' cosmic trail, Rollins proved
up-front and confrontational – eye-balling the listener with a full,
rounded tone that owed as much to Coleman Hawkins as it did
Dexter Gordon, plus an endless litany topped off with a perverse
sense of humour that often found Rollins deconstructing such
unlikely jazz vehicles as 'There's No Business Like Show
Business', 'Sonny Boy', 'I'm An Old Cowhand' and'Rock-A-Bye
Your Baby (With A Dixie Melody)'.

Away from Roach and Brown, Rollins gave the impression that the
more he diversed himself of all musical support the closer he would
get to realising his personal goal. Such albums as *Way Out West, A
Night At The Village Vanguard* (Blue Note CDP 7 46517/8 2), *The
Freedom Suite* (Riverside 258/OJC CD067), *In Stockholm 1959*
(Dragon 479003) and Aix En Provence 1959 (Royal Jazz RJ 502)
offer proof capturing him with just bass player and drummer.
'Surrey With The Fringe On Top' (*Newk's Time* Blue Note CDP 7
46517 2) becomes a free-wheeling dialogue between Rollins and
drummer Philly Joe and finally, 'Body & Soul' (*Sonny Rollins/
Brass/Trio* Verve 815 056) finds The Great Man home alone and
paying tribute to his original influence, Coleman Hawkins. Though
Miles would have prefered Rollins to Coltrane in his Quintet, the
fact remained Rollins saw Coltrane as a threat to his tenor Top Gun
status and quit for two years of serious woodshedding. His return,
in 1962 with *The Bridge* and *What's New?* (available as *Quartets* RCA
Bluebird ND 85643) both featuring guitarist Jim Hall in attendance, didn't herald quite the musical departure as many had
expected. In fact, it was all noticeably downbeat. Likewise,
encounters with Don Cherry (tpt).

A spell on Impulse! which produced the *Alfie* soundtrack failed to
resolve matters and so Rollins again chose self-exile and didn't
return until 1972 (*Next Album* Milestone 9042/OJC CD 312). In
concert, he may often consolidate his position as the greatest living
tenorman (*G Man* Milestone 9150), but far too often his studio
albums suggest a noticeable lack of commitment. It's as though
he's already said everything he could possibly say. Even the presence of Brandford Marsalis (ts) and Jack DeJohnette (d) (*Falling In
Love With Jazz* Milestone 9179) and Roy Hargrove (tpt) (*Here's To
The People* Milestone 9194) doesn't supply the necessary stimulus.
At this stage in his career, one doubts that the much-venerated
Rollins feels the need to return to the Williamsburg Bridge!

THE COMPLETE PRESTIGE RECORDINGS
(Fantasy/Prestige 7PRCD 4407) 7-CD

FRANK ROSOLINO

FREE FOR ALL
(Specialty 2161/OJC CCD1763)

Few knew of the torment Rosolino secretly suffered. Equal in stature to J.J. Johnson, Frank Rosolino was also a manic-depressive, who would unexpectedly disappear without warning, but not without first making sure he'd booked a suitable dep to cover in his sudden absence. The eventual tragedy had him fatally shooting his children before commiting suicide. A trombone player of dazzling technique and genuine humour who won international accalim with Stan Kenton (1952-54), Rosolino brought something extra to most record dates he was featured on. And there were hundreds. With his earlier Capitol/Stan Kenton Presents and Bethlehem albums now only available as limited edition Japanese imports, this West Coast date – which for no logical reason remained unreleased for 18 years until his death in 1978 – spells out his many virtues. Supported by a first-call team of Harold Land (ts), Victor Feldman (p), LeRoy Vinnegar (b) and Stan Levey (d) working on a set including 'Love For Sale', 'Don't Take Your Love From Me', 'Stardust' and 'There Is No Greater Love' it stresses all those virtues on which his reputation was founded. Not for Rosolino bumble-bee-under-a-glass-tumbler impressions, clean-cut phrasing and pin-point accuracy were his stock in trade. Be impressed. RC

JIMMY ROWLES

WE COULD MAKE SUCH BEAUTIFUL MUSIC
(Xanadu 157/EPM 5152)

SOMETIMES I'M HAPPY, SOMETIMES I'M BLUE
(Orange Blue 003)

Jimmy Rowles is not interested in musical rape. He is an accomplished improvising pianist who trades in the keyboard caresss; with him the parent theme is cossetted as it is re-shaped and its core beauty is devotedly retained. Despite this conviction, Rowles paid his dues in all departments of the business. Important, big band experience put the latent strength into his style but it was as an accompanist to singers such as Billie Holiday, Peggy Lee and Ella Fitzgerald that he made his name and established himself as a genuine tunesmith. *Beautiful Music* breathes new life into standards such as 'In The Still Of The Night' proving typical of the well structured piano style that made him a first call professional in New York during the seventies while *Happy* represents the face he showed to an expectant West Coast when he moved his trading post to South California in the eighties and features guest appearances by his trumpet blowing daughter, Stacy as well as that of Harry 'Sweets' Edison. In his honour, Los Angeles declared 14th September Jimmy Rowles Day – they certainly knew what they were doing. BMcR

HILTON RUIZ

A MOMENT'S NOTICE
(Novus 3123-2)

Named after the high-speed John Coltrane composition which is featured here along with the beautiful 'Naima', *A Moment's Notice* is one of Ruiz's most polished and exciting albums to date. As well as the energetic but sophisticated, exotic but earthy, salsa/jazz piano improvisations we have come to love from the leader, the record also gains from the presence of the formidable contemporary jazz saxophone duo of George Coleman and Kenny Garrett, and a breathtaking Latin rhythm section driven by drummer Steve Berrios and percussionists Daniel Ponce and Endel Dweño. This is a superb example of the pianist at his more jazz-orientated best, and should provide a very good introduction to his work. LC

HOWARD RUMSEY
& THE LIGHTHOUSE ALL-STARS

SUNDAY JAZZ A LA LIGHTHOUSE
(Contemporary 3501/OJC CD 151) [L]

LIGHTHOUSE ALL STARS VOL. 6
(Contemporary 3504/OJC CD 386) [L]

Second only to Birdland as America's most famous haven for all that was modern, this Californian beach front niterie may have played host to everyone from the MJQ and Miles to the Messengers and Mingus, but it's for its (Light) House Band that the venue is best remembered. Former Kentonite bass player Howard Rumsey inaugurated weekend sessions there in 1949, but in 1951, the jazz policy took on permanency when Rumsey elected to front Shorty Rogers (tpt), Jimmy Giuffre (ts), Frank Patchen (p) and Shelly Manne (d). It's this personnel with the addition of Bob Cooper (ts), Milt Bernhart (tmb), Hampton Hawes (p) and Carlos Vidal (cga) that features on *Sunday Jazz A La Lighthouse* scoring heavily on juke boxes with Rogers' 'Viva Zapata'. With a rapid change over of personnel, Teddy Edwards (ts), Art Pepper (as), and Max Roach (d) were but a few who became All-Stars, but it was to be the one that included former Kenton stars Conte Candoli (tpt), Frank Rosolino (tmb), Bud Shank (as), Bob Cooper (ts) and Stan Levey (d) that was the more stable, drew the biggest crowds and sold the most albums. It's fundimentally this line-up that's showcased on *Vol. 6*. Mixing Duke's 'Prelude To A Kiss', Basie's 'Dickie's Dream' and quality standards 'East Of The Sun' and 'Long Ago And Far Away' etc, with Cooper's 'Who's Sleepy' and 'Mad At The World' the formula of neatly arranged, breezy bop rhythms vividly reflected the affluent local sunkissed lifestyle and in every way quite the opposite to the urban hardness of its East Coast counterpart. Up until his death in 1994, Shorty Rogers and Shank toured a version of the Lighthouse All-Stars. RC

JIMMY RUSHING

THE COMPLETE VANGUARD SESSIONS
(Vanguard 622 093)

The ultimate big band singer, Jimmy Rushing was also one of the finest vocalists in all jazz, most famous for his bullfrog lyricism in front of the Count Basie Orchestra, where his contribution matched that of any of the instrumentalists aside from Lester Young. With Rushing, everything he sang was inimitably converted to his own musical world with a contagious enthusiasm which disguised the more profound ability to invest even the most facile lyric with meaning. The fact that he could handle blues piano informed his timing, which was peerless and an inspiration to the instrumentalists alongside him, whether in the Basie band or on the small group recordings he graced thereafter. Add to this a booting delivery of nonetheless subtly manipulated melodic lines and we have an interpreter of material of serious proportion. Of course, Rushing was himself of serious proportion, earning his nickname 'Mr Five By Five' with an eating talent as prodigious as that for singing. But, long after his death, he has left an important legacy of music, largely but not exclusively blues, with which he is indelibly associated, notably 'Evenin'', 'How Long Blues', 'Boogie Woogie', 'Goin' To Chicago' and 'I Want A Little Girl'. CS

GEORGE RUSSELL

EZZ-THETICS
(Riverside 9375/OJC CD 070)

NEW YORK BIG BAND
(Soul Note SN 1039)

SOULS LOVED BY NATURE
(Soul Note 1034)

An invitation to take on George Russell's *Lydian Chromatic Concept Of Tonal Organisation* is unlikely to thrill the casual listener. In practice, as pianist Russell transforms chords into scales and escorts his music into the area of pan-tonality, he is likely to take most listeners with him. *Ezz-thetics* is a typical example of his retreat from bebop and of the way he introduces his own scalar relationships. It also has soloists like Eric Dolphy (as/b-clt) and Dave Baker (tmb) to usher the new language to safety with their solo realities. Russell caught on both sides of the Atlantic and, in the sixties, embraced electronic aids for *Souls Loved By Nature*. It endorsed the Lydian theory rather than expanded it, although a revised edition *Electronic Sonatas For Souls Loved By Nature 1980* (Soul Note 1009) made no further progress. Russell began to lead larger aggregations in the seventies and actually had his own 'European Band'. The best of the recordings, however, used an American edition and the New York Big Band was just that. It is perhaps easier to read the Lydian message with smaller units but these New York stalwarts handle it very effectively especially when re-visiting Dizzy Gillespie's 'Cubana Be, Cubana Bop'. BMcR

LUIS RUSSELL

LUIS RUSSELL & HIS ORCHESTRA 1929-1930
(JSP CD 308)

Luis Russell's Orchestra was a maverick among those of the latter 1920s because it did not seek to follow the developments of such as Fletcher Henderson and Don Redman. Instead, it represented a more direct link with the music's New Orleans roots. It was a band of great fire and power, avoiding the more subtle tonal colourings and dynamic shadings of a Redman to erect a framework of solid riffs, stomps and blues over a backdrop of abandoned bass-slapping and drumming in the direct Crescent City tradition. Arrangements were mostly functional but, they showed off Russell's star soloists (trumpeter Red Allen, trombonist J.C.Higginbotham, clarinettist Albert Nicholas) to perfection. Eventually, its 'conservative' repertoire of blues and stomps proved unadaptable to the demands of the emerging Swing Era and, as key soloists departed for bands like Henderson's, Luis Russell was left to back Louis Armstrong's grandstanding routines through the '30s. CS

PEE WEE RUSSELL
PORTRAIT OF PEE WEE
(DCC Jazz 611)

JAZZ REUNION
(Candid CCD 79020)

Though most often lumped irrelevantly with the Dixieland school,
the lugubrious Charles Ellsworth Russell ('even his feet look sad',
commented one biographer) was in fact a master of many moods
and of the most individual of clarinet styles. It possessed such
elasticity that it succeeded in embracing a wide variety of jazz
movements, from the 1920s right through to post-Bop modality. A
Pee Wee Russell solo was therefore truly the 'sound of surprise'.
When he played, all matters of tone, pitch, rhythm and melody
were subject to spontaneous and unexpected variation. Each solo
seemed to see him as a man teetering on a tightrope, always taking
the risk rather than the soft option. Humorous passages jostled
against moments of starkly darker emotion; seethingly tense
phrases break into a shambling legato run or veer into knottier
shapes that disentangle unexpectedly. Rhythm is continually
stretched and compressed. His tone is first tart, then gruff, then
translucent; in the upper register it can be raspy or stunningly clear
in the lower it can be rich mahogany or dirty linen. Each time he
played, it was a story unique in the telling – next time would always
be different. CS

RHYTHMAKERS
(Riverside 141/OJC CD1708)

WE'RE IN THE MONEY
(Black Lion BLCD 760909)

EDDIE CONDON: WINDY CITY SEVEN
(CBS/Commodore 8.24054 2)

PAUL RUTHERFORD

THE HOLYWELL CONCERT
(Slam CD 302) [L]

Caution is not a word with which Paul Rutherford is totally conversant. His free playing is projected naturally, it is arrhythmically
designed and, despite being athematic in the accepted sense
traces a melodically consistent route. That does sound like rather a
heavy number to lay on the innocent listener coming across the
trombone/euphonium player's music for the first time. In fact, a
serious approach is invited by this master of extempore though
who overlays horn lines with vocalised sounds to create a unique
vocabulary of voice and trombone accents. Sadly, CD's of the
ground breaking Iskra 1903 group of the seventies or of master
works such as *The Gentle Harm Of The Bourgeoisie* or *Old Moer's
Almanac* are not yet available but the *Holywell* contains some fine
examples of the Rutherford magic. 'Half Pisced' has an oblique
story telling quality, despite his free intent, while on 'Ivory Horn'
he exploits the full range of the instrument. Of course, none of this
is recognise-the-tune time but it is the cue for any adventurous -
and open minded – listener willing to enter Rutherford's world o
voracious exploration. BMcR

DAVID SANBORN

CLOSE UP
(Reprise 7599 25715 2)

ANOTHER HAND
(Elektra Musician 7559 61088 2)

It's an irony that would not have been wasted on Miles Davis. Notwithstanding critical remarks about the apparent simplicity of Sanborn's playing, the emotional depth it evinces has made him probably the most imitated altoist of his generation. Modernisations of the infinite verities of the blues are the secret, and this is nowhere more apparent than in his masterpiece, the final work of his 'prepostmodern' period, the 1988 *Close Up*. This was the last unequivocally contemporary Sanborn album, raising funk counterpoint to the highest level and casing it in glassy, tightly compressed eighties production. Sanborn will surely never improve on the nerve-shattering example of his famous 'cry' which peals out 2.06 minutes into 'Pyramid'. Even the maudlin 'You Are Everything' seems an amiable enough indulgence. The 1991 *Another Hand* marked a sharp departure and a rapprochement between Sanborn's uptown commercialism and the Lower East Side artiness of the guitarists Bill Frisell and Marc Ribot, drummer Joey Baron, and the like. Sanborn gets plenty of chances to play jazz changes, but remains most eloquent at his simplest. But then, Sanborn has never claimed to be a jazz player, insisting his muse stems as much from Louis Jordan's jive as Eric Dolphy's cry. Nevertheless, he has many beautiful, elegiac moments, and luckily there are only brief intimations of the indeed rather shallow sixties rhythm and bluesreprises which occupied his next two albums, *Upfront* and *Hearsay*. MG

A CHANGE OF HEART
(Warner Bros 925 479 2)

DAVID SANCHEZ

THE DEPARTURE
(Columbia 476507)

David Sanchez was one of Dizzy Gillespie's last 'discoveries'. A Puerto Rican by birth, this remarkable tenor saxophonist attracted immediate attention when featured in Gillespie's United Nations Orchestra. The most fully realised debut of 1994, the success of *The Departure* is due in part to Panamanian pianist Danilo Perez whose solos effect a seamless crossover trip from jazz to Latin. However, Sanchez is the central attraction, and what makes him such an exceptional find is the highly-charged emotional content of every solo and his complete mastery of the two musical languages. Rhythmically and harmonically, he's all over his horn – jutting, strutting, playing a phrase, then repeating it, playing with it first, on the beat, then behind, then across the beat *ad infinitum*. 'I'll Be Around' may show off a tender, rhapsodic trait but a reverting, extended and harmonically restructured adaptation of Dizzy's 'Woody 'n' You' plus the title track and a molten mambo 'Cara de Payaso' finds Sanchez and his musicians striving towards a fresh fusion of ideas that conjures up the kind of unfettered creative vitality that once heralded the youthful flowering of both Rollins and Coltrane. TH

PHAROAH SANDERS

PHAROAH'S FIRST
(ESP 1003 2)

LIVE IN SEATTLE
(Impulse WMC 5 116) [L]

Pharoah Sanders' recording debut on the ESP label marked him out as a Coltrane disciple with a raucous tone and an unremitting attack that was to become a trademark. As such, he was an ideal companion for Coltrane, ironically looking for a helping hand in extending the emotional intensity of his music. They came together in 1965, their joint vehemence is captured on *Live In Seattle* and it demonstrates that master can be pupil in certain circumstances. Since that time, Sanders has remained true to the Trane colours, able to stay 'inside' with chord sequences or maraud 'outside' in what appears to be free form. In such cases, it is more likely to be a tortured extension of normal structures, as if he is a ballad player trying to get out. He was not very active on record in the seventies but almost any session from his busy eighties programme would serve as an example of his current work. The 1982 *Heart Is A Melody* (Evidence ECD 22063 2) is ideal; it is his working band, recorded live at Keystone Korner, delivering respects to 'Naima' and treating 'Rise And Shine' like a Sandersized 'Favourite Things'. Currently, embraced by factions of the Acid Jazz movement, The Pharoah does sometimes deal in excessive passion and over-statement but, at the heart of his style, there is a search for creativity and self expression. BMcR

MONGO SANTAMARIA

MAMBOMONGO
(Charly CD HOT 501)

MONGO EXPLODES!/WATERMELON MAN!
(Beat Goes Public CDBGPD 062)

A premier Cuban conguero who moved to the States at the beginning of the '50s, Santamaria began to experiment with the traditional *charanga* form with which he had grown up. Adding unorthodox instrumentation and jazz arrangements, he came to specialise in a soulful, danceable hybrid of jazz, salsa and soul musics and, in the process scored crossover hits such as a remake of Herbie Hancock's 'Watermelon Man' (*Mongo Explodes!/Watermelon Man!*). *Mambomongo* runs the stylistic gamut from the salsa-based 'Guajiro' to the funky (and brilliantly titled) 'Happy As A Fat Rat In A Cheese Factory', and features some deft soloing by its instrumentalists, while Santamaria's tight, propulsive percussion keeps things moving expertly throughout. LC

JOHN SCOFIELD

LIVE
(Enja CD 3013) [L]

SHINOLA
(Enja CD 4004) [L]

Fine though Scofield's post-Miles work is, one wonders if those who rated it his best were actually equipped to make the comparison. Long before Miles had brought him into the orbit of the broadsheet arts pages, Scofield was laying it down in no uncertain terms, and it seems unlikely he'll ever improve on the intensity and creativity of the 1977 *Live*. It shows that his main objective – the synthesis of polytonal jazz with the peculiarly guitaristic sound and energy of the blues – was already complete. Whether he's teetering outrageously on the brink of harmonic catastrophe (try 6.22 into Softly') or kicking over the traces with a knowingly bathetic B.B. King lick, every solo here is crammed with incident. As if any encouragement were needed, the CD reissue adds two extra tracks and leaves Richie Beirach's 'Leaving' unedited. *Rough House* (Enja CD 3033) a companion studio set from the following year, is marginally less amazing. Scofield's admiration for Jim Hall's lyricism was reflected in *Shinola* and *Out Like A Light* (Enja CD 4038), two live albums from Germany in 1981. However, the blues were still ingrained, not least in the exhilarating rock rave-up which closes *Shinola*. The 1979 *Who's Who* gave early notice of Scofield's interest in putting some funny notes in the funk, and the patchily brilliant *Still Warm* (Gramavision 18 8508 2) picked up where it left off, the polectic 'Protocol' a mid-eighties landmark. However, the 1986 *Blue Matter*, (Gramavision R2 79403) big on the blues but harmonically jazz, had consistently better tunes. The 1990 *Time On My Hands* (Blue Note CDP 7 92894 2) a post-modern assortment of bebop, Ornette and The Meters, confirmed Scofield's return to proper Jazz. It produced many fine moments, especially in the ballads, but nothing to eclipse the '77-'78 Enjas. The 1993 *Hand Jive* Blue Note CDP 8 27327 2) is also an update, chiefly of sixties soul-jazz especially so with tenorman Eddie Harris participating. The late seventies chromaticism is still missed, but Scofield is at his most direct for years, producing on 'I'll Take Les' (Les McCann?), the sort of blues solo which ought to come under a plain brown cover. MG

RONNIE SCOTT

NEVER PAT A BURNING DOG
Jazz House JC 012) [L]

The guv'nor, the wag who's always flown the flag, the man born Ronald Schatt is Mr Jazz U.K. A tenor-player who made it out of the ranks of the Ted Heath band in the late '40s, Ronnie became a resident of the groundbreaking Club Eleven in 1948, epi-centre for the then fledgling Brit-bop movement (Well documented in the Charly *Bebop In Britain* release). Following a brief spell with the Jack Parnell Band, he formed his own band in 1953, eventually double-heading the Jazz Couriers with fellow tenor titan Tubby Hayes for a couple of years. By 1959 Ronnie had moved on from mere musician to become the owner of a club that was to become the most prestigious in the world, a kind of combined Wimbledon and Wembley for jazzmen that not only provided a showcase for star-status American musicians but also acted as a platform to enhance the careers of homebase up-and-comers. Eventually someone on high actually had the nous to acknowledge his contribution to British music and in 1981 he became Ronnie Scott OBE. In the interim he'd continued to front bands that never failed to benefit from his direct yet fluid way with a horn, even if they sometimes threw up their hands at the array of one-liners their leader reserved for inebriates who foolishly attempted to trade insults with Ronnie at showtime. These days he operates a record label that acts as an extension of his club policy and provides sometimes neglected local talent a hearing outside the the confines of Frith Street (home to Ronnie Scott's Club since the mid-60s). As much icon as musician, Ronnie has but one major fault – a failure to realise just how fine a player he is, a flaw that has meant that little of his own playing is currently available on CD. But 'Burning Dog', recorded live at Scott's club in 1990, in the company of trumpeter Dick Pearce, saxman Mornington Lockett and a sympathetic rhythm section, proves that, on a reasonably diverse set that includes Cedar Walton's 'When Love Is New' and the Sinatra co-penned 'This Love Of Mine', Ronnie is as tasty-toned and alternatively tender and tough as many he admits to admiring between drinks at his own bar. FD

BEBOP IN BRITAIN
(Charly CD ESQ 100-04)

BUD SHANK

BRAZILLIANCE VOL. 1
(Pacific Jazz CDP 7 96339 2)

THE DOCTOR IS IN
(Candid CCD 79520)

Clifford 'Bud' Shank has been a consistently lucid West Coast flute and alto stylist for over four decades. His most significant contribution, however, was probably the early marriage of jazz and Brazilian music that he accomplished with guitarist Laurindo Almeida, long before its popularisation as 'bossa nova' in the early 1960s. With the 1954 *Brazilliance*, these colleagues from the Stan Kenton 'Innovations Orchestra' of 1950-51, combined the then fashionable 'cool' jazz of Southern California with the 'baia' and others rhythms Almeida had learned in his native San Paolo. The roots of bossa nova are most evident in 'Atabaque', 'Inquietacao' and 'Baiao', even if the rhythmic shapes are simpler and less refined. It's said, that on a visit to Rio, Almeida distributed a box of the resulting 10-inch LP to friends who assumed its contents to be the very latest jazz innovations and promptly copied it. Originally influenced by another Kenton colleague, Art Pepper and his replacement there, Lee Konitz, Shank – later a mainstay of The Lighthouse All-Stars – was capable of building long, articulate lines but with the somewhat fragile tone heard with Almeida. In contrast, his later work has grown more heated and bullish without losing any of the creative consistency that make nominating one recording above another so invidious. Over the last few years, Shank linked up with Shorty Rogers to co-lead the reformed Lighthouse All-Stars up until the latter's death in 1994. CS

HOWARD RUMSEY & THE LIGHTHOUSE ALL-STARS
VOL. 4: OBOE/FLUTE
(Contemporary 3520/OJC CD 154)

LIGHTHOUSE ALL-STARS VOL. 6
(Contemporary 3540/OJC CD 386)

ARTIE SHAW

BEGIN THE BEGUINE
(Bluebird ND 86274)

Artie never ceased searching. In 1936 he formed a band that utilised strings, then he headed for Mexico and came back to form a great late '30s big band that reeked class. Arranger Jerry Grey fashioned an arrangement of 'Begin The Beguine' spotlighting one of Artie's immaculately constructed clarinet solos and that was that. The single went to No.1 in the States and was still there six weeks later. After which the man born Arthur Arshawsky could hardly toot a note wrong. Not that he ever thought in terms of formulae.

If 'Frenesi' (1940) followed the 'Begin The Beguine' pattern and even exceeded the success of its predecessor by notching an unbelievable 13 weeks at the top, then there were other aspects to admire, sides like 'Lady Day' (in honour of Billie Holiday who once sang with the band) and 'Little Jazz', both heated statements from trumpeter Roy Eldridge, or more azure things such as 'St James Infirmary' and 'Two In One Blues', from 'Hot Lips' Page, another trumpet star who admitted to devouring the Armstrong textbook. The Gramercy Five too, was something else, a group that initially jumped to the sound of Johnny Guarnieri's harpsichord. Amid all this, there were other disbandments, other ideas taken up and dropped. By 1949, Artie still probing, was leading a fine, bop-influenced outfit. Then, after switching bands almost as often as he switched movie star-wives (the line-up included Ava Gardner, Lana Turner and Evelyn Keyes) he packed it in and, among many other things, wrote his autobiography (*The Trouble With Cinderella*). But, even now, when he feels like a change, he'll turn his hand to conducting. And, one day, maybe he'll lead the first swing band on the moon. Meanwhile, the Bluebird albums remember most of things worth remembering. FD

BLUES IN THE NIGHT
(*Bluebird ND 82432*)

WOODY SHAW

SOLID
(*Muse MCD 5329*)

IN MY OWN STREET WAY
(*In + Out 7003*)

Woody Shaw comes under none of the traditional classifications. He was a trumpeter of real talent, at home almost anywhere but a player who never made any niche his own. He worked with Willie Bobo and Eric Dolphy. He spent time in Europe, then fitted effortlessly into the 'hard bop' bands of Horace Silver, Jackie McLean and the Jazz Messengers. He essayed more adventurous work with Andrew Hill, Max Roach and Bobby Hutcherson and his mellow ringing tone and meticulous articulation always seemed to fit the surroundings. Surely with his own band in the late seventies he would settle into a coherent style that he could brand Shawspeak. Unfortunately, he rarely enjoyed the advantage of a settled band and he remained in his own musical limbo. Recordings under his leadership may lack a truly identifying personality but they are excellent jazz. His best team him with a challenging horn rival like alto saxist Kenny Garrett (Solid) or find him as the solo horn, as in the case of the splendid *In My Own Sweet Way*.

For those seeking CD versions of Shaw's long-deleted CBS albums, US mail order specialists have released a three disc set *The Complete CBS Studio Recordings Of Woody Shaw* (Mosaic MD3 142). Shaw suffered with a chronic eye condition and his sight deteriorated during the eighties. It is largely held to be the reason for his death, from injuries following a subway accident in Brooklyn in 1989. BMcR

GEORGE SHEARING

THE CAPITOL YEARS
(Capitol CDP 7 97170 2)

THE COMPLETE CAPITOL LIVE RECORDINGS
(Mosaic MDS 157) [L]

If you like to recognise the tune then you probably like George
Shearing, for George has never strayed too far from the melody.
Since leaving Britain in 1947 for the States the blind pianist has
travelled in some exalted company and always in First Class. His
early success in the US was assured when he hit upon the idea of
blending his piano sound with Margie Hyman's vibes using a
'locked hand' technique incorporated in a Quintet formula
rounded out by guitar, bass and drums. The success of 'Lullaby of
Birdland', 'September in the Rain' and other standards which he
recorded for MGM established the pianist as a popular entertainer
in the MOR market. *The Capitol Years* with lush arrangements by
Billy May framing the various Shearing Quintets in tasteful string
settings is an excellent example of the Shearing definitive style.
Breaking up the Quintet 'because we were getting nowhere' he
was immediately in demand as an accompanist to such as Peggy
Lee (*Beauty And The Beat* (Capitol CDP 7 98454 2)), Mel Torme
(*Top Drawer* (Concord CCD 4219)) and Nat 'King' Cole (a Top 10
hit with 'Let There Be Love'), again with enormous success. But
the best Shearing is not to be found on these albums where his
superb empathy with the singers tend to make him self effacing.
In spite of his immense popularity with a general public only the
most po-faced would query his committment to jazz. Thelonious
Monk never saw it that way, insisting that Shearing's success had
introduced a great many listeners to bop. Often criticised (unfairly)
as a copyist, Shearing is, instead, an eclectic performer borrowing
freely from many sources but always with that distinctive Shearing
touch. His many outings with bassists Brian Torff and Neil
Swainson are massively musical. His live set at the *Cafe Carlyle*
(Concord CCD 4246) is exceptionally good but catch the *Breaking
Out* (Concord CCD4 335) session with Ray Brown (b) and Marvin
Smitty Smith (d) where their extra musical weight stimulates the
amiable George into some of his finest solos in years. JM

ARCHIE SHEPP ✷ T

FIRE MUSIC
(MCA MCAD 39121)

STEAM
(Enja 2076) [L]

Poet, author and playwright, Archie Shepp is an outstanding saxophonist who, many felt, could so easily have become a great one. It
is not that there has been a conflict of interests. Shepp has pursued
his playing interests and been well represented on record, even if
important, early releases continued to evade the CD net. The
appropriately titled, *Fire Music* shows the early Shepp style as synthesis of gushing Ben Websterish romanticism and unremitting,
free outbursts. It accommodated the riffs of 'Hambone', the formal
focus of 'Los Olvidadas' and the balladeering of 'Prelude To A
Kiss'. Middle-period Shepp is well represented by *Steam*, recorded
at a 1976 Germany jazz festival with just Cameron Brown (b) and
Philly Joe jones (d) in support. It illustrates that, although the dash-
ing cadenzas still introduce Ellingtonian items like 'Solitude',

Shepp was simplifying his music. The title track has him at his swaggering best, however, and like 'Message From Trane' mines every vein of melodic advantage, before moving on to the next. Shepp retreated to more conservative areas in the early eighties, as if he had assumed the mantle of a one man history of tenor saxophone. He donned the cloak of Hawkins, Webster, Rollins and Coltrane and did it rather well. Into the nineties album such as *I Didn't Know About You* (Timeless SJP 370) find more common ground. They used standard jazz material and, although there was still a lurking trace of bathos, they carried well conceived new structures. Shepp is today his own one man Jazz At The Philharmonic; an historian with a taste for all eras. BMcR

ANDY SHEPPARD

RHYTHM METHOD
Blue Note CDP 8 27798 2)

DELIVERY SUITE
Blue Note CDP 8 28719 2) [L]

The marketing drive which followed the 'discovery' of saxophonist Andy Sheppard at the Schlitz Jazz Sounds competition in 1986 (his impassioned readings of Coltrane with Sphere at the 1981 Bracknell festival conveniently forgotten) turned him into a hot property at arts centres up and down the country, but the hyperbole did not impair a genuine ability. The elaborated funk and Latin grooves of *Rhythm Method* are nothing much as compositions, but they do provide serviceable platforms on which Sheppard generates a big-toned, Traneish head of steam without threatening individuality. The sister volume, *Delivery Suite*, designed to fit into the double-CD case which houses *Rhythm Method*, is Sheppard's biggish band in concert at Ronnie Scott's. Compositions echoing Carla Bley, Kurt Weill and Loose Tubes are to the fore, but the reduced space for the leader's engaging soprano and tenor is not wasted. Sylvan Richardson's electric bass gives both sessions a shape and momentum missing from earlier Sheppard albums.

WAYNE SHORTER

JUJU
Blue Note CDP 7 46514 2)

SPEAK NO EVIL
Blue Note CDP 7 46509 2)

ADAM'S APPLE
Blue Note 7 46403 2)

Shorter's big three for Blue Note seemed to come out of nowhere. There was little inkling in his work for Blakey's Jazz Messengers (1959-64) or in his own Vee Jay sessions (1959-61) of the startlingly fresh, carefully sculpted structures found in *Juju* in 1964. Shorter's spare, relaxed solos on these records are marvels of formal coherence, good enough to furnish melodies for a bookful of new tunes. Indeed, they are a reflection of his preoccupation with composition on every level. Miles Davis had set a precedent for minor keys and languid, lyrical moods at the end of the fifties, and Shorter's music has plenty of those, but what sets his sixties classics apart is an unusual yet logical disposition of chords (try 'Deluge' and 'Fee-Fi-Fo-Fum') and a close attention to rhythm throughout the ensemble, such that his pieces are defined as much by phrasing as pitch. The sound was unique, and the fertile imagination which so successfully negotiated the problem of new jazz forms in the mid-sixties was not under-employed in the revolution that was Weather Report a half-decade later. MG

HORACE SILVER

FINGER POPPIN'
(Blue Note CDP 7 84008 2)

SONG FOR MY FATHER
(Blue Note CDP 7 84185 2)

Art Blakey may have been the original life force, but it was pianist Horace Silver who not only helped shape hard bop but, through a seemingly endless series of highly percussive gospel-drenched finger-popping compositions, fashioned it into soul-jazz. From the Messengers' repertoire, 'The Preacher' served Jimmy Smith to good advantage while Ray Charles dabbled with 'Doodlin''. Aside from title tracks, all Silver's Blue Note albums contained at least one jukebox hit – 'Opus De Funk' *(Horace Silver Trio CDP 7 81520 2)*, 'Sister Sadie' *(Blowin' The Blues Away CDP 7 46526 2)*, 'Nica's Dream' *(Horace-Scope CDP 7 84042 2)*, 'Que Pasa' *(Song For My Father)* 'Filthy McNasty' *(Doin' The Thing At The Village Gate Blue Note CDP 7 84076 2)* while a TV commercial for Coca Cola's diet Tab helped pay the bills. Often, every bit as exciting as the Jazz Messengers, one has the suspicion that Silver felt himself to be in direct competition with his former colleagues for when, in 1956, he broke away from Blakey, he took with him the entire personnel and, with drummer Louis Hayes, launched his own instantly successful quintet *Six Pieces Of Silver* (Blue Note CDP 7 81539 2). Early personnel shifts had Art Farmer replacing Donald Byrd, Clifford Jordan taking over Hank Mobley's tenor chores, but following the introduction, in 1959, of Blue Mitchell (tpt) and Junior Cook (ts) on *Finger Poppin'* the frontline remained intact until 1964, when Carmell Jones (tpt) and Joe Henderson (ts) took over for the classic *Song For My Father*. Soon after the personnel began to change with predictable regularity. *Doin' The Thing* is a perfect snap shot of the intensity they could generate on location, one cut 'Filthy McNasty' proving positively menacing. Drawing on everything from blues and boogie to bop and beyond, Silver is an excitable pianist of immense vigour whose logical solos spill over in a tumble of stabbing riffs and repetative motifs positioned to highten the tension. Often constructed at a tangent, the tenor and trumpet top lines are shot through with easy-to-recall licks and dynamic extremes. After years running his own Silveto label, Silver is back with a major (Columbia) and earning his keep with *It's Got To Be Funky* (473877) and *Pencil Packin' Papa* (476979). RC

THE BEST OF HORACE SILVER VOL. 1 & 2
(Blue Note CDP 7 91143 2 & 7 93206 2)

NINA SIMONE

MY BABY JUST CARES FOR ME
(Charly CHARLY CD 6)

THE BLUES
(Novus ND 83 101)

Some say she's not jazz and consequently her records fail to appear in various jazz listings. But the Charly release, which includes her debut shots, proves that both vocally and instrumentally, Simone cooks in the right places. The title track, by which she's best known, may be umpty-rumpty old-timey, but set against this, there are many delights that include a knowing, expansive workout on Tadd Dameron's 'Good Bait' that even Bill Evans might have admired. And her blues interpretations, which swing from a tear-heart rendition of Buddy Johnson's 'Since I Fell For You' through to a downright churchy interpretation of 'The Pusher', once a favourite of Steppenwolf come kitted out with the kind of right-on angst that filled the best of Billie Holiday's low-down deals. Elsewhere, the pleading high drama of 'Don't Let Me Be Misunderstood' or the clenched-fist protest that is 'Mississippi Goddamn' places the artist in a league all her own. Simone may be a lot of things, High Priestess of Soul, and even a pain in the neck to promoters. But *not* a jazz singer? Phooey!   FD

AT THE VILLAGE GATE
(Roulette Jazz CDP 7 95058 2) [L]

THE BEST OF NINA SIMONE
(Philips 822 846)

ZOOT SIMS

LIVE AT RONNIE SCOTT'S 1961
(Fresh Sound FSR CD 134) [L]

ZOOT SIMS & THE GERSHWIN BROTHERS
(Pablo 2310 744/OJC CD 444)

ZOOT CASE
(Sonet SNT 1044)

The late Zoot Sims never liked to see a rhythm section go unemployed. He just loved to play which made him the ultimate performer. He played every concert, every club and every Festival as though it were his last. That's probably why he is the most consistent sax player of all. Almost all Sims albums are worth while buys. Zoot never short-changed anyone. A big Texan, with a blowsy manner and a devastating line in one-liners, he *attacked* an audience. In time, almost synonymous with the famed Soho niterie as the owner, *Zoot Sims At Ronnie Scott's* is an explosive unremitting assault. The British rhythm section raises its game and the angular, prodding piano of Stan Tracey fits surprisingly well providing an edgy, querulous foil for Zoot's muscular efforts while Kenny Napper (b) and Jackie Dougan (d) fall in behind on five familiar standards ('Stompin' At The Savoy', 'Gone With The Wind' etc) and a blues. *The Gershwin Brothers* is a mellower tribute to eleven of George & Ira Gershwin's best songs backed by the prodigious talents of pianist Oscar Peterson (an immaculate accompanist) and Joe Pass on guitar. Spilling over with some of the saxman's finest playing – an intensely bluesy 'Embraceable You' and a luxurious version of 'How Long Has This Been Going On?' – the latter suggesting that Zoot was an old softie at heart. As half of Woody Herman's legendary 'Four Brothers' sax team, Zoot's on-going symbiotic relationship with Al Cohn brought out the best in each player. Of their many encounters, *Zoot Case* is probably among the best if only for a searing chase on 'After You've Gone'. Sims, in later years, recorded almost exclusively for Pablo. Any of these discs are worth having. Take your pick! JM

FRANK SINATRA

SONGS FOR SWINGIN' LOVERS
(Capitol CDP 7 46570 2)

SONGS FOR YOUNG LOVERS/SWING EASY
(Capitol CDP 7 48470 2)

Sinatra is not a pure jazz singer. Ask him to scat and the result is laughable. Given a blues, he has more limitations than many. Even so, he's probably won more jazz vocal polls than any other male singer and though he's at his most potent on pure ballad albums such as *In The Wee Small Hours* (Capitol CDP 7 46571 2), *Only The Lonely* (Capitol CDP 7 48471 2) and *September Of My Years* (Reprise 901 014), he swings snappily in a manner acquired during his days as band singer with Tommy Dorsey and Harry James and knows how to hang dangerously on a phrase, in a way known only to the best in jazz musicians and singers. Big band-wise, *Songs For Swingin' Lovers*, with it's array of Nelson Riddle fashioned riffs and neat trumpet punctuations (Harry 'Sweets' Edison), is probably his masterpiece, though the *Sands* set, with the Basie band in full live flight, might gain the vote from those who prefer things mildly rougher.

Truth to tell, Hoboken's favourite son is happiest jazzwise when reaching out over a small group that provides him with room to move, as is the case with *Swing Easy*, an early whirl shaped by Riddle (once a trombonist with Dorsey), and the 1962 *Live In Paris* (Reprise 9 45487) on which a Goodman-styled combo provides an ideal musical springboard of the knowing kind. Elsewhere, for those who care to dig deeper, Sony have released *The Columbia Years* (Legacy CXK 48673) a 12-CD box-set that contains everything Frank fashioned in the post-Dorsey years up to the time he linked with Capitol. And though there's dross to be encountered, liasons with the likes of Harry James, the Phil Moore Four, Pearl Bailey, Billy Butterfield, the Metronome All-Stars and others provide suitable rewards for those who believe in blue-eyed swing. Additionally, RCA are responsible for *The Song Is You* (Bluebird 07863-663532) a 5-CD box-set featuring every side that Sinatra recorded while with the Tommy Dorsey band in 1939-1942, but it's really a momento of a man learning his trade and the set's most potent moments are those featuring Dorsey sidemen.

SINATRA AT THE SANDS
(Reprise 901 019) [L]

IT MIGHT AS WELL BE SWING – WITH COUNT BASIE
(Reprise 901 012)

COME SWING WITH ME
(Capitol CDP 7 94520 2)

A SWINGIN' AFFAIR
(Capitol CDP 7 94518 2)

JABBO SMITH

JABBO SMITH VOL. 1 & 2
(Retrieval CD FJ 1312)

Cladyse 'Jabbo' Smith was a trumpeter who combined rhythmic fluency with a strong dash of personal lyricism. The best of his work displays the compelling urgency of no less than a John Coltrane, using a fierce lead and biting upper-register attack to electrify his audience. Jabbo's solos are crammed with unexpected twists and turns, darting lyricism and 'modern' rhythmic devices. He may have been the first trumpeter to take note of the fluency achieved by saxophonists and, in emulating this, met problems whose solutions extended the flexibility of the trumpet. His phrasing became increasingly complex, reaching towards the future Roy Eldridge, as in his stop-time break on 'Till Times Get Better'. And by using passing chords and increased chromaticism, he hints ultimately at the young Dizzy Gillespie. An exhilarating example is 'Sweet & Low Blues', where his own fluency matches that of clarinettist Omer Simeon for facility and range. Nor did he abandon more traditional techniques. Note his voice-like bent notes on classics like 'Decatur Street Tutti', or the stomping excitement of 'Sau Sha Stomp', 'Jazz Battle' or 'Ace Of Rhythm'. CS

JIMMY SMITH

MIDNIGHT SPECIAL
(Blue Note B21/841E-84078)

BACK AT THE CHICKEN SHACK
(Blue Note CDP 74640 2)

In much the same manner as Coleman Hawkins transformed the tenor saxophone from a 'novelty' instrument into a legitimate jazz tool, Jimmy Smith took the lumbering electric organ out of the realm of bible thumping and chapels of rest, stuck a cold beer on the lid and frantically began pumping out the Devil's music! One of the few musicians to ever resurrect an instrument in his own image, he could be as rootsy as Ray Charles or Bill Doggett or as bop crazy as Bird. Blessed with a furocious technique, infinite stamina and a tap-dancer's skills on the bass pedals, he commenced at overkill and worked his way up, – all this being the reason why Jimmy Smith sold albums almost on a par with James Brown. And, in keeping with The Godfather Of Soul, also gave the impression of releasing a new album every other week.

Mostly, they showcased his speed *The Champ: A New Sound A New Star* (Blue Note 7 89391 2) or his deep blues feel, but it was when he was matched with a horn that Smith often proved the more interesting. Cut in a single session with Stanley Turrentine on tenor sax, *Midnight Special* and *Back At The Chicken Shack* warranted the crossover attention they received acting as a blueprint for the outbreak of Hammond 'n' Horn warfare. On Verve, Smith was indulged like few others, enjoying pop-style status, yet most of his back catalogue remains unavailable in any format. *Compact Jazz* (Verve 831 374 2) restores the hits 'Walk On The Wild Side' 'Night Train' and 'Who's Afraid Of Virginia Wolf?' while *Cat* (Verve 810 046 2) drips atmosphere as a result of Lalo Schifrin's big band charts. With the B-3 Hammond (once again) enjoying something of a renaissance, Smith remains the role model and, as *The Master* (Blue Note CDP 8 30451 2) a 'live' 1993 rerun of such party-pieces as 'The Preacher', 'Back At The Chicken Shack' and 'The Cat' attests, still working the same rich groove. RC

THE COMPLETE FEBRUARY 1957
JIMMY SMITH BLUE NOTE SESSIONS
(Mosaic MD3 154) 3-CD

SERMON
(Blue Note CDP 7 46097 2)

STUFF SMITH

LIVE AT THE MONTMATRE
(Storyville STCD. 4142) [L]

An indication of Hezekiah 'Stuff' Smith's status in the jazz hierarchy is indicated by the quality of musicians who stood in line to record with him – Dizzy Gillespie and Oscar Peterson plus fellow violinists Stephane Grappelli and Svend Asmussen being only four of such. Smith's early emergence was at New York's Onyx Club in 1936 with a trio which included Basie drummer Jo Jones who described his playing as 'taking the apron strings off the fiddle'. Although he acknowledged Joe Venuti as a fine player, Smith was influenced mainly by Louis Armstrong. Claiming he wanted to make his violin sound like a horn, Smith was the first to 'attack' the violin using an amplified heavy bow and by holding the instrument in the style of country fiddlers, he was able to create an almost cello like sound. With his natural talent for showmanship Stuff Smith was regarded as something of a joker and his talent as an genuine improviser of quality was overlooked for some time until the 60's when he was rediscovered and toured extensively in Europe. Although Stuff's style originated in the Swing Era, he sounds remarkably unfazed in the company of modernists and his head to heads with Dizzy Gillespie and Oscar Peterson , and others has him retiring unhurt. As an example of the mature Smith the *Live at the Montmartre* session, recorded in Copenhagen in 1965, just two years before his death, with the superb Kenny Drew on piano Niels Henning Orsted-Petersen (b) and Alex Riel (d) captures the exciting and unpredictable essence of this fine performer with an electrifying 'Take The 'A' Train' and a sensitive exploration of 'I Can't Get Started'. JM

SMITH-GILLESPIE-PETERSON
(Verve 521 676 2)

EDDIE SOUTH

EDDIE SOUTH
(DRG/Swing CDSW 8405)

One of the greatest of all jazz violinists, Eddie South's work has been matched in quality by perhaps only two others – Leroy 'Stuff' Smith and Leroy Jenkins. Known as the 'Dark Angel' of the violin, South was classically trained and musical director of a name jazz band by the age of 20. But extensive touring and studying in Europe during the latter 1920s diminished his immediate impact on the jazz scene. For sheer swing and emotional expressiveness, the recordings he made for the Swing label – alongside Django Reinhardt and occasionally Stephane Grappelly, whom he overshadowed – are among the finest in jazz. His dark, sometimes brooding tone and attacking phrasing were compelling, as was the near-rhapsodic nature of his ballad playing. Alongside the popular songs, elevated to minor artworks, 'Eddie's Blues' stands out, as does the early 'jazzing the classics' venture, Bach's 'Concerto For Two Violins', all the 78s of which were destroyed by the Nazis (during their occupation of Paris) as 'degenerate art'. South recorded little in the post-War period and eventually succumbed to heart trouble at the age of 57. But the legacy of his recordings for the Swing label lived on to touch more contemporary practitioners of the jazz violin. CS

MUGGSY SPANIER

AT THE JAZZ BAND BALL
(Bluebird ND 86752)

THE GREAT SIXTEEN
(RCA 13039 2)

In 1939, Muggsy Spanier, an aspiring Chicago-born white Dixieland cornettist and trumpet player, took a seven piece group of similarly respected but little known musicians called The Ragtimers into the RCA studios and created a 16 title masterpiece of Dixieland/Chicago music to be recognised, retrospectively as *The Great Sixteen*.

The impact of these Bluebird sides was enormous and contained some of the greatest ensemble work ever to be captured on wax. Classic recordings revered by jazz fans and copied by many other bands. Spanier, although a popular and sought-after sideman, for fifteen years, had never recorded under his own name and these inspired sessions caused a sensation in the jazz world. All these 16 classics are contained on *At The Jazz Band Ball* while *The Great Sixteen* comes up with eight alternative takes of the original titles. Spanier's hard driving lead with his precise timing and *hot* tone alternating with restrained and tight 'growl mute' work, fired a band whose brilliance was in their unselfish sense of involvement with the overall band sound. This is a soaring, joyous, infectious sound. The recording balance is perfect and the rhythm section bouyant. There is thesoaring King Oliver classic 'Dippermouth' and a beautifully heartfelt 'Relaxin' At Touro' – a tribute to the Chicago hospital where Muggsy almost died in the previous year. This is a magic moment in time, never again quite equalled. One year later, 1940, the Swing Era had arrived and the Ragtimers were as dead as last year's fashions. Up until his death in 1967, Spanier continued to play actively in various groups, but never achieved again the perfection of *The Great Sixteen*. JM

JOHN STEVENS

SPONTANEOUS MUSIC ENSEMBLE -KARYOBIN
(Chronoscope CPE 2001 2)

DEREK BAILEY – PLAYING
(Incus CD 14)

Laughably cubbyholed as a free music percussionist, John Stevens was a drummer of genuine versatility. He was brought into an unswinging Charlie Watts Big Band to add just that missing element and throughout all his cleverly conceived drum tutorials, emphasized the element of swing.

True he was a stalwart of Britain's free revolution and *Karyobin* is a monument to his totally open drum concept. In such circumstances, he was not the time keeper; his rhythmic flurries addressed his colleagues but gave them a buoyant base rather them calibratory guidance. His fusion group Away was one of the most impressive of its kind, but Stevens was at his most comfortable in a free improvisation situation. *Corner To Corner* (Ogun OGCD 005)is a case in point and it has the solo horn of Evan Parker taking full advantage of Stevens' fast hands and all-kit mobility . It is only topped by *Playing*, another duet, this time with guitarist Derek Bailey. Both masters of the terse statement, they emphasise the investigative nature of their creative art. Sadly, Stevens died in 1994, age 54. BMcR

REX STEWART

HIS BEST RECORDINGS
(Best of Jazz 4005)

Rex William Stewart was one of the most individual of trumpet stylists, possessing a repertoire of unique, even eccentric, effects using half-valve, embouchure and mutes. But, although he first came to prominence as Louis Armstrong's replacement in the Fletcher Henderson Orchestra, it was during his time with Duke Ellington from 1934-1945 that his playing truly blossomed.

As with others, Ellington exploited Stewart's eccentricities to tailor a series of compositions, notably the 1938 'concerto' for cornet, 'Boy Meets Horn'. The squashed and squeezed out notes exploited here are balanced elsewhere by a wide range of mood colours, including the exultant 'Trumpet In Spades', the sprightly 'Stingaree', the sly swing of his own 'Subtle Slough' (lost to Ellington in a card game) and the profound lyricism of 'In A Sentimental Mood' and 'Morning Glory'. His was one of the larger-than-life brass styles of all jazz, not without resonance in today's avant garde. That, however, was still in its infancy when Stewart died in 1967, a prolific author as well as musician whose latter-day recordings often failed to maximise his talents. CS

REX STEWART & THE ELLINGTONIANS
(Riverside 144/OJC CD 1710)

SONNY STITT

THE VERVE YEARS
(Verve Compact Jazz 513 632)

SITTIN' IN WITH THE OSCAR PETERSON TRIO
(Verve 849 396 2)

Come up with an original idea that will make millions, and, at that precise moment someone else on the planet, is having the very same thought! A point driven home by drummer Kenny Clarke's now famous statement: 'If there had never been a Bird there would have been a Sonny Stitt.' Unaware of Bird, so legend has it, altoist Sonny Stitt was beavering on an almost identical radical gameplan. Much the same thing would happen years later with free-formers Ornette Coleman (in the US) and Joe Harriott (in the UK) experiencing the same muse. Whereas, most proto-Boppers were forced to stretch themselves to their utmost limits or burn-out in an effort to meet the demands of bebop, earlier Prestige and Savoy recordings drove the fact home that Stitt (in common with trumpeter Fats Navarro) was sufficiently skilled to successfully arm-wrestle the form with power and inspiration to spare. At ease on both alto and tenor (he switched to the bigger horn for a number of years to stave off Bird comparisons), these mid-career dates, especially those with Oscar Peterson ('I Know That You Know' and 'Blues For Pres'), pay dividends for both the thought that went into their production and the realisation, that in convivial company, Stitt was very much his own man. Always contemporary, he was the original choice when Max Roach and Clifford Brown formed their trail-blazing quintet. So it was no real surprise, when, in 1960, Trane quit Miles, it was Sonny Stitt that the trumpet star turned to for a temporary replacement (*In Sweden*). RC

SONNY STITT/BUD POWELL/J.J. JOHNSON
(Prestige 7024/ OJC CD 009)

SUN RA

SUPERSONIC JAZZ
(Evidence ECD 22015 2)

JAZZ IN SILHOUETTE
(Evidence ECD 22012 2)

THE HELIOCENTRIC WORLD OF SUN RA VOLS. 1 & 2
(ESP 1014 2 & 1017 2)

Sun Ra was born on the planet Saturn, date unknown. He is reputed to have transferred to Earth, via Birmingham, Alabama in 1914. During childhood, he used the name Herman Blount but, long before confronting the world musically, had returned to Le Son'y Ra, or Sun Ra for convenience. His early, musical experience did not involve space crowns, giant chest suns nor huge cloaks. He did arrangements for Fletcher Henderson, played with Coleman Hawkins but does claim to have been using a form of electric keyboards in 1953. The world of Sun Ra is best approached with caution and *Supersonic Jazz* from 1956 employs a reasonably orthodox, big band. Orthodoxy ends there, however; 'India' adopts a modal route and on the solo 'Advice To Medics' we have Ra's electric piano, 'Living Sky' is a delicate tone poem and the sound is already uniquely Sun Ra. *Jazz In Silhouette* is another excellent example of the late fifties band but, as the sixties wore on, the leader looked increasingly at the freer attitudes in the jazz world around him. This is clearly illustrated on *Heliocentric World*, as carefully organised music takes on some deliciously incontinent freedom. Orthodox, musical development is sidelined, although even the most complex intermelodic laminations do seem to remain included. The story telling element is unquestionably removed but the sub-plots are a delight and soloists such as John Gilmore (ts) and Marshall Allen (as) continue to be supported. Sun Ra's retreat from the ESP's contained anarchy was gradual but, his interest in electronically induced sound increased. On *The Solar-Myth Approach* (Affinity AFF 760) the acoustic side remained pre-eminent; Art Jenkins 'plunger type' vocal on 'Realm Of Lightning' and the leader's headlong piano on 'Utter Nots' were more traditional eccentricities but more was heard, on titles like 'Pyramid', of Sun Ra's excellent keyboards. In the seventies, he began to embrace mixed media oddities, and dancers and fire eaters became part of the show in the eighties. Musically, they became less ambitious and a couple of swing era type arrangements found their way into most concerts. 'Stars Fell On Alabama' was the 'standard' choice for the 1989 studio recorded *Purple Night* (A&M 395 324 2)but it was just one item in a fine album of contemporary Ra-ish fare. The Arkestra was soon to be silenced when the leader returned to the planet Saturn on 30th May 1993. His stay on Earth had certainly given jazz something to remember. BMcR

JOHN SURMAN

THE TRIO
(Beat Goes On BGO CD 231)

THE AMAZING ADVENTURES OF SIMON SIMON
(ECM 1193)

The extremely musical John Surman dish is served with baritone, soprano, bass clarinet and sythesizer on the side. The problem for this master musician is which one to feature most prominently. In the sixties, he won critical polls for his baritone, as an innovator at the head of the instrument's vanguard. His fine soprano and bass clarinet can be compared on *The Trio*, a superb issue that shows his ground breaking work on all three but leaves no doubt that it is the baritone that dominates.

It was his first choice with Mike Westbrook and Brotherhood Of Breath, as well as in Mumps, S.O.S. and in work with Stan Tracey, Karin Krog and Miroslav Vitous. While with the saxophone trio S.O.S., Surman began to experiment with synthesizers and the electronic side of his music became increasingly important to him. It was of special value on the delightful suite *The Amazing Adventures Of Simon Simon* where multi-tracking, a programmed background, adds an extra dimensions. Similarly, the best moments of *Such Winters Of Memory* (ECM 1254) are achieved when synthesizer, saxophonist and singer Krog are musically merged. The drawback comes only when attention to the electronics is at the expense of his number one horn, because it is the baritone that assures Surman his place in the jazz pantheon. BMcR

STEVE SWALLOW

SWALLOW
(XtraWatt 6)

The balmy, mellifluous Latin textures of the 1992 *Swallow* might a first suggest that Steve Swallow had converted to 'lite jazz', but the record turns out to be a stylish showcase for his distinctive plectrum-bass playing and a light, melodic compositional style he has rarely essayed before. Although Jaco Pastorius quipped 'Steve Swallow' when asked in the early eighties about promising young players of the electric bass, this set proves that though not a virtuoso or innovator on the level of Pastorius (and hardly young any more), Swallow has become one of the most immediately recognisable of electric jazz bassists. There are also fine solos from pianist Steve Kuhn and Karen Mantler doubling on keyboards and harmonica plus guests Gary Burton (vib) and John Scofield (gtr). A later set, *Real Book* (Xtra Watt 7)has him pedalling back on the solos to produce a pad of hard bop originals for a band with Tom Harrell (tpt) and Joe Lovano (ts). MG

BUDDY TATE ✶ T

BUCK & BUDDY
(Swingville 2017/OJC CD 757 2)

George Holmes Tate came to prominence as replacement for his hero, the late Herschel Evans in Count Basie's 1939 Orchestra, and was the next in a long line of Texas Tenors that has also included Basieite Illinois Jacquet and Booker Ervin. This means a direct emotional approach, bolstered by a big-toned, swaggering style of phrasing that always swings with authority. It won him appreciation when Herschel Evans was still sorely missed and Tate's sheer consistency has retained that ever since.

After leaving Basie at the end of the 1940s, Tate bucked the trend against Swing by maintaining an excellent little band at New York's Celebrity Club for nearly a decade, subsequently touring with former Basie colleague Buck Clayton's band. In later years Tate's playing continued to evolve, assimilating something of Coleman Hawkins' latter-day bluntness, but he never surpassed the quality of his work on the *op cit*, where the empathy between

trumpet and tenor is extremely fine. This is most notable on 'High
Life', a compelling performance redolent of the best of Clayton's
lauded *Jam Sessions*. CS

SWINGING LIKE . . . TATE!
(London 820599 2)

SACKVILLE ALL-STARS
(Sackville SKCD2 3028)

THE TEXAS TWISTER
(New World NW 352 2)

ART TATUM

CLASSIC EARLY SOLOS 1934-1939
(MCA GRD 607)

THE COMPLETE PABLO SOLO MASTERPIECES
(Pablo 4404)

THE COMPLETE PABLO GROUP MASTERPIECES
(Pablo 4401)

Four decades after his death in 1956, at the age of 46, pianists are
still trying, unsuccessfully, to emulate Art Tatum. Fats Waller,
cited by Tatum as his main influence, paid him the ultimate com-
pliment one night by promptly halting his set when Art walked into
the club to announce, "Ladies and gentlemen, I play piano but
God is in the house tonight." It wasn't as extravagant a quote as
one might imagine. One of the major innovators in any field of the
arts, Art Tatum's extraordinary talent is genuinely overwhelming.
It's not just jazz players who feel intimidated when measuring their
own accomplishments against Tatum's. Technically daunting and
equal to any legendary concert hall virtuoso, Tatum, who was blind
in one eye and practically sightless in the other, made everything
sound so incredibly easy from his playful tinkerings with Dvorak's
'Humoresque' through to the characteristic manner in which he
would frequently restructure familiar standards from half-a-dozen
different angles as evident on his hits singles 'Body And Soul' and
'Tea For Two'.
The fine-sounding MCA collection of solos depicts Tatum in his
mid-'20s, in dazzling form – those majestic flourishes, the fleet-fin-
gered bursts of speed, his finite sense of swing and sheer invention
revolutionised jazz piano playing. The two Pablo boxes constitute
the real motherlode in that they cover the latter period of his extensive career from 1953 to 1956. *The Solo Masterpieces* are the result of
marathon sessions held between December 1953 and January 1955,
and comprise 125 tracks originally released on Clef, plus 'Someone
To Watch Over Me', 'Begin The Begine', 'Willow Weep For Me'
and 'Humoresque', which stem from a Hollywood Bowl concert in
August 1956 just three months before his death. All seven discs are
available separately and of such uniformed slack-jaw excellence,
that it's down to a question of which selection(s) of tunes one finds
the most attractive. *The Group Masterpieces* cover the period from
June 1954 up until a few short months before Tatum's death.
Again, available as individual discs, Lionel Hampton performs on
three of the eight sessions, but it's *Vol. 3* (Pablo 2405 426) and *Vol. 4*
(Pablo 2405 427) where he and Tatum are joined by drummer
Buddy Rich for an event that many enthusiasts believe was akin to
the Gods at play. JF

CECIL TAYLOR

THE WORLD OF CECIL TAYLOR
(Candid CCD 79006)

UNIT STRUCTURES
(Blue Note BCT 8 4237 2)

SILENT TONGUES
(Arista Freedom FCD 41005)

For the newcomer, pianist Cecil Taylor's music is 'difficult'. He has no time for the cosy rebuilding of themes. He is the explorer, sailing from the haven of a stated theme and then wave clipping in the uncharted zones of the melodic ocean. As the solos on *The World Of Cecil Taylor* show, once he is free, no reference is made to his thematic home port*. Earlier classic albums, such as the 1958 *Looking Ahead* (Contemporary 7562/OJC CD 452) retained some contact with structural improvisation and its 'Excursion On A Wobbly Rail' and 'Wallering' illustrate his 'point of departure' for the sceptic. The wonderful *Live At The Cafe Montmartre* is yet to appear on CD but an important aspect of Taylor's music is to be found on *Unit Structures*. It offers the formal organisation of 'Enter Evening' and the perambulating freedom of the title track. The whole is a controlled complex that both promotes solos and then supports them and it is as important to an understanding of C.T.'s music as are any of his headlong solo tirades.

The finest of those was *Silent Tongues*, another Taylor suite and, like *Unit Structures*, a performance with its own formal organisation. Taylor's piano is as exciting as it is brilliant. His articulation at breathtaking speed is phenomenal but he is not dealing in empty, pointillistic flurries. His roaring clusters, as well as his orthodox arpeggios, are part of the total, melodic continuum. Together they progress his entire melodic movement and are in total contrast to the way that traditional chordal systems redirect improvisational thrust. The Taylor story is brought up to date with the 1989 *In Florescence* (A&M 395282 2). Its basis remains the energy of William Parker (b) and the fast hands of Gregg Bendian (pc). It also documents Taylor's multi media interests with poetic inserts, vocal chants and, one suspects, dance parts, without the dancers. It was Taylor's first recording for a U.S. domestic label for more than ten years and confirms his continued inspiration.

*US mail order specialists Mosaic have assembled a limited edition 4-CD set containing much rare and hitherto unreleased material recorded in 1960/61 under the title *The Complete Candid Recordings Of Cecil Taylor and Buell Neidlinger* (Mosaic MD4 127). BMcR

JACK TEAGARDEN

THAT'S A SERIOUS THING
(RCA/Bluebird ND 90440)

B G & BIG T IN NEW YORK
(MCA/GRP GRD 609)

Jack Teagarden's laid-back, avuncular image belies his status as one of the key trombonists in jazz and a uniquely original stylist. Indeed, he was *so* individual that he influenced no identifiable school of trombonists, probably because his own inspiration came not from other brass players but from the piano, combining its rippling, *legato* phrasing with the slide instrument's gruffer 'smears'. Something of the surprise he generated on arrival in New York can be felt from the way he bounds from the strictly '20s ensemble on 'She's A Great, Great Girl'. The obvious characteristic shining through Teagarden's solos was a 'singing' quality, derived from the Texas bluesmen he heard in his youth. Allied to a flawless rhythmic sense, his lines could float over the beat to give his work an especially spacious air. Unfortunately, his easy-going nature meant that he paid too little attention to business matters, and this quickly saw the demise of the big band he led at the end of the Swing Era. It also meant that he often kept bad company, recordingwise, and too many of his performances were buried by commercialism. It disguised his harmonic boldness and exaggerated his tendency to sentimentalise. This became stronger in the post-War period, which is dominated by a relatively brief association with Louis Armstrong's All-Stars (*Pops/The 1940s Small Band Sides*, RCA/Bluebird ND 86378). He soon went off to lead his own Dixieland sextets whose work was efficient but, in the nature of repertoire, dull, repeating the same old warhorses. Consequently, Teagarden's legacy was indirect, but crucially important by demonstrating that the seemingly impossible was possible, an example heeded later by Jay Jay Johnson. CS

JACK TEAGARDEN'S BIG EIGHT
(*Riverside 141/OJC CD 1708*)

IT'S TIME FOR T
(*Jass 624*)

EDDIE CONDON: WINDY CITY 7
(*Commodore CD 8.24054 2*)

JAMMIN' AT COMMODORE
(*Commodore CCD 7007*)

CLARK TERRY

COLOUR CHANGE
(*Candid CD 9009*)

THE POWER OF POSITIVE SWINGING
(*Mainstream 474415*)

A flawless technician, Clark Terry became the most lyrical trumpeter ever to mess with bebop. A Charlie Barnet, Count Basie and Duke Ellington alumnus, he has played just about everywhere. His style, aptly presented on *Colour Change*, was a meeting place for Dizzy Gillespie's bop concept and Rex Stewart's colourful tonal shading. At other times, he played two horns at once, trumpet upside down but, despite all the gimmicks, was still a superlative jazz soloist. His appearances on the *Tonight* show in America made his 'mumbling' vocal style a household (near) word and a Terry/Red Mitchell album (Enja 5011) provides a fine example of his unique form of scatting. The aptly titled *The Power Of Positive Swinging* showed how easily he fitted into a mainstream groove. It contrasted valve trombonist Bob Brookmeyer's carefully conceived solos with Terry's sociable jive and, in the process, made a point for spontaneity. It is difficult to choose a 'best' from the Terry catalogue but *Memories Of Duke* (Pablo Today 2312/OJC CD 604) from 1980 or *Live At The Village Gate*, recorded at the age of 69, could replace the chosen two. BMcR

LIVE AT THE VILLAGE GATE
(*Chesky JD 49*) [L]

LUCKY THOMPSON

TRICOTISM
(GRP/Impulse 11352)

LUCKY STRIKES
(Prestige 7365/OJC CD194)

Eli 'Lucky' Thompson is an important transitional figure whose most beautiful tenor saxophone tone disguises undercurrents of artistic bitterness that have disrupted his career. Gaining his first exposure with the 1946 Count Basie Orchestra, he moved on to Charlie Parker's West Coast Bebop band (and the Dial session that produced 'Yardbird Suite', 'Ornithology', 'A Night In Tunisia' etc,), for a time becoming one of the most prolifically recorded musicians of the day. Thompson built his style originally on the examples of Coleman Hawkins and Don Byas, combining something of the former's swing rhythmic sense with the latter's harmonic adventure, itself extended by the lessons of Parker. The principal legatee of his style has been Benny Golson. Thompson thus conveys his emotional message directly to the listener, even while negotiating passages of harmonic complexity, as most notably on 'Body & Soul' *Tricotism*. This, despite its strong Hawkins associations is made totally his own. After this, he abruptly left the USA for Europe because he felt 'frozen out'. In France he was able to make many fine recordings with local bands (*Lucky Sessions*, Vogue 743211 1510 2), before returning to the USA in the early 1960s. There, as *Lucky Strikes* reveals, he was among the first to follow John Coltrane's example by taming the soprano saxophone, which seems further to have had the effect of simplifying his style, though not the depth of its message. One of the truly original voices on both instruments, Thompson made few records thereafter and now lives a reclusive life. CS

MILES DAVIS: WALKIN'
(Prestige 7076/OJC CD 213)

HENRY THREADGILL

RAG BUSH AND ALL
(Novus P1 83052)

Henry Threadgill grew up musically in the free jazz environment of sixties Chicago. He toured with a gospel group for almost two years but there is little store-front, chapel bombast in his saxophone work. His 1971 group Reflection, with Steve McCall (d) and Fred Hopkins (b), became Air in 1975. *Air Mail* (Bluebird ND 86578) was a typical album; the music polished yet consistently virile. The leader's solo work displayed a good sense of organisation and he delivered preaching tenor on 'RB' to contrast with graceful flute on 'BK'. In the eighties, Threadgill led a seven strong Sextett (sic) and made some very fine music. *Rag Bush And All* was its most successful album. Each title echoed his 'writing from the rhythm section' theory and each took a cohesive route away from the theme and solo ideal. In the 90's came Threadgill's Very Very Circus. Despite a line-up with two tubas, it was not circus music. The only similarity being that, like a three ring circus, different musical interludes occurred concurrently. It sounded unlikely but it worked. A common state of affairs in Threadgill's world. BMcR

SPIRIT OF NUFF ... NUFF
(Black Saint 120134)

CAL TJADER

MAMBO WITH TJADER
(Fantasy 3-202/OJC CD 271)

JAZZ MASTERS: 39
(Verve 521 858 2)

A former Brubeck drummer, Cal Tjader's decision to switch to vibes and then work out of a (fashionable) mambo bag quickly put him in the same preppy big league as his former piano pounding boss and, on the charts with the dance floor-friendly *Mambo With Tjader. Los Ritmos Collection* (Fantasy FCD 24712) demonstrates that when going latin, Tjader wisely hired on the best available help in percussionists Mongo Santamaria, Tito Puente, Willie Bobo, Armando Peraza and the lock-chorded pianos of Charlie Palmieri and Eddie Cano. When, the mood called for less exotic rhythms *Stan Getz/Cal Tjader Sextet* (Fantasy 3266/OJC CD 275) supplied a credible amount of jazz juice. Whereas, with the introduction of new fads many careers level out then tail off, Tjader's popularity increased from campus favourite to international acclaim. And, while never a threat to Milt Jackson his slightly-muted lightly-swinging style was instantly recognisable, Tjader's skills were his ability to appeal to a mass audience by pioneering a fusion of mood-making latin boogaloo and soul jazz which, on Verve, dripped sophistication when framed by the colour rich arrangements of Lalo Schifrin, Claus Ogerman and Clare Fischer. While *El Sonido Nuevo* (Verve 519812-2) should not be ignored, the specially-priced *Jazz Master* compilation is an expansive introduction to Tjader's work. The familiar 'Soul Sauce' sets Tjader's vibes against a heady combination of muted trumpets and flutes. Horace Silver's 'Tokyo Blues' and Bobby Timmons' 'Moanin'' are afforded a new slant, while the heavily exotic 'China Nights' and 'Borneo' are not dis-similar to those Swingin' Sixties soundtracks that underscored widescreen all-action full-colour maverick cop and superspy movies. RC

MEL TORME

LULU'S BACK IN TOWN
(Charly CD 5)

MEL TORME, ROB McCONNELL AND THE BOSS BRASS
(Concord CCD 306)

Mel Torme's transition from child film star to fully paid up Jazz Vocalist came as a surprise to everyone. We knew he was a talented musician, played piano and drums, had played in Harpo Marx's band (really!) and had formed the vocal group the Meltones. So he was respected, but the arrival in 1956 of the material contained on *Lulu's Back In Town*, amounts to a fully formed classic set with arrangements by pianist Marty Paich and performed by his (almost-big band), the Dek-ette; that included Pete Candoli (tpt), Bud Shank (as), Bob Cooper (ts), plus two french horns and tuba. Paich's deft, clever scores which personified the West Coast 'sound' of the time, pointed up the smooth airy delivery in a voice which has, onomatopoeitcally, earned him the description of the 'Velvet Fog'. The choice of some fairly neglected, but quality standards 'I Like To Recognise The Tune', 'Sing For Your Supper' and 'When The Sun Comes Out' showed an adventurous streak. Since 1956 Torme's career has proved fertile and consistent. The standard is astonishingly high and the output prolific only occasionally showing signs of slight fatigue. He tackled, with great charm, the *Swings Shubert Alley* (Verve 821 581 2) again, with Paich on board and premier league songs of the quality of 'Too Darn Hot', and *The Ellington and Basie Songbooks* (Verve 823248 2) which established his singing as a benchmark for other vocalists. His long stay at Concord delivered several more classics the best of which is probably *An Evening with George Shearing and Mel Torme* (Concord CCD 4190) an inspired coupling with Shearing's sensitive accompaniments leaving the singer with the kind of space he relishes and producing a cozy 'after hours' atmosphere.

Of the later Torme, the Big Band set with Canada's Rob McConnell and his Boss Brass is a stimulating association. Torme's admiration for McConnell's upfront sound and arrangements caused him to seek the trombonist out. The result is a free-wheeling, dynamic set which allows Torme to take on the Band, alternatively engaging with them in chase choruses, or phrasing in unison with the sections 'Just Friends' is a spirited revelation and the unlikely 'Cow Cow Boogie' is an object lesson in assured performance. Although he would rather be known as a 'Musicians' Singer' he still remains a touchstone for jazz vocalists and the best exponent yet of scat. JM

MEL TORME IN HOLLYWOOD
(GRP 1617 2)

COMPACT JAZZ: MEL TORME
(Verve 833282 2)

STAN TRACEY

UNDER MILK WOOD
(Blue Note CDP 789 449 2)

STAN TRACEY PLAYS DUKE ELLINGTON
(Mole CD 10)

Stan Tracey is a major jazz figure on the British jazz scene. House pianist at Ronnie Scott's Club from 1960 to 1967, he played with the world's greatest. His style was genuinely unique, initially nodded into idiosyncrasy by the playing of Thelonious Monk, it became a rich mixture of the rhythmically unpredictable and the harmonically adventurous. There were, however, far more weapons in the Tracey arsenal; he was an effective leader and an imaginative composer and in 1965 he took a quizzical look at Dylan Thomas' play *Under Milk Wood*. With the aid of saxophonist Bobby Wellins, Tracey wove very un-Welsh magic into its textures.

In the early seventies, Tracey became involved with the British free jazz scene and brought his own brand of logic to its wilder elements. From 1976 to 1985, he led an all star octet. It recorded successfully on his own fine Steam label. (Much of this material will be reissued on CD as part of Tracey's recent Blue Note deal). He also led big bands of quality and the combination of Duke Ellington's music, Tracey's arrangements and a quality band made *We Still Love You Madly* a special event. The pianist works well with all groups but his style, his musical attitudes and his sense of priorities are never better displayed than in the unprotected atmosphere of a duo, as on *Plays Duke Ellington*. BMcR

WE STILL LOVE YOU MADLY
(Mole CD 13)

LENNIE TRISTANO

LEE KONITZ – SUBCONSCIOUS-LEE
(Prestige 7004/OJC CD 186)

LENNIE TRISTANO/THE NEW TRISTANO
(Rhino/Atlantic WE 835)

Lennie Tristano was reputed to be jazz's cold shower at the end of the bebop sauna. He held that the creative process did not need to sell itself with over-emotional bolt-ons. He had the ability to double distill standard tunes, firstly recomposing, using the original chord sequence and then subjecting the 'new' theme to an orthodox, improvisational survey. He held that this was enough. His like-minded repertory band that included Lee Konitz (as), Warne Marsh (ts) and Billy Bauer (gtr) concurred. As *Subconscious-Lee* shows, he was served by a prodigious technique but did not always need to put it to his service. Being able to play as fast as Bud Powell or Art Tatum was a talent to hold in reserve. In fact, technique played no real part in 'Intuition' and 'Digression' on which he invited his sextet to play without chord sequence, melody or key centre. They were effectively jazz's introduction to free form, and that in 1949! Significantly, greater exposure to his music acquaints the listener with his latent sensitivity. On *The New Tristano*, 'Requiem' is his answer to those who question his commitment to the blues and perhaps alerts the sceptics to an emotional strength not overtly on show. That 1955 album also looks to the future in its mechanical adjustments to the tapes on 'Line-Up' prior to issue. But then, Tristano was always looking ahead. BMcR

FRANKIE TRUMBAUER

BIX & TRAM VOL. 1 C-melody
(J.S.P. CD 316)

There was a certain risibility about Frankie Trumbauer if only because of his choice of instrument. Even for his era, the C-melody saxophone was unusual but with Tram, the element of the farcical ended there. Despite being somewhat overshadowed by the brilliance of his cornet playing cohort Bix Beiderbecke, he was a player with a point to make and he made it. For most of the recordings they made together, Trumbauer was the band leader and, as *Bix & Tram* shows, he made a very good job of it. He was an adept arranger and the four piece reed section here takes on the cadence and, to some extent, the tone of his instrument. As a soloist, he was better when he did not parade his technique, as on the showboating 'Trumbology'. He is happier with the lyricism of 'Singin' The Blues' or the grace of 'I'm Coming Virginia'. On this release, there are also two chamber trio tracks, with Beiderbecke mainly occupied on piano, Eddie Lang on guitar and with Trumbauer making the most positive improvised statements. Dare it be said, he was the greatest of all C-melody men. In fact, almost the only one. BMcR

BRUCE TURNER

HUMPHREY LYTTLETON – MOVIN' AND GROOVIN'
Black Lion BL 760504)

Although it sounds somewhat incongruous, Bruce Turner studied alto with Lee Konitz and played alto and clarinet with traditionalists Freddy Randall, mainstreamer/traditionalist Humphrey

Lyttelton, led his own similarly inclined Jump Band and once turned down an offer to join Count Basie. Compromises were required but they were accommodated rather well. His clarinet playing picked its way through paths laid by Pee Wee Russell and Lester Young, his soprano (when used) was on the Kenny Davern/Bob Wilber route and his alto, while keeping its loyalties with Konitz, followed its own inclinations. Very little of his work has reached CD status but he fitted the mid-fifties Lyttelton band better than the 'anti-saxophone brigade' would have. On *Jazz At The Royal Festival Hall* (Dormouse DM22 CD) he plays only three solos, yet still manages to sound the band's most eloquent voice. Later in his career he was to rejoin Lyttelton and the strange situation was that the band had stylistically 'caught him up'. *Movin' And Groovin'* enjoys the fine trombone of Roy Williams, the still reliable trumpet of the leader but, with Turner, it has the best of three good saxophonists. BMcR

STANLEY TURRENTINE

LOOK OUT!
(Blue Note CDP 7 46543)

UP AT MINTON'S
(Blue Note CDP 8 28885)

JOY RIDE
(Blue Note CDP 7 46100)

Like many '60s 'soul' jazz players, Turrentine honed his robust tenor style and fatback tone from endless onenighters with R&B road-star Lowell Fulsom (1950-51), then, after a year long stint with Tadd Dameron, 'Flamingo' hit star Earl Bostic (1953-54). Having gained attention with Max Roach's Quintet (1960), the big break came when, upon signing to Blue Note, he partnered Jimmy Smith on a monumental state-of-the-art Hammond 'n' Horn session produced both *Midnight Special* (Blue Note B21/841E-84078) and *Back At The Chicken Shack* (Blue Note CDP 7 46402) in just one day. From that moment Turrentine was deemed a big league player. His own debut as a leader *Look Out!* was acoustic and cut on a straight ahead soul bias with Horace Parlan on piano, likewise his themed pairings with pianists Gene Harris *Blue Hour With The Three Sounds* (Blue CDP 7 84057) and Les McCann *That's Where It's At* (Blue Note B2 84096). With a programme that includes luxurious readings of 'I Want A Little Girl', 'Gee Baby Ain't I Good To You' and 'Since I Fell For You' *Blue Hour* is bang on the money. Thereafter, Turrentine teamed with then-wife organist Shirley Scott, taking turns as leaders on a succession of formularized albums recorded for Blue Note, Prestige and Impulse! By the '70s, Turrentine, like fellow hornman Grover Washington Jr, regularly eased himself into the more undemanding jazz-funk charts. (*The Best Of Mr.T* Fantasy 7708). *The Best Of Stanley Turrentine: The Blue Note Years* (Blue Note CDP 7 93201) is as good as any place to start in that it also includes Oliver Nelson's evocative big band arrangement of 'River's Invitation' from *Joy Ride*. RC

NEVER LET ME GO
(Blue Note CDP 784129)

LET IT GO
(Impulse! GRP 1104)

29TH STREET SAXOPHONE QUARTET

YOUR MOVE
(Antilles 314 512 524-2)

Towards the end of the '80s the 29th Street Saxophone Quartet was enjoying the results of something of a vogue for this unusual and demanding 'rhythm section-less' format, taking up the more popular, bop-orientated room left by the mighty Rova and World Saxophone Quartet. Largely a vehicle for the exciting, virtuoso voice of alto saxophonist Bobby Watson, the group nevertheless developed an impressive rapport, that enabled them to combine an adventurous mixture of improvisation and arrangement, sometimes at stunningly high speeds. After a series of albums featuring additional guests, *Your Move* represented a return to the original four-horn format, the baritone taking care of the bass-line, two horns suggesting the harmonies while the fourth improvises. It is gripping stuff. LC

McCOY TYNER

THE REAL MCCOY
Blue Note CDP 746512 2)

THE TURNING POINT
Birdology 513 163 2)

McCoy Tyner is a pianist who takes the musical bull by both horns and the tail as well. A Benny Golson/Art Farmer Jazztet trainee, he blossomed to his full flowering with the legendary John Coltrane Quartet (*Live At The Village Vanguard* MCA 39136). At the same time, he made his mark as a composer and recording date leader in his own right. His grasp of modal principles and his astute use of African rhythmic flavours, made him a distinctive player. A master in the trio situation (*Supertrios* Milestone MCD 55003), his authoritative piano was even more coercively applied on *The Real McCoy*, a quartet date (with Joe Henderson on tenor) superficially like the Trane sessions but (on 'Four By Five' and 'Search For Peace') actually showing greater Tyner flexibility and suggesting that, for him, intensity is only one of his pianistic tools. His big band offers yet another different means of expression. *Turning Point* shows how he ignores tradition and uses single instruments and sections in a totally novel way. From the elegant 'Angel Eyes' to the ferocious 'Fly With The Wind' is a long trip but it is one that has Tyner as a guide for the entire journey. BMcR

SARAH VAUGHAN

SARAH VAUGHAN WITH CLIFFORD BROWN
EmArCy 841 641)

AT MISTER KELLY'S
EmArCy 832 791) [L]

SWINGIN' EASY
EmArCy 514 072)

A diva, a true diva. Well able to soar where no other jazz singer had ever gone before. Technically, Sarah was the best equipped chanteuse ever to make it out of 52nd Street. Her range was awesome and she possessed so much control that she left most of her rivals back at the starting blocks. Her grand entrance was of the kind that stays in the mind forever – immediately turning 'Lover Man' into a standard while merely a small-print-on-the-label singer with the 1946 Dizzy Gillespie Sextet. There's been earlier stints, with Earl Hines and the Billy Eckstine Orchestra, but 'Lover Man' turned out to be the blind date that sticks in the memory. There's a later version of the song on *Swingin' Easy*, a trio album that allows Sassy room to move, to have fun and kick both swingers like 'Shulie A Bop' and such ballads as 'Polka Dots And Moonbeams' into unique shape. *In The Land Of Hi-Fi* (EmArCy 826 454) is an Ernie Wilkins thing, brash and big band, with a four man trumpet squad, an ever-urgent Cannonball Adderley and such an array of powerhouse tracks as the bluesy 'Don't Be On The Outside' and the run-for-the-hills 'How High The Moon' (with Cannonball and Sarah joyfully swapping fours) that the listener is forced to gasp for breath. *Mr Kelly's* is arguably the perfect live portion of Sassy, relaxed and in your lap, though the session with trumpet legend Clifford Brown has to be the desert island choice. Every member of the band from the brilliantly inventive Brownie through to drummer Roy Haynes is in superb form and the resulting album, built around just nine standards, is packed with perfect moments. Al four recommendations are mid-'50s shots from a period when Sarah was able to do her coloratura thing without the Callas element that pervaded some of her later work leaving any trace of blemish. FD

SASSY SWINGS THE TIVOLI
(EmArCy 832788 2) 2CD

EDDIE 'CLEANHEAD' VINSON

CLEANHEAD AND CANNONBALL
(Landmark 1309 2)

KIDNEY STEW
(Black & Blue 233021)

Immaculate clothes, black silk socks and expensive shoes, Eddie Vinson was the archetypal, blues dude. This limited classification ended there; Vinson was one of the best jazz based blues shouters and an alto saxophonist with a lot of Charlie Parker coursing through his musical bloodstream. On his 1961/2 recording with Cannonball Adderley he does not lose face to the daunting challenge of his fellow altoist and he weighs in with a version of his beloved 'Kidney Stew' as well as a fine reading of 'Just A Dream'. 'Kidney Stew' was something of a hit for him and, as such, make an ideal title track for the Black & Blue compilation. It also contains Cleanhead classics like 'Juice Head Baby' and 'Alimony Blues' and features blues majors T-Bone Walker, Jay McShann and Hal 'Cornbread' Singer in support. A bonus is provided by two instrumental titles with Eddie 'Lockjaw Davis' on tenor and organist Bill Doggett. Vinson remained in constant demand on the festival circuit but it was in the intimacy of the small club that he scored most readily. His explanation for his 'baldness' in 'Cleanhead Blues' remained an audience winning classic until the end. BMcR

MIROSLAV VITOUS

FIRST MEETING
(ECM 519 280 2)

ATMOS
(ECM 513 373 2)

Czechoslovakian double bassist Miroslav Vitous was one of the founder members of the now legendary fusion band Weather Report. However he remains most associated with the subtle, introspective, Eurocentric and often folk-influenced improvised music that characterises the ECM label. *First Meeting* features the brilliant new international quintet he formed on leaving Weather Report. Recorded in 1979, it is a record of beautiful, enigmatic themes, tinged with a lovely, pastoral melancholy. Soprano saxophonist/ bass clarinettist John Surman, pianist Kenny Kirkland and drummer Jon Christenson play with a fine rapport. *Atmos* was recorded 13 years later in 1992, but shares the previous release's characteristic ECM aesthetic. It consists of nine compelling duet tracks with brilliant tenor and soprano saxophonist Jan Garbarek, and features percussive effects played on the body of the bass and triggered orchestra samples. By this time Vitous had developed a stunning language of chords and harmonics that give these duets the textural variety they need. Miroslav Vitous must be considered one of the most profound voices on his instruments today. LC

MAL WALDRON

THE SEAGULLS OF KRISTIANSUND
(Soul Note 121148)

It is conceivable that Mal Waldron's early classical training is responsible for the chordal strength of his jazz style. He is a player who develops his solos in an uncomplicated but powerful way, aware of the original theme but never tightly harnessed to it. His use of riffs sometimes hides the subtleties that go on in his creative process although, on a bad day, he can be rather leaden in his delivery. Thelonious Monk is an influence, even if the final Waldron, stylistic product is not particularly like him. Waldron's compositions and the organisation of his various groups observe similar structural principles and, like the bop pioneer, Waldron functions best in fast company. The 1986 *Kristiansund* is typical, uses his own material and shows how well he backs committed horn players – in this instance Woody Shaw (tpt) and Charlie Rouse (ts). It's three tunes are very different; 'Snake Out' shows how he builds his melodic frames, 'July' takes the hard bop route and the title track has the insistent tension to remind us that Waldron was also an effective, Charles Mingus sideman. Following a nervous breakdown in the early sixties, he had to relearn his jazz. He made the wise decision to use his own records as a text book. BMcR

FATS WALLER

FATS WALLER 1934-35
(Classics CD 737)

PHENOMENAL FATS
(Parade PAR 2011)

FATS AT HIS FINEST
(Parade PAR 2003)

Fats Waller's desire to be loved was insatiable. He projected this by being everyone's friend – a loveable, cuddly, clownish rogue. He was happy to be recognised as The Court Jester and in his time, he made a lot of people smile. Behind this public front much of what he recorded was unworthy of his talents, junk songs which publishers felt he could deliver. Generally, he did. His sheer incessant energy and good humour covering the weakness of this material. Waller's great success was with the three minute vocal aimed at the Juke Box market of the thirties and forties, so that on these 20 track compilations there's is such persistent jollity that sometimes it feels like being locked in a room for a week with Mel Brooks. It is as a pianist that one realises that Waller is an enormous force. For a big man he had a surprisingly delicate touch. The *1934-35* sessions are the start of Waller's most productive period and features the usual team of Herman Autrey (tpt), Gene Cedric (as/clt) and the dependable Al Casey (gtr) and guest appearances from the majestic Bill Coleman on trumpet. A varied disc with four brilliant solo performances (check *Turn On The Heat* Bluebird ND 82482) for further solo sides) and a twinkling 'Not The Only Oyster In The Stew' replete with some of the gorgeous descending right hand runs.

Phenomenal Fats concentrates on the lesser known titles, while *Fats At His Finest* concentrates on his most popular material. Both are exuberant showcases for his bubbling performances. He is in great form in both encouraging Autrey and Cedric (not really first division musicians) to play above themselves. As a force for sheer joy in jazz, Thomas 'Fats' Waller was incomparable and, if he didn't stand still long enough for us to fully evaluate his formidable talents, then that was our loss but was the nature of the man. And, he couldn't change that, could he? JM

JACK WALRATH

OUT OF THE TRADITION
(Muse MCD 5403)

A year dot crunching with Ray Charles can be a salutary musical experience. Jack Walrath had that experience and, shortly afterwards spent four years with Charles Mingus to face a very different discipline. He emerged chastened but not scarred and, in the eighties, toured worldwide and began to make a name for himself as a leader. His trumpet style is distinctive, pitches its stances on the irreverent side of bebop and, as befits a late sixties Berklee student, it shows Walrath to be cognizant of the free revolution, if not in its pocket. *Out Of The Tradition* is a useful place to start an investigation of his style. With Larry Coryell (gtr) and Benny Green (p) on the team, Walrath uses a trumpet mouthpiece for a little chromatic mayhem on 'Clear Out', acknowledges the Chazz background with a 'So Long Eric' and on 'Stardust' remains reasonably respectful. The origins are not disguised, the fine, brassy tone makes its points well and, with some of the bop licks slightly factured, the album title is just about right. BMcR

CEDAR WALTON

AMONG FRIENDS
(Evidence ECD 2023 2)

Pianist Cedar Walton was thirty three before he cut his first album as a leader. Since then, he has cut more than thirty, although their high quality hardly equates with the number available on CD. In the fifties he recorded with Kenny Dorham, J.J. Johnson and Blue Mitchell. He was later in demand for countless sessions with Milt Jackson, Clifford Jordan and Houston Person and had more than one productive spell with the Jazz Messengers. Strings of trio albums have affirmed his all purpose technique, his fine touch and his ability to swing. They demonstrate his avoidance of cliche and ensure that the attentive listener retains contact with the theme in hand. *Cedar Walton* (Timeless SJP 223) is a perfect example of the integration to be found in his trios, with the pianist making musically, fruitful dissertations and David Williams (b) and Billy Higgins (d) becoming third and fourth hands. *Among Friends* merely adds the superb vibraphone of Bobby Hutcherson on 'My Foolish Heart' to further winch up the quality and to produce a quartet performance which, like the rest of the session, sets its own challenges and meets them with style. That he was first choice for the Timeless label's Timeless All Stars was perhaps inevitable. BMcR

DINAH WASHINGTON

DINAH JAMS
(EmArCy 814 639 2)

IN THE LAND OF HI-FI
(EmArCy 826 453 2)

THE DINAH WASHINGTON STORY
(Mercury 514 841 2)

Dinah was everything to everybody. She was a soul queen, a blues lady and jazz singer of highest quality, though she rarely improvised. Her voice had a little of Billie Holiday and something of Bessie Smith in quality and was rarely better utilised than on *Dinah Jams*, which pitted her earthy vocals against the skills of a band that featured a trumpet triumvirate of Clifford Brown, Clark Terry, Maynard Ferguson plus Harold Land (ts) and Max Roach (d), among others. And if *In The Land Of Hi-Fi* doesn't quite duplicate the cut and thrust of Sarah Vaughan's similarly titled encounter with Cannonball Adderley (who to a lesser degree provides the instrumental foil on this album) then it's still a happy thing. The *Dinah Washington Story* twinset does what it sets out to do and encapsulates the singer's years with Mercury, though true believers are pointed in the direction of the series of five Euro-Mercury's 3-CD sets (*The Complete Dinah Washington On Mercury* that seeks to comprehensively detail the same period. A warning though – Vols 1 and 2 are available only as expensive Japanese imports. *Drinking Again* (CDP 7 93270), is an underrated release from Dinah's later years with Roulette and wins through simply because the choice of songs ('For All We Know', 'I'll Be Around', 'Loverman' etc.) is superb, while Don Costa frequently provides the kind of settings that made his liaisons with Frank Sinatra so memorable. She charted again in the '90s via a TV-ad revival of 'Mad about The Boy'. FD

WEATHER REPORT

WEATHER REPORT
(Columbia 468212 2)

MYSTERIOUS TRAVELLER
(Columbia 471860 2)

NIGHT PASSAGE
(Columbia 468211 2)

Both of Weather Report's first two albums furnish persuasive if dated examples of the multi-cultural collective improvisation which made its name. The 1971 *Weather Report* focusing on *In A Silent Way* introspection, the 1972 *I Sing The Body Electric* often recalling the ferocious rock-inflected jams of Miles Davis's 1969 concerts. *Weather Report* is marginally the more successful record, rallying strong compositions and a wide range of mood – from the exquisite impressionism of 'Orange Lady' to the sinewy but sensitive freebop of 'Eurydice' – into a cohesive, well-recorded programme. After the first two albums the music became less obviously radical, though no less revolutionary. Under the guidance of keyboards maestro Joe Zawinul, the emphasis shifted from open rehearsals of musical sketches towards through-composition (thus sustaining the ensemble principle which first inspired the group), from loose pulses towards explicit Latin and funk beats, from occasional free-playing to tonal harmony and riffing pentatonics, and from standard jazz instrumentation towards electrification, but as *Mysterious Traveller* (1974), *Heavy Weather* (1977) and *Night Passage* (1980) show, the group's deployment of superficially commercial ingredients was as ingenious as anything in its earlier work. Even at its populist peak, exemplified by *Heavy Weather* (Columbia 4682112) the treatment of texture and dynamics was extraordinarily resourceful: the opening strain of 'Birdland' is as hackneyed now as 'Autumn Leaves', but Zawinul's arrangement, propelled by Jaco Pastorius's vibrant bass lines, is a masterpiece of dramatic development. Zawinul's co-principal, Wayne Shorter, a striking writer and player in his Blue Note years, was less prominent in Weather Report, but 'Palladium', a driving samba again carried superbly by Pastorius, shows his compositional powers undiminished. *Night Passage* also nods to the swing era, and although no single item approaches the compact genius of 'Birdland', overall it's one of Weather Report's best-written albums. Pastorius is at his finest, and the record is a comprehensive inventory of Pastorius's unique style, from the perpetually inventive four-four of 'Night Passage' to the harmonic mastery of 'Three Views Of A Secret'. MG

I SING THE BODY ELECTRIC
(Columbia 468207 2)

CHICK WEBB

SPINNIN' THE WEBB
(MCA GRP 16352)

The diminutive Chick Webb was the undoubted King of New York's famous Savoy Ballroom ('home of happy feet'), leading a very definitely *hot* band, whose heat was sparked by his own influential drumming. Yet, for all the joyous spirit of his music, he was one of the idiom's tragic figures. Born with a tubercular spine, it left him hunchbacked, little over four feet tall and in constant pain. Yet the seamless surge of his music was the essence of Swing, with such landmarks as 'Don't Be That Way' (a hit later for Benny Goodman), 'Blue Lou' and 'Liza'. Also here was the music's first flute player, Wayman Carver (*cf* the Little Chicks' barnstorming 'I Got Rhythm'). His own work quickly established him as the third great drummer in jazz after Baby Dodds and Zutty Singleton – a crucial link to the modernists, notably Art Blakey. But he did not have long at the top. He discovered the young Ella Fitzgerald, whose success left few instrumental recordopportunities, his illness caught up with him, and he died, aged barely thirty, in 1939. CS

RHYTHM MAN
(HEP CD 1023)

ON THE AIR 1939
(Tax CD 3706 2)

BEN WEBSTER

THE TATUM GROUP MASTERPIECES VOL. 8
(Pablo PACD 2405 431 2)

COLEMAN HAWKINS ENCOUNTERS BEN WEBSTER
(Verve 823 120 2)

Ben Webster was unusual in developing one articulate tenor saxophone style, then promptly abandoning it to develop something altogether more individual. His early development, as a roughneck follower of Coleman Hawkins, can be traced through the 1932 recordings of Bennie Moten and the 1934 Fletcher Henderson sides; the stylistic renewal came with Duke Ellington's classic 1940s band. Essentially, his playing became less hurried and more epigrammatic, built on a uniquely expressive tonal manipulation and trombone-like smears. This was supported by improvising based on thematic, rather than harmonic possibilities, auguring the approaches of such as Sonny Rollins. Nowhere was his art more perfectly displayed than during his 1956 encounter with Art Tatum. Webster countered Tatum's tendency to overwhelm any soloist he accompanied by cruising over the tides of grandiloquy with a tellingly contrasting grace. That he should have coped with Tatum when so many proved unequal was probably because his only formal training was as a pianist, and he often played Fats Waller and James P. Johnson records as 'waking up music'. Through many recording dates, Ben Webster proved remarkably consistent, and their value was not lost on a whole generation of important tenor voices, from Paul Gonsalves to Eddie 'Lockjaw' Davis, Chico Freeman and David Murray. CS

KING OF THE TENORS
(Verve 519806 2)

MEETS OSCAR PETERSON
(Verve 829167 2)

SOULVILLE
(Verve 833551 2)

BOBBY WELLINS

THE NEW DEPARTURES QUARTET
(Hot House HH CD 1010)

Scottish tenor player Bobby Wellins' first major appearance on record was five years into his professional career with the New Departures Quartet. Formed in 1961 and also comprising Stan Tracey (p), Jeff Clyne (b) and Laurie Morgan (d), it's *raison d'etre* was to improvise with radical British jazz poets Pete Brown and Michael Horowitz. Away from wordsmiths, Wellins contributed three of the five originals on the quartet's album, displaying a grasp of the situation which distanced him from most of his contemporaries and placed him in seemingly good stead with his peers on both sides of the Atlantic. Unfortunately, this recognition has, three decades on, still to be echoed by the public who are infinitely more familiar with local tenormen Ronnie Scott, Tubby Hayes, Don Rendell and Dick Morrissey. Stateside, great sax players were in such abundance that Wellins simply got lost in the shuffle. His first real breakthrough came in 1965 with the release of *Under Milk Wood* – by any standards an album of classic dimensions – it took the form of a jazz-suite composed by pianist Stan Tracey and based on Dylan Thomas' play of the same title. With only Jackie Dougan replacing Laurie Morgan, the line-up was identical to that of New Departures. But, four years down the line, Wellins had matured into a most adventurous artist able to articulate himself with a certain grace. *Under Milk Wood* should have opened all doors. As it transpires, his future was as a jazz academic at such venerated establishments as Chichester and The Guild Hall. Recorded in 1992, *Nomad* (Hot House HH CD 1010) mixes Wellins originals alongside Monk's 'Little Rootie Tootie,' Timmons' 'This Here' and Hank Mobley's wonderous 'This I Dig Of You', The outcome being that Wellins was warmly greeted like the long lost friend he has been for far too many years. JF

DICKY WELLS

SWINGIN' IN PARIS
(Le Jazz CD 20)

Were it not for one comparatively brief interlude in jazz history, Dicky Wells would probably be judged as an outstanding trombonist who contributed fine solos to the bands of Luis Russell, Benny Carter, Teddy Hill and, most especially, Count Basie. In fact, while with Hill in Paris in 1937, he made a series of recordings, some in the company of Belgian guitarist Django Reinhardt, that earn him a place in the pantheon of small group mainstream gods. *Swingin' In Paris*, with eight bonus tracks featuring trumpeter Bill Coleman, presents them all and has Wells giving an object lesson in solo construction, effortless swing and heartfelt blues playing. His halcyon years with Basie spanned, on and off, from 1938 to 1950 but he was on hand to play a considerable part in the mainstream revival of the fifties and, although none of his recordings of the period aspire to the 1937 heights, *Bones For The King* (Limelight 820 601 - 2) shows that he remained an impressive musician often in the company of the Countsmen – a gaggle of Basie alumni. BMcR

ALEX WELSH

CLASSIC CONCERT
(Black Lion BLCD 760503) [L]

It would be a tragedy if the late Alex Welsh was to be remembered more for his drinking capacity than for the fact that he led, probably, the greatest little Chicago style band in the world. Americans guesting with the band from Earl Hines to Bud Freeman all extolled the qualities of the band claiming it was the best of its kind, anywhere. A small, smiling man with unbounded energy, his hot, fiery cornet drove a band of like-minded musicians with a fierce committment. His campaign for small band Dixieland began in Edinburgh in the early 50's, long before the 'Trad Jazz' boom of which he was never a part. He steered a devoted and single minded path, parallel to, but separate from, the British Trad Jazz Revival. The Dresden Concert captured on one classic night in 1971 is a fine example of the Welsh band in full throttle. All the soloists especially the immaculate Roy Williams on trombone and Johnny Barnes on saxes, are in rousing form. Alex is an effervescent lead. The late Fred Hunt reminds us that he was arguably the finest stride pianist Britain ever produced and the drumming of the irrepressible Lennie Hastings punches the band along. Temperature is close to boiling, especially on 'Chinatown' and the pace never lets up. The audience is estatic. A golden record. JM

MIKE WESTBROOK   *Guitar*

CITADLE/ROOM 315
(Novus ND 74987)

Mike Westbrook is one of those individuals who seems startled by his success. In fact, he played a major part in the British modern jazz scene in the late sixties and seventies, leading a band of gifted players and writing and arranging in an imaginative way for orchestras of various sizes. Following in the path of Release and Marching Song (at the time of writing not yet on CD), Citadel/Room 315 is a fine, major work. The plaintive soprano on 'Tender Love' or the powerful baritone on 'Outgoing Song' establish saxophonist John Surman as the leading soloist but, as always, Westbrook's melodic vision and apt arrangements draw fine offerings from trombonist Malcolm Griffiths and from the flugel horn of Henry Lowther. Westbrook was not as prolific in the eighties but the quality of his work for medium or large groups remained high. The 1984 Duke's Birthday (hat Art 6021) was a joy, no attempt was made to re-discover Ellington but the depth and spirit of his music was stylishly captured on 'East Stratford Too-Doo' and the title track. His fine 1986 flirtation with Rossini transformed Italian opera into pure Westbrook (hat Art 6002) and, it is fair to say, prepared a septet reading would have left an unprepared Glyndebourne in a total state of shock. BMcR

KENNY WHEELER

MUSIC FOR LARGE AND SMALL ENSEMBLES
(ECM 1415/6)

Kenny Wheeler is a Canadian born Londoner and a trumpeter who has been in pole position for many of Britain's jazz developments. He was a member of John Dankworth's bop orchestra, a pioneer spirit on the Spontaneous Music Ensemble's *Karyobin* (Chronoscope CPE 2001 2) and, in Europe, an infighter with the Globe Unity Orchestra – at present only represented on CD by *Rumbling* (FMP CD 40), and that with a pared down edition of the band. Wheeler was a regular with Mike Gibbs and his trio work with vocalist Norma Winstone and pianist John Taylor in Azimuth was always rewarding. All were ideal platforms for a player with such a wide, emotional range and each provided a different style of building brick to complete Wheeler's own construction kit. The scope of his trumpet playing is never better displayed than on *Large And Small Ensembles*. It mixes total consonance with free flow, calm resolve with fiery outcry and, in the process, presents different size units playing Wheeler's compositions quite superbly. BMcR

BOB WILBER

SUMMIT RE-UNION
(Chiaroscuro CR3 1 CD)

Bob Wilber is so good, so accomplished a musician that he is often forgotten. No-one has served a longer apprenticeship or explored every avenue of jazz quite so thoroughly as Wilber yet even the most exhaustive reference books occasionally overlook him. His playing, as befits a man who studied with such diverse figures as Bechet and Tristano, is dedicated and open minded. Early photos from the 40's seem always to show the young bespectacled Wilber in college boy haircut in the company of various middle aged luminaries as Bechet, Teagarden, Goodman and Condon, although we were not always aware of it, or were rather suspicious of this interloper who seemed to be so accepted in such good company, Wilber was there because he had earned it. Always a pioneer, he has fronted combinations from modernist Tristano's group to Bechet and King Oliver Tribute bands. He has written for films including recreating the Ellington score for *Cotton Club* and he is active in Jazz Education programmes. His partnership with Kenny Davern – spotlighted in a series of *Soprano Summits* in which Wilber also plays clarinet, (his first choice) and alto – brought him a new audience in the Eighties. Of these the most exciting is *Summit Re-Union*, a joyous, stomp of a record with the wonderful Dick Hyman on piano, Bucky Pizzarelli (gtr) Milt Hinton (bs) and Bobby Rosengarden (drs). The up-tempos 'Can I Reveal' and 'Limehouse Blues' are masterly examples of small group jazz at full stretch and Wilber's, Hodqes-tinged alto is a model of fine interpretative playing on the Blues numbers. The presence of Davern provides an excellent spur but this is perfect team work not ego-driven skirmishes. One would have to search long and hard to find a better example of exhilarating music and if you prefer to have two for the price of one, then Wilber with Davern is the best buy. JM

MARY LOU WILLIAMS

MARY'S IDEA
(MCA/GRP GRD 622)

The first woman to achieve an international reputation as a jazz performer, Mary Elfrieda Scruggs, later Mary Lou Burleigh (the Williams came when she married) was not only an outstanding pianist but also an outstanding composer/arranger. Without her, Andy Kirk's 12 Clouds Of Joy would have remained a minor territory band based in Kansas City. Their first recordings only came about because Decca's boss insisted that Mary replace the regular pianist. She was then the alto saxist's wife and already a promising arranger. Noted for being neat and swinging, with an identifiable sense of melody, Mary Lou's charts were also commissioned by no less than Benny Goodman ('Roll 'Em', 'Camel Hop') and Duke Ellington ('Trumpets No End'). But she remains best-known for putting the swing into Andy Kirk's band through vehicles like 'Walking & Swinging' and 'Bearcat Shuffle'. In the late 1940s, she retreated into religion, re-emerging in the 1970s with a series of religious works and, in 1977, a concert with Cecil Taylor. But she was also persuaded to play her distinctive piano in trio settings from time to time. Anytime, she was the soul of the band. CS

THE LONDON SESSIONS
(Vogue 743211 1516 2)

TONY WILLIAMS

LIFE TIME
(Blue Note BCP 84180 2)

THE TONY WILLIAMS LIFETIME/EMERGENCY
(Polydor 849 068)

Forget about any front line tactics, with rare exception, it's only when the drummer kicks in on the same wave-length that innovation can said to have occured. It doesn't happen too often. Max

Roach driving Bird and Diz, Elvin Jones exploding behind Coltrane, Ed Blackwell shadowing Ornette Coleman and, in 1963, a 17-year old Tony Williams colluding with Herbie Hancock(p) and Ron Carter (b) to give Miles a veritable rollercoaster ride. Immediately, the youthful Williams caused many drummers to reconsider their role. Not content to deliver a perfunctory exercise in timekeeping, this firebrand relentlessly worked on the beat, across it, checked out every possible angle to create a polyrhythmic maelstrom for others to ricochet off. The problem is that having contributed to the success of one of the greatest groups ever – as well as further participating in a number of equally innovative record dates (i.e. Eric Dolphy's *Out To Lunch*) – where do you go to from there? His own mid-'60s albums for Blue Note *Life Time* and *Spring* (B21Y 46135) were both sax led by tenor tearaway Sam Rivers (with Wayne Shorter turning up on the second) and yet, surprisingly, looked inward. Intrigued as much by Cream and the Jimi Hendrix Experience as anything else, Williams quit Davis in 1969, to form Lifetime, a frenetic power trio featuring Larry Young (org) and John McLaughlin (gtr) with the sole aim of noisily revising the sound of the organ combo while staking out jazz-rock. Ultimately, Lifetime imploded. By the late-'70s, Williams seemed preoccupied with unfinished business. The spectre of the pre-electric Miles Davis quintet refused to fade away and began to overshadow anything else that either Williams or the post-Weather Report/Headhunters projects former Davis alumni were involved in. Finally, Herbie Hancock, Ron Carter, Wayne Shorter and Williams gravitated towards one another, with Freddie Hubbard in the role that once had been Miles'. First as the Yen-grabbing V.S.O.P and more recently with Williams as the driving force, the *Miles Tribute* was convened with Wallace Roney now subbing for Hubbard. However, it wasn't just a return to familiar terrain but an excuse to search for something new. Though Williams recent bands have been staffed with the more promising pupils of the Messengers last intake, (Roney, tenorman Billy Pierce and pianist Mulgrew Miller), ultimately he both lacks the charismatic depth of Blakey and the knack of sparking his players to produce a band truly worthy of himself. RC

CASSANDRA WILSON

SHE WHO WEEPS
(JMT 834443)

BLUE LIGHT 'TIL DAWN
(Blue Note CDP 7 81357 2)

American jazz singer Cassandra Wilson's work is both refreshing and profound, and currently represents perhaps the most interesting steps forward in the jazz vocalist's art. Initially associated with saxophonist Steve Coleman's M-Base school of melodically angular, rhythmically complex contemporary funk, Wilson has gone on to develop a unique setting for her dry, smoky voice. *She Who Weeps*, from 1990, still contains some of the funkier M-Base elements, but they never distract from the strangely cloudy yet direct effect that characterises her singing. The record's best moment is an enigmatic performance of the beautiful 'Chelsea Bridge'. *Blue Light 'Til Dawn* sounds so natural in its unorthodoxy that it is easy to overlook its creative achievement. Highlights include a powerful 'You Don't Know What Love Is', accompanied by just acoustic guitar, and compelling arrangements of the Robert Johnson blues classics 'Come On In My Kitchen' and 'Hellhound On My Trail'. BMcR

GERALD WILSON

PORTRAITS
(Pacific Jazz CDP 7 93414 2)

Although one of the least fashionable big band names around, Gerald Wilson's work is probably more widely familiar than most bigger names – because he stamped his musical style on hundreds of Hollywood-made TV crime and spy movies from the early 1960s. Nonetheless, Wilson proves to be a *jazz* writer/arranger with a sharp ear for catchy melodies and danceable rhythms, a trait born of his apprenticeship in the late Jimmie Lunceford's orchestras of the mid-1940s (for whom he wrote the forward-looking 'Yard Dog Mazurka'). Whether framing Miles Davis's 'So What', Thelonious Monk's 'Round Midnight' or his own 'Caprichos', he manages to stamp his own individuality on them in a style that, because of the TV work, has been much copied in the commercial world.

Yet, despite the success of his TV writing, his jazz recordings have been consistently of the highest, uncompromising standard, using the finest available soloists on the West Coast. Wilson himself rarely soloed, giving the space instead to younger Turks – here, trumpeter Carmell Jones. Saxists Jimmy Woods and Harold Land and guitarist Joe Pass are also impressive. CS

MOMENT OF TRUTH
(Pacific Jazz CDP 7 92928 2)

ORCHESTRA OF THE '80S/LOMELIN
(Discovery DSCD 947)

TEDDY WILSON

TEDDY WILSON 1937
(Classics 531)

TEDDY WILSON 1937-38
(Classics 548)

TEDDY WILSON 1938
(Classics 556)

AND THEN THEY WROTE
(Columbia 476524 2)

Teddy Wilson's quiet, dignified and cultured demeanour always seemed slightly out of place in the jazz world, almost as though a concert pianist had wandered in to the wrong party. Basically, Wilson brought a classical consideration to jazz. Everything he played seemed thoughtful. He was a brilliant artist, but never used pyrotechnics. He was an object lesson in how to play less and say more. Most of Wilson's best work was with Benny Goodman's Orchestra whom he joined in 1936, to create Goodman's memorable trio and quartet. His other involvement was with Billie Holiday where his guidance was a key factor in the singer's success. Wilson started out partnering Art Tatum (talk about starting at the top!) and while other less mortals might have succumbed to wrist-slashing faced with Tatum's awesome technique, Wilson held his own. Sadly, no recordings of this partnership exist. *1937, 1937-38* and *1938* are but three in a series of around nine CDs available on the Classics label covering the years 1934 to 1941: the same period is also anthologized by Hep, sometimes with superior mastering. The Classics sets are simply magnificent. Wilson was in pioneering form and the list of Greats who rushed to record with him and

Holiday included Cootie Williams, Harry James, Buck Clayton, Bobby Hackett (tpt), Johnny Hodges (as), Lester Young, Chu Berry (ts), Red Norvo (xy) – even Goodman, and crammed with unforgettable performances of the quality of 'Mean To Me', 'I'll Get By', 'Just A Mood' etc. Very few records of Wilson playing solo or with just a rhythm section which reflects a man who carried self-effacement almost to the point of invisibility. One marvellous example of his range and ingenuity, is encapsulated on a 1959 recording *And Then They Wrote* where Wilson tackles the signature tunes of a dozen disparate pianists from Jelly Roll Morton to Stan Kenton, taking in Shearing, Basie, Ellington, Garner, Hines (a big influence) and others. In every way a *tour de force*,the end result has Wilson reinventing them brilliantly in a way that avoids slavish copying, but retains the essence of the individual players. JM

NORMA WINSTONE

SOMEWHERE CALLED HOME
(ECM 1337)

At a reception at Ronnie Scott's Club in London to celebrate winning *Melody Maker*'s 'World's Best Jazz Singer' catagory, Norma Winstone conjured up a picture of Ella Fitzgerald meeting Sarah Vaughan in New York and saying "Norma Who?" She actually has no need of such modesty. Not that anyone really pays regard to such polls but, within her field, Winstone is a singer of outstanding ability. It was her discovery of Eric Dolphy and John Coltrane that led her into her specialist, vocal area and ultimately to her becoming a role model for many who essayed the art of improvised, word-less expression. In the sixties, she worked with Michael Garrick and Mike Westbrook and, in the seventies, formed an intimate trio called Azimuth with husband John Taylor (p) and trumpeter Kenny Wheeler. *Azimuth* (5230102) is a three CD issue that gives a comprehensive insight into their music but an augmented edition with Tony Coe on reeds presented an even more colourful *Somewhere Called Home*. On it, Winstone transforms the trite 'Hi Lili, Hi Lo' into pure poetry to show her power with words, while she makes 'Tea For Two' something entirely different. It is the work of an outstanding jazz singer. Norma who? BMcR

PHIL WOODS   ✳ B·B

PHIL & QUILL
(Prestige 7115/OJC CD 215)

INTEGRITY
(Red VPA 177)

Few jazzmen have maintained such consistent standards over forty years. altoist Phil Woods was a Charlie Parker disciple who never fully digested the rule book. His solo construction flies with the Bird but his line allows the wind to take it; the approach is more smoothly contoured, elegant but never remotely foppish. Studies with Lennie Tristano, experience with Charlie Barnet and Dizzy Gillespie presented, at the *Phil & Quill*, a well rounded performer, free from rhetoric and with Gene Quill (his alto playing partner) presenting already coherent styles and on 'A Night At St. Nick's' making it a concept quintet that worked in practice. Woods spent much of the sixties in Europe leading his European Rhythm Machine but it was the quintet that he led from 1984 to 1990 that marks out (*Integrity*) his finest combo work. The lyrical trumpet of Tom Harrell complemented his own well tempered bebop. The Hal Galper (p), Steve Gilmore (b), Bill Goodwin (d) rhythm section seemed to have been together for ever but, in any case, they played as if they had on a diverse selection that embraced the writings of Duke Ellington ('Azure') through to Wayne Shorter ('Infinite Eyes'). Despite such stalwarts, Woods remains the charismatic leader who does not need charm to sell a style full of grace, melodic good sense and rhythmic aplomb. BMcR

WORLD SAXOPHONE QUARTET

W.S.Q.
(Black Saint BSR 0046)

Hamiet Bluiett, Julius Hemphill, Oliver Lake and David Murray formed the New York Saxophone Quartet. The original NYSQ complained of plagiarism and seemed no more pleased when the four suggested the New New York Saxophone Quartet. The alternative was obvious and the World Saxophone Quartet came into being in 1977. There were certainly no problems musically, four 'loft movement' modernists combined brilliant solos, strong counterpoint and superbly executed unison passages. The excellent *Point Of No Return* (Moers 01034) launched them on record but W.S.Q. marked a high point. It shows that these four men were champions of melody, both in their compositions and in their improvisational realisation of them. Their musical journey takes in the declamatory on 'Sundance', a trip through beautiful harmonies on 'Plain Son', collective complexity on 'Pillars Latino' and sobriety on 'Connections'. James Spaulding replaced Hemphill in 1991 and was himself replaced by Eric Person in 1993 but the W.S.Q. tops a long succession of saxophone quartets , evoking the ghost of Savoy Ballroom dancing in modern day New York. BMcR

JIMMY YANCEY

IN THE BEGINNING
(Solo Art SACD 1)

JIMMY YANCEY COMPLETE WORKS VOL. 1-3
(Document DOCD 5041, 5042 & 5043)

All the elegant simplicity and beauty of the blues abound in Jimmy Yancey's piano playing, yet this was a man who did not play full time. From 1925 until his death in 1951 he was groundsman at Chicago's Comiskey Park, home of the White Sox baseball team. For this reason, his discography is slender (much of it ignored by CD reissues), but almost all his recorded works are remarkable for their emotional expressiveness despite limited material – many of his compositions were based on the same themes or only slight variations of them. His secret, as with much of the very greatest jazz, however sophisticated harmonically, melodically or structurally, was rhythmic. Every solo brims with phrasing that is felicitous in its timing and therefore expressive power. Reflecting the current paucity of reissues, the *op cit* contains all Yancey's performances for Victor in 1939 and 1940, and is therefore rounded out by the work of others. This has the happy consequence of affording direct comparisons with Meade Lux Lewis, Albert Ammons and Pete Johnson which, despite the latters' power, reveal Yancey's peerless mastery of the boogie woogie style. CS

THE YELLOWJACKETS

THE GREENHOUSE
(GRP 9630 2)

Paradoxically, given GRP's reputation as a lite-jazz label, The Yellowjackets began to take themselves far more seriously with *Greenhouse* than they did in their period with Warner 8rothers in the early eighties. The treatment of the changes to 'I Got Rhythm' is a revealing index of the shift in their position: Their 1983 album *Mirage A Trois* straightened out the swing and cut the tune into funky blocks, but here, underpinning a spiky, Monkish theme by Steve Khan called 'Brown Zone', the sequence 18 taken four-to-the-bar, with jazz solos from Russ Ferrante on 'acoustic' piano and new boy Bob Mintzer on bass clarinet. However, while a return to jazz is the main news, the warm, synthesised brass chords and flexible Latin beat of Ferrante's 'Freedomland' and the McCoy Tyner-meets-The-Dubliners jazz-reel of 'Freda' show the group still striving to stand outside the mainstream. MG

LARRY YOUNG

UNITY
(Blue Note CDP 84221 2)

By the mid-'60s, the distinctive electric rumble of the Hammond Organ had become the most marketable soul jazz sound. Jimmy Smith might have been the instruments best salesman but, as *Unity* demonstrated, not everyone was overshadowed by 'The Incredible' one's presence. In the company of drummer Elvin Jones, Larry Young looked elsewhere for devine inspiration: their quest took them to Elvin's boss, John Coltrane. The pair had already had previous nailed their intentions to the door in the company of guitarist Grant Green on *Talkin' About JC* followed by three more albums in rapid succession all of which are included on a CD six-pack *The Complete Blue Note Recordings Of Larry Young* (Mosaic M 137). As the essential one disc *The Art Of Larry Young* (Blue Note CDP 7 99177 2) corroborates, not only did they anticipate Larry Young's later dazzling work alongside John McLaughlin (gtr) and Tony Williams (d) in the latter's (short-lived) jazz-rock power trio Lifetime, but sessions with Jimi Hendrix and an appearance on Miles Davis' barricade smashing *Bitches Brew*. But that was still in the future. By the time Young and Jones teamed up with Joe Henderson (ts) and Woody Shaw (tpt) for 1965's *Unity*, (for which Shaw provided most of the charts) they had reshaped a new approach to the Hammond's position in jazz. However, the arrival of a whole new arsenal of electronic hi-tech keyboards, sidelined the Hammond and its latest innovator. Frustration followed, wrong career moves taken, finally resulting in Young's death at 37. RC

LESTER YOUNG

LESTER YOUNG & FRIENDS
(Commodore CCD 7002)

THE COMPLETE LESTER YOUNG
(Mercury 830920 2)

PRES & TEDDY
(Verve 831270 2)

Lester Willis Young, the President of all the Saxophones (or simply Pres) as Billie Holiday dubbed him, was one of the four or five greatest soloists in the history of jazz. Only Armstrong, Parker (whom he influenced) and Coleman equalled his best work, which was so original that it brought, first, denunciation, then the slavish admiration of an entire generation of post-War saxophone players. The reproval began as early as 1934, when Coleman Hawkins travelled to Europe, having left the tenor saxophone established as a new, tempestuous jazz voice with a specific style being emulated across the USA. It was ironic then that, as his replacement in the Fletcher Henderson Orchestra , the one man was chosen who was immediately out of step with the accepted practice. And Lester Young remained deliberately out of step for the next decade – the first jazz artist consciously ahead of his time. A critical bruising from fellow musicians continued for several months before he and Henderson parted company – but not before Henderson had told his own men that Young was the better musician. Young had underlined that the previous year by cutting Hawkins in a jam session in Kansas City. Influenced unusually by Bix Beiderbecke & Frankie Trumbauer, Young burst on to the scene with a fully mature style that reached its apotheosis in the Count Basie Orchestra. His immediately obvious innovations included a light, dry, airy sound – full-bodied but avoiding the heavy vibrato and buzzy effects of the Hawkins style. Where Hawkins phrased in an arpeggiated, almost *rococo* fashion, Young played in a rangy, *legato* manner, floating over the rhythm yet simultaneously revealing exciting cross-rhythms through rhythmic displacement. The shifting rhythms of Young's solos were a significant feature of his work and a clear function of his early schooling as a drummer. Countless solos from his work with Basie or Billie Holiday reveal a preoccupation less with harmony (*vide* Hawkins) than with the natural evolution of the melody. However, he had such melodic gifts that, while pursuing his aims, he was able constantly to make harmonic innovations to a degree where his phrasing seemed to rely more on scales (as, later, in Coltrane's modality) than on specific chordal patterns. Evolving melody also meant that he made startling use of rests to create asymmetric phrase patterns of unusual, attractive and often breathtaking length. Gone was the old reliance on two and four-bar phrasing; in its place was a bubbling lyricism of compelling quality. After Lester left Basie in 1940 (returning for most of 1944), his style began to change. Some have blamed abuse by the US Army, but the changes, like those in the Basie band's own style, were evolutionary. In Lester's case, they were a reaction to the death of sectionmate Herschel Evans in 1939; Young's tone gradually deepened and the sorrows of this and later problems seeped into his playing. Not least was the discovery on return from service that 52nd Street was full of young saxophone players aping what he had invented – from Dexter Gordon to Stan Getz, Allan Eager to Sonny Stitt. Suddenly the master was slightly passe, and that hurt sparked a process of withdrawal until his untimely death, aged 49, in 1959. In between, the energy that marked his finest pre-War achievements was matched less and less frequently. CS

THE PRESIDENT PLAYS
(Verve 831670 2)

LESTER YOUNG & THE JAZZ GIANTS
(Verve 825672 2)

JAMMIN' WITH LESTER
(Archive of Jazz 3801.182)

Jazz Record Shops and Distributors

ACORN MUSIC
P O BOX 17, Sidmouth, Devon EX10 9EH
01395 578145

CADILLAC DISTRIBUTION *(John Jackson)*
61-71 Collier Street, London N1 9DF
0171 2787391

CRAZY JAZZ
5 Prospect Road, Cheshunt, Herts EN8 9QX
01242 677257

GOOD PRICE
23 Raindeer Court, Worcester WR1 2DS
01905 619649

HARMONIA MUNDI JAZZ *(distributor)*
19-21 Nile Street, London N1 7LR
0171 253 0863

HONEST JON'S RECORDS
278 Portobello Road, London W10 5TE
0181 969 9822

JAZZ MUSIC
Glenview, Moylegrove, Cardigan, Dyfed SA43 3BW
01239 86278

J & M RECORDS
P O BOX 276, Taunton TA3 6YZ
01823 481234

MOLE JAZZ *(inc James Asman's Record Centre)*
291 Pentonville Road, London N1 9NP
0171 278 8623

MONTPELLIER
23a Church Road, Bishops Cleeve, Glos GL52 4LR
01242 677257

NEW NOTE *(distributor)*
Unit 2, Orpington Trading Estate, Sevenoaks Way, Orpington, Kent BR5 3SR
01689 877884

RAY'S JAZZ SHOP
180 Shaftesbury Avenue, London WC2
0171 240 3969

THE RECORD CENTRE
45-46 Loveday Street, Birmingham B4 6NR
0121 359 7399

SOUL BROTHERS RECORDS
1 Keswick Road, Putney, London SW15 2HL
0181 875 1018

SPOTLITE *(Tony Williams - distributor & label)*
103 London Road, Sawbridgeworth, Herts CM21 9JJ
01279 724572

TEMPLAR RECORDS
9a Irving Street, Leicester Square, London WC2
0171 930 3579

KAY JAZZ PRODUCTIONS
Dept KJ, 29 May Road, Rochester, Kent ME1 2HY
01634 405698

Jazz travel agency

JAZZ TOURS
37 Wood Street, Stratford-Upon-Avon CV37 6ES
0789 267532